Poetic Creation
Inspiration or Craft

POETIC CREATION
Inspiration or Craft

By Carl Fehrman
Institute of Literary Research
University of Lund, Sweden

Translated by Karin Petherick
Department of Scandinavian Studies
University College, London

UNIVERSITY OF MINNESOTA PRESS
Minneapolis

The Swedish edition of this book appeared
under the title *Diktaren och de skapande ögonblicken*
and was published by P. A. Norstedt and Sons,
© 1974 by Carl Fehrman.

Library of Congress Cataloging in Publication Data

Fehrman, Carl Abraham Daniel, 1915-
    Poetic creation.

    Translation of Diktaren och de skapande ögonblicken.
    Includes bibliographical references and index.
    1. Poetry, Modern —History and criticism.
2. Creation (Literary, artistic, etc.) I. Title.
PN1116.F413   808.1   79-17901
ISBN 0-8166-0899-7

Preface

The enterprise of writing a book on the creative craft of poets may appear to have little connection with the mainstream of current literary criticism. During the reign of the New Criticism, nothing but the finished work of art was considered worthy of scholarly analysis. And among Marxist critics, the productive forces of society are thought to be of more fundamental importance to literary history than the creative power of artists. Today, when in many parts of Europe the reception of literature is regarded as the central task of literary historians, interest in the creator has been replaced by interest in the receiver. It is an obvious fact, nonetheless, that in the chain of communication there can be no receiver without a transmitter, nor a re-creator without a creator.

During recent decades, there have been signs of a growing interest in the creative process as well.[1] Interesting material is presented in the volume *Writers at Work*, published in the well-known series "The Paris Review Interviews." New manuscript collections in Europe and the United States have been established with the sole purpose of making possible intensified study of the creative process. Psychologists like Julius Bahle in Germany and Frank Barron in the United States have devised new methods of investigating the working habits of composers and writers. Literary scholarship has devoted numerous studies to periodicity in the life

cycle of creative writers. The theme of creativity (and its counterpart, blocked productivity), often concealed behind religious and
erotic metaphors, await more extensive investigation as part of
the hidden themes of literature.

The various myths of creativity have changed from period to
period in Western literary history. During the romantic era, people
cherished the idea of creativity as a spontaneous, unpremeditated
act. Georg Brandes, the Danish critic, rebelled against this myth
with the famous words: "A man of genius is not an idler but a
worker." In the twentieth century the myth of the writer as a
worker among other workers has competed with the Surrealist
myth of the spontaneous author who writes in a sort of trance.
Myths vary. But there can be no doubt that the creative process as
such, *the act of creation*, is transhistorical. The study of this act—
as an isolated phenomenon—is the subject of this book.

The volume comprises ten chapters or essays. After an introductory chapter on the various types of documents and experiments
used to investigate the poet's work habits, there is a chapter dealing
with the phenomenon of improvising music and poetry in front of
listening audiences. The three following chapters are case studies
in literary creativity. The first two deal with Samuel Taylor
Coleridge's writing of *Kubla Khan* and Edgar Allan Poe's composition of *The Raven* respectively. These two well-known descriptions
can be seen as thesis and antithesis in a dialectical chain, the final
link of which is Paul Valéry's account of his prolonged work on
the poem *Le Cimetière marin*, amply corroborated by his manuscripts. The next two chapters deal with literary works that underwent genre transformations: Henrik Ibsen's play *Brand* began as an
epic poem, and Selma Lagerlöf's *Gösta Berlings saga* passed through
no less than three stages of development, from poem to play to
novel. Two concluding chapters summarize the results of the foregoing studies, introducing new material from the fields of music
and the visual arts, and providing a sketch for a general theory of
productivity. The final pages have as their title a quotation from
Kierkegaard: "Concluding Unscientific Postscript."

My background as a Scandinavian scholar may account for
numerous references to authors and authorities unknown to readers
outside the Scandinavian countries. For this book I excluded a

substantial number of quotations and references that appeared in the original Swedish version; those that remain will, I hope, seem naturally integrated in the context. Translations of all other non-English texts are by the translator unless attributed to a specific source in the corresponding note.

It should be pointed out that as an author I have followed a path in Swedish aesthetics that since the beginning of this century has attracted philosophers, art historians, and literary scholars intent on problems connected with "the birth of the work of art." If the term does not sound too pretentious, I should like to offer this book about the creative process contribution to the discipline of comparative aesthetics.

The translation of my book (originally published in 1974 by Norstedts, Stockholm, under the title *Diktaren och de skapande ögonblicken*) was made possible by a grant from the Swedish Humanities Research Council.

Finally I wish to record my profound gratitude to Dr. Karin Petherick, University College London, for translating the Swedish version, to Victoria Haire of the Editorial Department, University of Minnesota Press, for her unending labor with the manuscript, and to the University of Minnesota Press for publishing the volume.

Lund, Sweden   Carl Fehrman
August 1979

Contents

Poetic Creation
Inspiration or Craft

Documentation
and Experimentation

Investigating the creative process is exceedingly
difficult. In fact it is impossible to observe
the inner development of this process from the outside.
It is useless to attempt to follow the various
phases of somebody else's inner work.

Stravinsky
Der schöpferishe Akt in der Musik

1

Scholars have proceeded along a variety of paths in their attempts to gain knowledge of the creative process.

They have used the actual words of writers and artists in letters and autobiographical works.

They have then compared these pronouncements with available sketches, working papers, and successive manuscripts.

Professional psychologists have taken another approach. They, in interviews and experiments, have sought to trace the creative process and to investigate its conditions. Particularly in the United States creativity research has become something of a fashionable science.

Starting from different premises, linguists, aided by computers, have conducted experiments with the word mass a poem contains: they have shaken up the words more or less like dice. By imitating the creative process in this way—with the help of chance and certain programmed rules—they have sought to gain insight into the workings of the human mind at the moment of literary creation.

Comparative aesthetics offers yet another path. Scholars doing research in music and the visual arts have amassed and systematized a considerable body of material on the genesis of works in these two fields. This material and conclusions derived from it can to some degree be used to shed light on the writing of literature.

The subject of this introductory chapter are the five paths to knowledge outlined above.

2

Not until the romantic era did writers manifest a significant interest in the genesis of individual works of art. Rousseau is the first to be self-revelatory in this manner. His account in *Confessions* of the origin of his first prize-winning essay is the prototype of the accounts of inspiration that became so common among the romantics and succeeding generations.

In our time a considerable selection of authorial accounts and reflections have been collected in volumes with titles like *Poets on Poetry* or *Writers at Work*. In addition to providing an account of the authors' experiences, these reports offer interpretations of the creative process, and frequently they provide a perspective into the wellspring of the creative act. Yet the scholar has to deal warily with this material. For there can be a long period intervening between the genesis of a particular work and the account of this offered by its author. Such was true of Rousseau. Temporal distance facilitates rationalization and fantasy. For the memory of artists—perhaps particularly so—is selective. How the facts are then interpreted is determined by the public's expectations and by prevalent aesthetic conventions.

When writers, artists, and musicians wish to indicate how a work of art is created, they often have recourse to images. It is possible to identify two recurrent types of image. One, prevalent in the aesthetics of romanticism, consists of images taken from the world of growth, from organic life. The other belongs to the world of craftsmanship, industry and artifacts, and became common during the second half of the nineteenth century.

Metaphoric language derived from organic nature is already fully developed in the work of Edward Young, one of the founders of romantic aesthetics. In his 1759 essay *Conjectures on Original Composition*, he writes, "The mind of a man of genius is a fertile and pleasant field," and he continues, "An Original may be said to be of a *vegetable* nature: it rises spontaneously from the vital root of genius; *it grows, it is not made.*"[1] In Sweden Johan Henrik Kellgren, a leading critic and poet, used similar, more or less embryonic imagery in the 1790s when in his preface to *Fredmans epistlar* he spoke of Bellman's poems as though they had "sprung forth fully fashioned from the womb of a fiery imagination." Alfred de Vigny, a last-generation romantic, wrote in his *Journal d'un poète* (1836): "Je ne fais pas un livre. Il se fait. Il mûrit et croit dans ma tête *comme un fruit.*"[2] It is worth noting that the Vigny who here speaks so enthusiastically of creativity as a spontaneous act occasionally when he composed a poem first wrote a prose version, which he subsequently "translated" into poetry. This once again demonstrates that aesthetic convention and poetic reality are not always coextensive.

Two more examples of metaphorical language derived from the "organic" reasoning of the romantics are found in the work of a philosopher and a composer. Schopenhauer writes in *Parerga und Paralipomena*: "Das Werk wächst . . . wie das Kind im Mutterleibe. . . . So entsteht ein organisches Ganzes und nur ein solches kann leben."[3] Tchaikovsky writes in a letter (to N. v. Meck): "The seed of a coming work usually arises suddenly, quite unexpectedly. When the soil is favourable, that is to say when one is in the mood for work, the seed begins to root itself with amazing power and speed, it grows up from the soil, shows stem, leaves and branches, and finally flowers. I cannot describe the creative process by any other means than these images."[4] The metaphor has been absorbed into common linguistic usage when we speak of a literary work being *conceived* and of the *birth* of a work of art.

Comparisons and images of the second type are taken from the world of craftsmen, workshops, and artifacts. When Edward Young wishes to describe other, inferior literary works, which were *not* original creations but copies, he writes: "Imitations are often a sort of *manufacture*, wrought up by those *mechanics, art* and *labour*, out of pre-existent material not their own."[5] Young's use of technical metaphor is clearly derogatory.

In his book *Culture and Society* (1958), Raymond Williams draws attention to the sociohistorical background of the imagery and terms used by Young in a pejorative sense: "mechanics," "a sort of manufacture," "labour." Williams sees in them a reminder of the new industrial processes in society, from which the romantic poets from Young's generation on firmly dissociated themselves even to the extent of denying the importance of methodical work in artistic creativity. Instead they stressed the "organic" process of both literature and history.

It is an observable fact that the generations succeeding the romantics did not shrink from charging technical images with positive value. Flaubert, the indefatigable creative worker on the boundary between romanticism and the realist movement, gives the following testimony about his novels in a letter from 1857: "Les livres ne se font pas comme les enfants, mais *comme les pyramides*, avec un dessin prémédité et en apportant de grands blocs l'un par-dessus l'autre, à force de soucis, de temps et de sueur."[6] This is the writer on his/her way to becoming the equal of Sisyphus, or rather, an architect, a master builder, a constructor. That Flaubert happens to be a prose writer is of little consequence here. After his time, lyric poets like Edgar Allan Poe and Paul Valéry voiced the same view with similar imagery and did everything to sweep away the jargon of romantic aesthetics. Valéry repeatedly—and he is speaking of the lyric poet—calls the author an "engineer," an "unerring calculator," and he praises the architectural characteristics of Poe. Seen in this perspective, the poem itself becomes a mechanical product: "a sort of machine, designed to produce (in the reader) the poetic state with the help of words."[7]

Imagery deriving its comparisons from the technical and artifactual sphere has also been absorbed into common linguistic usage. The contemporary writer descends—both literally and metaphorically—to the shop floor. As early as 1914 Selma Lagerlöf published some manuscripts to *The Coachman (Körkarlen)* under the title "A Look into *the Workshop*." When Horst Bieneck in 1962 edited a collection of interviews with modern German authors he gave it the fitting contemporary title "Werkstattgespräche mit Schriftstellern." It is obvious that the two types of images—the organic and the technical—reflect basic dissimilarities in the aesthetic views of different generations of artists or different types of artists. During the romantic period the writer's creative activity was assumed to belong to a level of the personality not dominated by the intellect and calculation, in short, to the level of dreams and the subconscious. Technical imagery, on the other hand, seizes upon conscious artistic effort, on planning, craftsmanship, and literary technique. "Es dichtet in mir," declares Jean Paul,[8] the romantic, and the words have been repeated by many poets who have declared their allegiance to spontaneous inspiration. "Ein Gedicht entsteht sehr selten, ein Gedicht wird gemacht," replies the twentieth-century writer Gottfried Benn antithetically.[9] If one sought to harmonize the apparently irreconcilable opposites indicated by the metaphors, it would be possible to maintain that the two types of image relate to different stages of creative activity: the inspirational as opposed to the work stage, often two clearly discernible phases.

Besides the two contrastive types of image mentioned, a third type of metaphor has become common when speaking of the genesis of a work of art. A work of literature, visual art, or musical composition is said to have arisen through a *creative act*. This somewhat pale image owes its origin to mythological and theological beliefs.

The image of the writer as creator became common in the beginning of the eighteenth century. It implies an analogy between the activity of the writer and the cosmic powers. According to the Bible the first creator was God, who made heaven and earth out of nothing; according to Plato in his dialogue *Timaeus* the world's creator was the Demiurge. When the writer is seen as *creator*—and no longer as *imitator*—she/he is placed on a par with the cosmic creator. The writer becomes a god, albeit a smaller version of one. This view unites the eighteenth-century Platonist Anthony Ashley Cooper Shaftesbury, who called the poet "a second maker," and Edgar Allan Poe, who a hundred years later declared that human imagination to some extent corresponds to "the creative power of God." The analogy between poet and deity has lived on; in our century the Brazilian lyric poet Vincente Huidobro claims the role of a minor god on behalf of the poet.[10]

But this is mythical language. In a scholarly context the complex of ideas concerning the writer as creator has long since been demythologized. Whenever we still speak of the writer's creative moments, there are behind the words no cosmic or metaphysical claims on his/her behalf. They entail only the idea that a writer, with some degree of liberty, shapes a new poetic cosmos out of available material—words. The writer's creative act consists of this, and this alone.

3

The most direct evidence we have of writers' and artists' creative activity is found in sketchbooks and manuscripts, material more objective than stories and myths of creation. The literary scholarship of many nations contains a wealth of studies of the notebooks and manuscripts of individual writers. On the other hand, it can hardly be said that any generally accepted methodology has been arrived at for the manuscript study that aims to reveal the genetic processes or the writer's work habits.

Nevertheless, an attempt to systematize observations arising from such study has been made by Rudolf Arnheim. This is found in an essay in the book *Poets at Work*, written as a presentation of what at the time was the largest collection of contemporary literary manuscripts, The Modern Poetry Collection in Buffalo. In his theoretically based study, "Psychological Notes on the Poetical Process," Arnheim touches on a number of interesting approaches and problems.[11]

The very first impression of a manuscript is given by the handwriting. Arnheim observes that poets and writers are the last people to have mastered the dying art of writing by hand. His observation, made in 1948, probably still has some, albeit decreased, validity. "I write poetry by hand; prose I can easily type," the Danish author Klaus Rifbjerg told an interviewer a few years ago.[12] When Lawrence Durrell, also a few years ago, was faced with an interviewer's suggestive question "It's impossible to write a poem on a typewriter, isn't it?" he confirmed the impossibility of such an undertaking for his own part. He said that the poet George Barker was the only person he knew who provided an exception to the rule. T. S. Eliot was one of the exceptions; he explained in connection with his work habits that he too at certain times typed his poetry manuscripts.[13]

Undoubtedly, handwriting provides the scholar with more direct contact with the moment of creation than does the typed manuscript. Handwriting has its own system of signs, which occasionally can tempt one toward psychological interpretations. Manuscript scholars made an observation about Yeats, which doubtless has a more general application; his handwriting is often "an index of his inspiration;" after hesitant and uncertain—also calligraphically uncertain—lines with many crossings out and variants, there emerges, for instance in the poem *Sailing to Byzantium*, a firmer handwriting toward the end of the stanza, proof of the speed and confidence with which the poem was brought to a triumphant conclusion.[14]

Naturally, however, this calligraphic aspect applies only to a superficial level of the poem. The most important questions follow and concern what we can learn from the different, successive versions of a poem, from the author's alterations and reformulations. When Arnheim outlines the various types of alteration that a text undergoes at the hands of a writer, he draws attention to what might be called the law of binary alternatives. A lyrical text can be recast in a more subjective or objective form, become more private or more universal in its application, more compressed or expansive, more concrete or abstract in its attitude.

If we were to believe Freud, the earliest stages of the shaping of a poem would be those closest to the level of private daydreams and fantasies. Examination of many contemporary poets' manuscripts have proved Freud right to the extent that they demonstrate how the poet gradually strives to eradicate or minimize traces of his/her most private self. This can be done in a variety of ways, for instance, by the simple expedient of a pronoun change: an original "I" can be transformed into "you," whereby the poet can be said to include the reader in his/her experience and give the poem a general appeal it did not initially possess.

The reworking of a poem can of course—in direct opposition to Freud's belief—also proceed in the opposite direction, from a more generalized to an increasingly concrete private stance, to a naked disclosure of the original experience. The poem can become a form of private psychoanalysis, in which the poet drills deeper and deeper toward the center of his/her experience and has no hesitation in impressing upon it a highly personal mark. So over against the "general relevance factor" one can place the opposite, perhaps as frequently observable, possibility—the individualizing factor. Arnheim reminds us that a special case of this tendency occurs when contemporary visual artists deliberately leave a trace of their own hands' creative activity in the work of art, as when Rodin left the imprint of his chisel on a finished sculpture. It might be possible to discern an example of a similar tendency in the doodlings of concrete poets, seemingly identical with the text in the manuscript stage: a desire to allow the momentary private sphere, even including the stamp of a personal handwriting, to live on in the poem offered to the reader.

As already noted, other possibilities of poem transformations discussed by Arnheim include a move toward increased abstraction or concreteness in the presentation of reality. In addition, he suggests the possibility of tracing the growth and transformation of metaphors with the help of manuscripts. He also presents the case for a study systematically directed toward a poem's acoustic level, where alterations often—in connection with vocal harmonies, rhythmic effects, and rhyme—are extremely central. Arnheim's schema also gives prominence to the study of material that has been rejected as superfluous during the course of writing the poem and, conversely, of the new elements that have gradually been integrated into the final totality.

More than twenty-five years have passed since the appearance of *Poets at Work*, with Arnheim's essay. The intensive research that one might have expected on the extensive material systematically collected in The Modern Poetry Collection in Buffalo as well as on the even more extensive material of a similar nature now held by the University Library in Texas has—broadly speaking—failed to appear.

The difficulties of dealing with such overwhelmingly rich manuscript material are of course numerous. Even if the tens of thousands of alterations in the manuscripts were to be fed into a computer, there might still be doubt about what results would emerge of general relevance for the study of the creative process. On the other hand, it is not impossible that sufficient comparative material might provide new insights into writers' habits during different periods and in different literary movements. An extreme case amenable to such investigation would be the surrealists' alleged or genuine "automatic writing."

4

The majority of studies in this field deal with the manuscripts and work habits of individual writers. As a rule they permit no conclusions of a general nature. Yet they do in a number of instances allow us to compare the aesthetic pronouncements of certain poets with their poetic practice. Adherents of what in Scandinavia is called the "Aladdin myth" of the romantics, which prizes the person upon whom Fortune smiles as opposed to the "Noureddin" type, who toils and schemes in vain, are particularly interesting in this regard.

Shelley is a good example. We find ourselves in the rare research situation of possessing not only many of his manuscripts but also the notebooks in which he jotted down his initial poetic impulses. In other words, this material enables us to follow individual poems from original lines, which are frequently extremely fragmentary, through a series of alterations. Shelley had appealed to the greatest poets of his age and asked whether it was not a mistake to claim that the most beautiful passages of a poem had been created out of "labor and study." What have the unequivocal record sheets provided by the manuscripts to say on this point?

In his book *Shelley at Work* (1956), Neville Rogers carried out the taxing but rewarding work of examining in detail the twenty-six notebooks containing much of the raw material of Shelley's great poetry as well as his other manuscripts. The results are interesting. Two manuscript versions exist of the poem *To a Skylark*. Behind these lie the early impulses, recorded in the notebooks, in which the sporadic, often arbitrary nature of these impulses is strikingly demonstrated. It would appear that it was not the first stanza which occurred first to the poet—or was written down first—but instead some lines in what was to become the sixteenth stanza:

> Heaven is all above
> Yet that in thy joyance
> Langour cannot be.

This is followed in the notebook by the lines of the stanza that was to become the first, immediately followed by the stanza that would be the fifteenth. Here is the fragmentary form of the latter:

> Oh what thou art we know not
> But what is like to thee
> From the moon these flow not
> Clear
> The Silver
> As from thy presence showers quick melody.

This stanza truly can be described as being *in statu nascendi* both rhythmically and verbally, with mere verbal indications and numerous gaps. Shelley later returns to the stanza, fills in the gaps with new word combinations and euphony, and gives to the final line the rhythm which apparently was either not hit upon or not used in the initial stages:

> As from thy presence showers a rain of melody

—a closing line which has been said to possess something of the bird's own soaring flight.

Shelley's *Ode to the West Wind* shows the same sort of discontinuity in its generative stages, the same slow and gradual process toward completion. Neville Rogers found material for this poem in no fewer than five of the notebooks. To begin with, there are single short phrases that in a slightly changed form were to appear in the poem: "meeting branches," later to become "tangled boughs," "dead leaves" which become "the leaves dead." Sometimes single lines appear. One page bears the lone line:

> Lulled by the silence of his crystal streams.

The line is better known to us in another version and is one that might well be thought to provide a good example of what Valéry called a *vers donné*—if, that is, we did not know that it is a *vers calculé*:

Lulled by the coil of his crystalline streams.

Shelley's first thoughts were, if we are to judge by the words jotted down, swift, brief, and little formed. "When my brain gets heated with thought it soon boils and throws off images and words faster than I can skim them off;" Shelley's own description has the ring of truth about it. On the other hand, we should not entirely overlook the possibility that some of the words noted down by Shelley were primarily intended as mnemonics and that his inner flow of words might have been more connected and organized than the graphological signs indicate.

After the many single words, lines, and stanza fragments we come upon a preliminary, connected version of the *Ode to the West Wind* in the notebook Neville Rogers labeled the third. By now the earlier blank verse lines have been assembled into a *terza rima* pattern, and a draft of some fifteen to twenty lines has been written down, a draft which as yet has little resemblance to the finished poem. Later, in the same notebook, the poem is found at a crucial stage. It is a pencil sketch of the first three stanzas. The order of succession between them is clear and the final form seems to be in sight. If we are to speak of a definite breakthrough, it will most nearly apply to this stage of the poem's development. In the following notebook, which Neville Rogers numbers the fourth, we find these penciled stanzas neatly copied out. But it is not until a later notebook, number five, that the two final stanzas appear in a rough sketch. The closing line of the poem, "If Winter comes, can Spring be far behind?" has not yet been given its self-evident rhetorical form. It has the tamer, more trivial formulation: "When Winter comes Spring lags not far behind."

"Labor and study" show themselves, despite Shelley's contention, to lie behind the most famous lines of his major poems. There are other, private remarks by him that clearly indicate his awareness of the role played by work in the poetic creative process. He writes in a letter to Medwin, a friend who had noted his hypercritical attitude toward his own products: "The source of poetry is native and involuntary but requires severe labour in its development."[15] In its ostensibly simple formulation, this dictum says something essential about the dialectic involved in all poetic creation. Side by side with the aesthetics of inspiration, the mystique of the organic, to which the romantic poets professed verbal allegiance, is to be found a sure insight into the calculation, planning, and work entailed by poetry. In poems like *Ode to the West Wind*, all that was sporadic and discontinuous in its development has been entirely eliminated in the well-ordered shape of the final product, with its almost geometrically perfect structure.

5

Representatives of an "aesthetics of work"—a Valéry, a Yeats, an Auden—are less prone to the type of contradiction between the respective testimonies of mouth and hand mentioned above. Extant manuscripts of their work provide unequivocal testimony of "labor and study."

Yeats is a typical example. There are several studies of Yeats at work; the most thoroughgoing, written by John Stallworthy, is entitled *Between the Lines* and was published in 1963. The pattern of Yeats's creative activity, which Stallworthy examines, varied little during the course of his life. He often wrote preliminary prose drafts for his poems. (This practice is by no means uncommon among lyric poets; we know that Vigny did the same; we know from his own account that a poet like Robert Lowell, for some of his poems, used quite detailed prose drafts, containing some of the phrasing intended for inclusion in later poems.) After Yeats's prose version would come one or more verse drafts with a wealth of variants and excisions. Finally there would be a fair copy and first publication in a magazine, usually followed by further revisions before first publication in a book.

What makes Yeats's work so instructive and illustrative is that he appears, as Stallworthy points out, to have thought with his pen on paper; this provides the opportunity of following the play of associations, the growth of images and acoustic considerations at uncommonly close quarters. Throughout, Stallworthy makes the following observation: there is often a phrase, a couple of words, a line—a sort of nucleus—that is there from the very beginning and that Yeats clearly is at pains to find the right setting for. Another fact emerging from Stallworthy's investigation and that of others is that Yeats, like many contemporary poets, often during the course of working with a poem eliminates oversubjective elements, the direct traces of his private self.

Although Yeats' manuscripts contain a wealth of material, and although he decidedly thought with his pen, we cannot draw the simple conclusion that we have in front of us the total word-material behind his poems. For although with Yeats—as with Hebbel and the Goncourt brothers—we have access to a succession of notes from the first flashes of thought down to the final form, intermediate links and underlying intermediate stages, about which we can know little, are still missing. The same thing applies to the sketches of visual artists; here, too, we are confined to the stages that have been manifested to the eye. As a warning against exaggerated belief in what manuscripts can teach us, it may be worth recalling what Stravinsky once said: "Investigating the creative process is exceedingly difficult. In fact it is impossible to observe the inner development of this process from the outside. It is useless to attempt to follow the different phases of somebody else's inner work."[16] What we can observe are the footprints in the sand, not the runner, not the elasticity of the movement.

There are privileged instances in our own time when we have not only the writer's manuscript but also his/her commentaries to outlines and drafts. In a famous essay called *The Making of a Poem* (1946), Stephen Spender describes the notebooks into which he used to copy his poems, from the first impulses, through the various reworkings, up to the final version. He quotes extracts from his lyrical manuscripts and comments on the textual variants. "The method which I adopt", he writes, "is to write down as many ideas as possible in however rough a form in notebooks."[17] Spenders technique can be compared to what creativity psychologists call "brainstorming," a collective process in which all members of a group are given the chance to throw out ideas and suggestions, without an assessment of individual suggestions during the course of the flow. Stephen Spender gives free rein to his impulses and ideas, and does not subject them to critical scrutiny until the flow has ceased. Behind this process lies, as in all similar cases, the poet's conviction that his/her text can be improved, can attain a definitive form, faced with which s/he believes that nothing remains to be altered. Stephen Spender illustrates his method by setting out a series of images, each of two lines, in eight different versions. They are taken from a poem, which in turn has gone through twenty versions. Not until the final version did he succeed in recreating his vision, he tells us.

Spender is of course conscious of the fact that not all poets work in this way, just as his own method can vary from poem to poem. He draws parallels with the composing of music and refers to contrasting creative types represented by Mozart and Beethoven. It is known that Mozart claimed to receive his musical inspiration in the shape of whole pieces of music, which he wrote down as such. Beethoven, on the other hand, jotted down fragments of themes in his notebooks and worked on them for years, shaping and recasting them. Musicologists have had reason to wonder at how imperfect and even clumsy his first impulses appear to be—and how wonderfully they are transformed by the process of work. Stephen Spender's method is the opposite of Mozart's. He works deliberately, heavily, and methodically. For every poem he completes after many attempted variants, there are seven or eight that he never completes.

One observation remains concerning manuscripts and their investigation. The poems that by virtue of their genesis are the most remarkable—i.e., spontaneous poems, recorded improvisations—are the least interesting as manuscripts. Faced with one of them, we feel we are looking at a fair copy. The only difference appears to be calligraphical; the original may show signs of greater haste. The spontaneous poem never allows itself to be exposed by calligraphic means, however. Nor does it reveal itself by any particular structure. It simply exists. It is a rare specimen, but it would be unscientific to deny its existence.

6

A third path to knowledge of poetic creation was touched on earlier: psychological experiments and systematic interviews by optimistic creativity researchers in this century.

An early example of this kind of research is found in a small work by Catharine Patrick from 1935, *Creative Thoughts in Poets*. It is an attempt to study experimentally the writing of poetry, in part under laboratory conditions. Patrick, who evidently wrote poetry herself, collected a group of fifty-five poets and a control group of forty-eight nonpoets. The "poets" were to some extent professionals: they had all had one or two poems published in magazines. The control group consisted of people who had never written any poetry. Patrick's method was the following: she presented her subjects with a picture of a "romantic" landscape, with clouds, snow-capped mountains, waterfalls, and a foreground of pine forest and a plain. The experimental subjects were now told to write a poem about this landscape—painted in tones of green and blue—or about anything else that occurred to them as they gazed at it. Strangest of all, they were urged to speak aloud the whole time and articulate whatever occurred to them. The experimenter sat at a discreet distance and noted down in shorthand words and ideas and finally the completed poem, which—as had been agreed beforehand—should be at least four lines long. There was no time limit.

In addition to the poetry session, the subjects had the opportunity of filling in a questionnaire. The "poets" were asked if they normally completed the essential structure of a poem in one sitting or allowed the poem first to undergo an "incubation period," and if so, for how long. Another question concerned the "poet's" normal state of mind when composing; was his or her mood emotionally colored or cool and detached? Did some of the lines come spontaneously, of their own accord, as though they could not be expressed in any other way (Patrick had perhaps read one of Valéry's essays), and to what extent did the poets revise their products? Judiciously enough, this questionnaire was submitted only to the group of "poets" and not to the group whose members were making their first attempts at writing poetry.

Nobody would expect remarkable results from an experiment conducted under such crude conditions, nor were any forthcoming. According to Patrick, the most important result was that she thought she could discern certain temporally distinct stages in the act of poetic composition.

As a result of comparing the group of supposed poets with the control group, it emerged that the former produced poems "of greater artistic merit"—and who would have expected anything else? Two members of this group subsequently published, without revision, their poems written under these experimental conditions—which suggests a favorable publishing climate in 1935. Images, metaphors, and allegories proved to be more common amongst those who had written poetry previously; they were also at pains to open and close their poems with "stronger" lines; they were quicker and more dexterous at revising; and they were less bound by the stimulus provided by the picture itself. All except one of them claimed previous experience in producing the essential structure of a poem during one sitting—which is surprising; 90 percent felt that part of the experimental poem had come "automatically," 10 percent of the group did not feel this. Over 80 percent said they had been in an emotionally charged condition; the remainder had felt cool and detached.

Patrick's book is more of a curiosity than anything else, but it has been mentioned in the creativity literature ever since it appeared. During the 1960s and 1970s the creativity researcher Frank Barron has made use of considerably more sophisticated methods. For his investigations—which he has presented in a number of books[18]—he chose fifty-six professional writers and ten students attending a course in "creative writing." Of the professional writers, thirty had by common consent achieved recognition as writers of quality; the remainder were successful commercial authors. We are not told the names of the writers; Barron accords the epithet "creative" only to the thirty quality writers.

Frank Barron writes in his book *Artists in the Making* (1972), "By creative writing, then, we mean the composition of stories, essays, novels, poems or plays whose intent is to communicate the author's distinctive interpretation of experience." The definition assumes, Barron points out, "that individual differences be found in style, intent, quality, and reception of the work. In this presentation, however, we shall not be concerned with individual differences but with characteristics of creative writers as a class; or rather as representatives and agents of the creative spirit."[19]

When Barron set aside a group of thirty "creative" writers from the main group of "productive" ones, he had clearly made a value judgment. What the purely *literary* qualities of the thirty were, we have no means of knowing. Creative geniuses are rare in every generation and in every country; it would scarcely have been possible to trace thirty writers in this class (who in addition agreed to answer questions) at one and the same time in America. A group that had been classified as serious writers, not professional entertainers, by contemporary American critics, had to suffice.

With the aid of a list of one hundred statements, calculated to allow a clinical argument or diagnosis, Barron concludes that the thirty creative writers had five characteristics that distinguished them from the other group. They all appeared to have a large intellectual capacity; they genuinely valued intellectual and cognitive matters; they were verbally fluent; they enjoyed aesthetic impressions and were aesthetically responsive. Lower down on the scale of determining characteristics come such talents as getting things done (which publishers are likely to corroborate). Still farther down is a concern with philosophical problems, a high aspiration level, a wide range of interests, unusual ways of associating new ideas, and unconventional thought processes altogether.

These results, too, are unsensational and on the whole correspond with the generally accepted picture of authorial talent. That writers—compared with architects—are more verbally fluent and express their ideas more easily says little more than that they work with words as their material and have domain over the universe of words; whereas their colleagues, the architects, are sensitive to physical materials and to sense impressions of the world around them.

Faced with a test consisting of various figures, authors—like visual artists—preferred figures that were freely composed, asymmetric, or just generally provocative. Faced with a "symbol equivalence test," for which subjects were required to react to a stimulus picture by thinking of a symbolically equivalent one, the writers proved very original. A picture of leaves blowing in the wind could result in the symbolic equivalent: a civilian population fleeing chaotically from an armed attack. It is obvious during what period the experiment was conducted.

The creative writer group also gained a high score, which Barron specifically notes, for pathological indications and ego strength, and for such characteristics as flexibility, self-acceptance, achievement through independence. On the other hand, they achieved attractively low scores for "achievement through conformance," as well as for "socialization" (roughly a tendency to subordinate oneself to a dominating society or group).

Barron found that the most striking difference between writers and other creative groups was in the imaginative life of the writers and their intuitive and perceptive modes. Dreams proved to be of particular interest in the writer group. Writers dreamed more frequently than any other group, and they often dreamed in color. They tended to have recurrent dreams, repeated throughout their life. About 20 percent claimed to have dreams of a "prophetic" type, some of which Barron classed as examples of "precognition," whereas he more cautiously interpreted others as examples of dreams with an intuitive grasp of future possibilities. The writer group also provided a number of telepathic phenomena, of hallucinatory experiences, feelings of mystical oneness with the universe, but also of feelings of foresakenness and horror. Barron shows an interest in the possible creativity-intensifying power of certain hallucinatory drugs, used by some writers and artists. Let it once more be pointed out that Barron was writing in the United States of the 1960s and 1970s.

How far-reaching are the conclusions that can be drawn from Barron's material about the peculiarities of the creative writer group? A factor he never discusses or takes into account is what could be termed the generation factor. All his thirty, indeed all fifty-six, writers are *contemporary* authors, hence greatly influenced by the society, aesthetic conventions, and psychological situations of our time. A scholar with a historical perspective immediately asks to what extent Barron's results are conditioned by their period and to what extent they have a more general relevance. Would a writer from the classicist period, *le grand siecle,* have immediately preferred the asymmetrical figures to the others? Would a writer during the high tide of rationalism in the eighteenth century—the period of Voltaire—have demonstrated such marked divergences regarding telepathic phenomena, clairvoyance, feelings of desolation and alienation? Even if the reply in this case is hesitant, it is probable that writers in other climes and periods would have demonstrated marked verbal skill and imagination, aesthetic sensitivity, the gift of wide-ranging associations and of creative symbolism. For it is scarcely possible to conceive of an authorial talent lacking these characteristics. We may have known this before, but now with Barron's help we know it experimentally, which according to some currently favored theories of knowledge is regarded as an advantage.

In addition to his main undertaking of describing the creative writer group in comparison with other groups of individuals, Barron expressed another aim for his investigations: that of examining the creative process by means of detailed study of these writers' works, by means of interviews and through tests that required the ability to compose and that provided the opportunity for creative perception or production. Important components of the creative process were to be scrutinized: the author's conscious intentions, his/her preconscious and unconscious intentions, the significance of the writer's productivity in relation to his/her whole life cycle. Plus the choice of form for a literary work, important revisions, the role of self-criticism with particular regard to unfinished works, unexpected or unplanned alterations in the intentions or form of a literary work, sudden inspiration, time factors and emotional factors within the process, work intensity and emotional intensity, obstacles to creative work, periods when writing came more easily, the feeling that a work is finished or unfinished, and finally attitudes toward a work after its completion and publication.

The above list, published by Barron in the periodical *Money*, 1971, is a more or less complete inventory of interesting features forming a part of the creative process. An account of the results of *this* part of the investigations conducted on the fifty-six professional writers does not, at the time of the writing of this chapter, appear to have been published. Even without these results it is fair to say that creativity research has given and continues to give literary scholars occasion to reconsider their traditional approaches and possibly to relocate or shift the emphasis within a field like that of literary biography. In an account of a writer's life the scholar should more deliberately consider the factors in the environment, i.e., childhood, home, and society, that favor and increase—or paralyze—

the writer's creative powers. The findings of creativity researchers should also lead literary scholars with an interest in psychology to seek to establish the rhythm of productivity and improductivity within a life cycle, often connected both with outer factors and with an inner, biological rhythm. A long row of questions await answers: when, at what age, does a writer produce his/her best works, when are the writer's creative powers at their peak—once, twice, or on several occasions during his/her lifetime—and when and how slowly do they diminish?

Creativity researchers recommend two methods for sparking the creative process. One of them is "brainstorming," already mentioned; the other is the "synectic" method.

In brainstorming, as has been indicated, all members of a group are urged to throw out a constant stream of ideas to find a solution for a particular problem. The salient point is that the stream of ideas is allowed to flow freely, unhampered by assessment from individuals or the group, and that no contribution may be subjected to criticism or self-criticism. A parallel was drawn in the previous section between the collective form of brainstorming and Stephen Spender's individual strategy of opening the sluice gates for his free-flowing ideas. The manuscripts of many other writers suggest the application of a like method. Manuscripts by the Swedish poet Gustav Fröding, for instance, with lists of rhymes jotted in the margin, mechanically listed on acoustic principles, seem proof that he worked in a similar way: on the free flow principle. Not until he had tested and evaluated the resources of the language—in this instance the limited frame of possibilities afforded by rhyme—did he pick a rhyme and then proceed with the poem.

In creativity terminology "synectics"[20] means the strategy which in the solving of a problem renders the unfamiliar familiar, while that which is accustomed becomes strange. What is aimed at is a complete shift of perspective, which enables a new and unusual solution. The strategy called synectics is reminiscent of what is known as "deformation" in formalist-structuralist literary aesthetics. The word "deformation" has no pejorative connotation in this connection: it merely observes that a neutral material has been reshaped in order to gain an aesthetic function. One of the first scholars who drew attention to this factor was Viktor Shklovskij, in his essay "On the Devices of Art." There he writes that "the function of art is to communicate a feeling of the object as vision, not as recognition; art's mode of procedure, its device, is 'alienation' of the object and the 'deliberately complicated form'."[21] Shklovskij illustrates his theory of how the familiar is rendered unfamiliar with examples from prose literature, for instance, works by Tolstoi and Gogol. He also hints that metaphor in poetry can be seen in the same light. An image can make the accustomed seem strange, or the unfamiliar familiar, simply by changing the perspective. Particularly innovative literary works that have broken with tradition could with advantage be studied from the angle that in creativity research is called "synectics" and in formalist theory "deformation."[22]

7

The fourth type of experiment consists of computer-aided attempts at "simulating" poetic creativity; in short, letting computers write poems to see what can be learned about the stream of words that have been organized into poetry.[23]

A computer is provided with a so-called random number generator, which the computer-poet utilizes. The scope allowed to chance is, however, limited from the start by the rules embodied in the programming. In other words, this is "directed" or "programmed" chance.

If a computer program produces a number of sentences that are syntactically well formed and then gradually introduces arbitrarily selected words in syntactically correct positions in the sentences, a certain semantic glide, which strongly resembles poetic effects, will be the result. If the computer programmer wishes the text to approximate poetry, it is not sufficient, however, to produce isolated sentences. For the rules of poetry place certain demands on rhythm or meter, style and imagery. The mathematician Theo Lutz of Standard Electric's Computer Center in Stuttgart has by means of deliberate aesthetic programming, which takes some account of these factors, produced the following computer poem:

Not every glance is close. No town is late.

A castle is free and every living is remote.

Every stranger is remote. One day is late.

Every house is dark. An eye is deep.

Not every castle is old. Every day is old.

Not every guest is raving. A church is narrow.

No house is open and not every church is still.

Not every eye is raving. No glance is new.

Every road is close. Not every castle is slow.

etc.

The words in the poem are from the first page of Kafka's *The Castle.* The actual volume of words is relatively limited. Words are played out against each other in changing constellations. The text has a certain structural coherence owing to the repetition of its various elements and the tension arising between them; it can be seen that all the sentences have been formulated as logical assertions. The semantic effects in the poem are the same as those in much late twentieth-century poetry; the rise of the computer industry coincided by chance with a point in time when poetry had assumed a form copyable by a computer.

It appears to be more difficult for a computer to produce logically coherent poems in set meters. One of the Anglo-Saxon specialists on "poetry generation," Louis T. Milic, based an experiment on a four-line rhyming stanza by Blake. Rhymes from rhyme lists were fed into the computer, and in the short form of four lines composed of two sentences, the machine wrote an acceptably coherent poetic text. With longer texts, the trouble appears to be that the computer repeats itself more than human beings do. Innovative, meaningful, in the true sense of the word "creative" impulses appear to be, at least for the time being, the prerogative of the human brain. Or to put it more humbly, humans have an advantage in their selective and judgmental faculty.

In an essay in the journal *Computers in the Humanities*, Milic summarizes some of the theoretical results of experiments in computerized poetry composition to date. He does not overestimate the poetic worth of the products; he harbors no illusions, as he puts it, that he with the aid of these computerized poems will gain a place beside Pope, Shelley, and the other inhabitants of Mount Parnassus. The greatest appeal and value of this kind of poetry derives from what it can teach us about the shaping of poetry, the conditions and prerequisites of the poetic word stream.

In his experiments Milic starts with poems already written and completed by humans. For instance, he takes a poem by Dylan Thomas in order to generate a new poem, letting noun change place with noun, verb with verb, adjective with adjective. He can do this with some justification, since Dylan Thomas is reported to have proceeded at times along similar, experimental lines. An early friend of Dylan Thomas's says that he sometimes was concerned simply with producing pure word patterns, poems whose effects were based on unusual word combinations and word positioning. He might even start with a rhyme series and then fill in the remaining words. He sometimes sketched out a stanza, leaving a few gaps. He had a notebook, which he called his dictionary and in which he noted down a host of quite ordinary, frequently short words. When he wished to fill in a gap in a stanza, he would look in his dictionary and try one word after the other. If nothing would do, he might try to find a word listening to the conversation of others, and as a final expedient he might open a book at random and try the first word on each page. One could even go so far as to say that Dylan Thomas—and no doubt a number of other poets—unknowingly "simulated" a random creative process resembling that of a computer. Or perhaps it would be truer to say that since humans have built computers, the latter's manner of functioning has certain similarities with that of our own brains and hence of course with the way a poet's brain works.

In one of his experiments Milic, as stated, uses a Dylan Thomas poem, which the computer alters by a series of permutations. With the help of a sufficiently sophisticated method, it might be possible, he suggests, to produce new "poems" by Thomas, which could pass as genuine examples of his style and work. The same method has in fact been used to produce computer-composed music in the "style" of Mozart and Haydn.

One of Milic's colleagues produced a number of poems of Japanese haiku type. He used a vocabulary garnered from an anthology of haiku poems and instructed the computer to observe syntactical rules and to produce three-line verses of seventeen syllables. The result was four thousand haiku. The experimenter sent some of the ones he considered best to a student literary magazine; they were not printed, whatever the reason for this may have been.

In his last experiment Milic started with a poem by a contemporary writer, Alberta Turner, entitled *Return*. Milic fed its words, both singly and in phrases, into the computer. During the course of the experiment these words appeared in new combinations—still in accordance with the programming, grammatically and syntactically impeccable but naturally with bolder word combinations, with little or no meaning in ordinary language. A few concrete examples can illustrate the mutations undergone by the poem.

In the original poem, *Return*, one line read:

> Hemlocks are nearly round,

another:

> Have I planted crowbars under my porch?

a third:

> Yesterday I saw the weathercock

and a fourth:

> Apple twigs are cut.

Redisposed, but still syntactically correct, these lines are turned by the computer into a poem, which Milic humorously calls, *Returner three*:

> Yesterday hemlocks planted all the apples at home yet
> They often turn crowbars
> Today.

Possibly the most interesting aspect of the experiment is that Milic believes that he, after a sufficient number of sophisticated maneuvers, would be able to *reproduce* the poem *Return* in its original version! The computer would then undeniably have done its utmost. But not only that. Milic assumes—with some justification—that on the return journey to *Return 1* he would have produced all possible early stages of the poem, including the original, alternative versions that the manuscripts would provide if they were still in existence; on the other hand, it is self evident that the computer would not be able to say *which* stages the poem had in fact undergone. There is of course a shortcoming in this hypothetical experiment, which Milic does not appear to have considered. For the experiment presupposes that Alberta Turner worked with a fixed and constant vocabulary throughout, the one found in the final poem, and that during the various stages of the poem's inception the words merely changed places. This in itself is a highly unlikely supposition. If all words present in Turner's consciousness, in her brain and on paper when she was shaping her poem, all tested and rejected words, were to be reproduced, it would obviously require the further feeding of a large number of synonyms into the computer. One asks oneself how this could be done, and to what purpose. From the standpoint of work efficiency, a study of the manuscripts—if available—would undoubtedly be simpler.

One can take experiments of this kind with greater or lesser seriousness. It is not inconceivable that at some future time they, in conjunction with structural linguistics, may be able to lead to new insights into the manner in which poets arrange words into poems. We can perhaps already venture to say this much as a result of computerized verbal experiments: all poetry arises from the interplay of rational rules and irrational chance. The history of literature shows us the rules. Chance has had a variety of names: at times it has been ennobled by the name inspiration; at other times it has simply been called chance—as, for instance, when Strindberg wrote a programmatic essay entitled *Du hasard dans la production artistique*. In it he recounts that carpet weavers have used kaleidoscopes to discover new patterns, and he draws conclusions about the role of chance in the writing of literature. So far, however, computer composed poetry better illustrates the concept of imitation than the concept of creation.

8

The fifth path to knowledge about the process of literary creation, as noted at the beginning of this chapter, involves insights derived from comparative aesthetics, primarily in the fields of musicology and art history. That the laws followed by literary creation should be the same as, or resemble, those governing artistic and above all musical creation is a very likely hypothesis.

The German musicologist Julius Bahle has examined the process of musical creation. In 1936 he published the work *Der musikalische Schaffensprozess*; three years later came the book *Eingebung und Tat im musikalischen Schaffen*. He covered the same field in a 1936 article in *Acta psychologica*.[24] Bahle's method is experimental yet avoids the pressures of a laboratory atmosphere. He calls it "remote experiment" (Fernexperiment). He has collated the results of his experiments with remarks on the creative process by composers from different periods.

Bahle sent a letter, in which he suggested that a poem be set to music, to a number of German and foreign composers. He had selected eight modern German poems, by authors such as Max Dauthendey, Hermann Hesse, Kurt Klaeber, Georg Trakl, and Manfred Hausmann; these were fairly short texts, suitable for setting to music. He asked the composers who undertook the assignment to give a detailed account of how their musical composition took shape, and he gave as his motive a desire to get beyond current, often speculatively theoretical and very general hypotheses about artistic creation. At the same time he provided the composers with a list of items for self-analysis. They were to state what had moved them to their particular choice among the texts; in what way the poem appealed to them; and which were the most important formative stages (*Entstehungsphasen*) in the composition of their *Lieder*. They were also to describe the relationship of their composition to the text, for instance, the ways in which the text had stimulated their creativity—rhythmically, acoustically, melodically—and to what extent the new tone-poem sought to reflect the mood and ideational contents of the poem. The composers were to note to what degree musical material, which already had been of interest to them, was embodied in the new composition; if during the process of composition they had felt themselves dependent on and inspired by earlier or contemporary composers or had drawn on earlier works of their own, if they had consciously observed any particular aesthetic norms or principles.

The letter was sent to some thirty contemporary composers, including Casella, Honegger, Krenek, Schönberg, and R. Strauss, and in reply Bahle received twenty-seven new compositions. Eighteen composers had used one of the suggested texts as a basis for their work; the remaining nine had taken advantage of the option, provided by Bahle, of choosing a text themselves. In addition, Bahle received self-analyses of the creative process from most of the composers; he had referred to André Gide's *Logbook of the Coiners* as a model of the sort of accounts he deemed it possible for a creative artist to provide. Having received the compositions and the *Schaffensberichte*, Bahle proceeded by means of further written questionnaires, followed by conversations with the composers, in which he also touched on their instrumental music and the composition of works already finished by them as well as works in progress.

According to Julius Bahle, the main finding of his study was that the psychological side of musical composition shows greater uniformity than might have been expected. To check the validity of available results and posited hypotheses, Bahle assembled extensive historical material that throws light on the creative activity of famous composers. He collected items, from letters, diaries, and autobiographies, describing the development of specific musical works. Above all, he sought out accounts that were contemporaneous with the composition of the pieces in question and that thus had a certain likeness to material from his interviews. Bahle's aim was consistently to give an authentic picture of musical-artistic creativity and to analyze a number of concepts in musical aesthetics, like "impulse," "inspiration," and "unconscious growth," that had not previously been closely scrutinized.

One could object—and this has indeed been done—that Bahle with his method dealt only with an assignment situation, with how composers work when subject to an external stimulus—in this instance the texts provided. On the other hand, he did give them the option of choosing their own text for a *Lied*. Moreover, it is a musical as well as a literary fact that many works have been generated by external commissions. So the situation was not entirely artificial.

It is of course a limitation of Bahle's study that on the whole he had to confine himself to observing how *one* already finished artistic impulse—of a literary nature—was transformed into another medium—that of music. But this does make it possible to observe composers' attitudes toward texts from which they choose and reject material, and to what extent they feel bound by the mood or form of the texts. In these respects the composers provided interesting answers. They also recounted a good deal about their external working conditions, about the rhythm of their creativity within the twenty-four-hour span, and about existential experiences connected with their work.

Bahle's most interesting observations from our point of view, since they have direct equivalents in the sphere of poetic creativity, are those about the process itself, about the nature and length of creative impulses, and about the relationship between impulse, inspiration, and work.

Phenomenologically speaking, the musical impulse appears, to the person subject to it, as something sudden, surprising, and inexplicable; it presents itself "like a spirit at a seance," in the words of one of the interviewees. The literary impulse has often been described in similar terms. Clearly the "mystical" nature of these impulses has led to all manner of fantastic assumptions and mythologies in the history of both music and literature. Bahle takes it upon himself to demythologize the creative process. It appears that musical impulses are always short: a phrase, a motif, or a theme of two to four bars, say those questioned; Beethoven's notebooks suggest a similar state of affairs. It is characteristic of the impulses to arise suddenly. But the suddenness is not in itself a criterion of their worth: there are worthless musical impulses, just as there are valuable ones. Selective and corrective artistic reason later decides what can be utilized. Impulses are not always fully fashioned when they arise; there are primitive *Vorformen*, which cannot be retained in their original form. On the other hand, it is also not uncommon to find premusical, abstract-schematic *Gestaltüberlegungen* preceding musical impulses when setting a text to music.

Bahle regards the musical "translation" of a text—or of an experience—as a *Gestaltübertragung* in line with the creation of symbols. In several reported cases a linguistic rhythm gave rise to a musical one; words or word groups became the nucleus from which a musical impulse was developed. The view held by Bahle, as against a number of older aestheticians, for instance Volkelt, is that the best impulses arise from previous deliberation, as a result of work already commenced. Within the musicological field such impulses are termed "disciplined improvisation." One of Bahle's well-founded cardinal tenets is that conscious, preconscious, and unconscious levels, spontaneous impulses, as well as technical expertise and work, all merge in the composer's activity.

Finally he devotes a largely semantic analysis to what the composers mean by the so frequently used and abused word "inspiration," a word representing many different experiences and types of experience during the creative process.

Bahle's experimental methods and sober observations have not gone unchallenged. The composer and music theoretician Hans Erich Pfitzner responded in a work called, programmatically, *Über musikalische Inspiration*. He dissociated himself strongly from the method of presenting composers with texts in order to investigate inspiration. The born composer has creative impulses because s/he is born to compose, declared Pfitzner; impulses do not arise because someone *wants* to compose and exerts her/himself to do so. He quotes Max Reger, who claimed that one creative impulse is dearer to him than a hundred thousands tons of musical work. Pfitzner altogether defends the aesthetics of inspiration as opposed to that of work; he quotes Goethe's words in *Zahme Xenien 3: "All unser redliches Bemühn/Glückt nur im unbewussten Momente"*; and he contends that roses would not bloom if they had knowledge of and insight into the nature of the sun. From Schopenhauer's *Parerga und Paralipomena* he quotes a passage about the work growing like a child in its mother's womb, without the mother understanding what is going on inside her, and he lets Ibsen second this with words from his play *The Pretenders*: "Indeed, my lord, no poem is born in day-light; it can be written down in sunshine, but it writes itself in the still of the night."[25]

The sort of objections raised by Pfitzner against the artificiality of the experimental situation has already been noted and answered above. When Pfitzner bombards us with quotations about the mysterious night of creation, about the role of the unconscious and the organic nature of creativity, he has one-sidedly chosen quotations to represent his point of view. Clearly he himself is the type of artist who finds his creativity best expressed and interpreted by "organic" metaphors and images, of which he quotes a large number. But it goes without saying that had he been another variety of artist and belonged to a different artistic tradition, he could have found an equal number of quotations describing works of art as artifacts, as products of conscious labor and artistic planning. Bahle's methodology cannot be challenged by such simple means as a collection of metaphors.

More interesting are Pfitzner's views on some of the historical documents used by Bahle. This applies, for instance, to Bahle's comments on Beethoven's famous notebooks and the information to be gained from them. Can one, asks Pfitzner, regard them as a means of getting to know Beethoven's musical impulses, as Bahle inter alia has tried to do? Pfitzner quotes the editor of the notebooks, who stresses that these working papers do *not* reveal the "inner" law by which Beethoven was guided during composition, as follows: "We must therefore make it clear to ourselves that they are silent about a great deal, and that we least of all can expect to derive from them experiences of all that (in creativity) is termed organic."[26] Pfitzner himself believes that the composer's notebooks allow us to see a grappling with form rather than any creative impulses. The same could justifiably be said of many extant *literary* drafts. They allow us to observe the shaping, development, and alterations of a work of art rather than its genesis and "birth."

In addition to musicology, the history of art provides material and arguments of considerable interest to those who wish to study the processes of literary creation. I have in mind particularly the book by Ragnar Josephson, the distinguished Swedish art historian, entitled *The Birth of the Work of Art (Konstverket födelse)* and published in 1940. Already in the 1930s Josephson had laid the foundations of the museum of sketches and preliminary studies that was to become the Archive for Decorative Art in Lund. His plans and strategy had a certain similarity to those of Charles Abbot, who—at exactly the same time—built up the huge collection of literary manuscripts in Buffalo. These two gentlemen were almost certainly unaware of each other's existence and plans, but the temporal coincidence of their projects is worth thinking about. Ragnar Josephson collected sketches for subsequently completed works of visual art, i.e., sequences of drawings, paintings, and models for sculptures. Initially the material was primarily Swedish and Scandinavian, but the geographical boundaries were later extended.

In his book *The Birth of the Work of Art*—his crowning achievement, which his museum work had led up to—Ragnar Josephson examines the process of artistic creation by using concrete material, supplemented by the artists' own observations. Ragnar Josephson's purpose is not only to trace the genesis and developmental stages of individual works of art, but if possible to discover or approach the inner laws that apply to and partly govern the processes of creation. He is above all interested in the successive transformations undergone by a work of art between the stages of sketch and completion. These phases are fairly easily discernible in the artists' sketches. Josephson groups the various stages under these telling titles: transformed model, the creative moment, displacement, crossing, filling in, rearrangement, and cohesion.

In the chapter about the transformed model he examines the way in which an artist during the initial act of copying makes discoveries that lead him/her to a new, independent vision. An example of this is provided by van Gogh's *The Sower*, which ultimately derives from Millet's painting of the same name. In the literary field the same or similar types of shift, from a predominantly imitative stance to an independent conception, is found very often in motif research. Folktale material or a mythological theme taken from traditional sources can be used by the author in new and surprising ways. Later generations of poets have not only copied but also transformed the Faustian material of the folk legend as well as the stories in Ovid's *Metamorphoses* of Narcissus, Icarus, and a host of other well-known figures.

In his chapter "The Creative Moment," Josephson studies those elements of movement and gesture in the sketches which with sudden and seemingly inevitable naturalness lead to completely unexpected solutions; he gives examples from, among others, Leonardo and Michelangelo. The creative moment is the moment of "illumination," found in numerous accounts in biographies of inventors, writers, musicians, and visual artists.

By "displacement" Josephson means the not unusual situation in which a secondary motif is pushed aside or even eliminated, since there is no room for it in the work in question, but then crops up again and becomes the main motif in a later work by the same artist. The history of literature is full of examples of this. To give one: Thomas Mann recounts in brief a legendary tale from the medieval collection *Gesta romanorum* in his novel *Doktor Faustus.* When he soon afterward builds an entirely new novel, *Der Erwählte*, on the same story, this very "displacement" which Josephson speaks of in *The Birth of the Work of Art* has taken place. By "crossing" or fusion he has in mind a phenomenon similar to the one Freud studied in dreams and called condensation: two persons, two unrelated styles, are merged into a new unity. When Lowes in his well-known book *The Road to Xanadu* (1927) studies Coleridge's poems and shows how he threw into his poetic melting pot a series of fragmentary memories from a number of old travel accounts, Lowes, too, has undertaken a study of crossing and fusion, of the conscious and unconscious condensatory processes of the imagination.

It might indeed be claimed—and the idea was not foreign to Josephson—that a majority of the methods he tried out in *The Birth of the Work of Art* had already been used and developed in the genetic study of literary works. But what he did was to clarify these methods with exceptional precision by applying them to highly tangible and visible material, i.e., artists' "manuscripts." In this way he was able to pass back insight to scholars dealing with literary creation.

Improvisation — Rite and Myth

*I had scarcely expected to see poetic rapture
so vividly enacted.*

> G. G. Adlerbeth
> (eighteenth-century Swedish author)
> *Letter from a Swede about
> His Visit to Italy*

1

Are there any other means of gaining knowledge about a work of literature at its moment of inception, apart from the ways indicated in the first chapter?

At a certain stage of its genesis a literary work, whether prose or poetry, consists of a stream of inner words. Admittedly, these words are already to some extent structured rhythmically, acoustically, and figuratively, but they still have to overcome the barrier of being written down. Is it possible to know anything about the word stream before it becomes set in its written form? The attempt, described in the previous chapter, of an American psychologist to acquire knowledge about the spontaneous word flow of poets was hardly a success; she let a number of people who had been directed to write a poem think aloud while she sat discreetly in a corner and took notes. This was before the era of the tape recorder, but even with one the experiment would have smacked too much of an artificial laboratory atmosphere.

There is one situation, however, in which a poet or musician spontaneously communicates his/her work at the moment of its creation—and this is when s/he improvises. In the annals of literary history only cursory interest has been demonstrated in the art of improvisation. Yet the neglect is understandable, since the material, i.e., the improvisations, by their very nature are gone with the wind.

The concepts "to improvise" and "improvisation" are defined in the same way in musicology and the literary field. That person improvises who simultaneously composes and executes an unwritten piece of music or literature, and all genuine improvisations have in common speed, spontaneity, and an absence of premeditation. This is stressed in the terminology of a variety of languages: *all'improviso, impromptu, ex tempore, sur le champ, aus dem Stegreif.* Improvisation is essentially the opposite of the slower, reflective composition anchored in a visible medium; on the other hand, an improvisation can, of course, be a preliminary stage or exercise prior to composition. The Swiss musicologist Ernst Ferand, who has studied the technique and history of improvisation in many weighty works, describes musical improvisation as a sort of "musical reflex action."[1] He also stresses that the most gifted improvisers in the musical field are likely to have auditive-motor talents. Their inner auditory images are immediately transformed into a pattern of movement, for example, the play of fingers on keyboard or strings. There is every likelihood that the gift of improvisation in words is also an auditive-motor talent.

But an improvisation never arises in a vacuum. Improvisation, be it literary, musical, or visual, requires two things: a technique and a tradition. The two concepts frequently go together: the improviser has learned his/her technique from tradition. Even improvisational artists need a certain degree of knowledge and experience in arranging sounds, words, forms, or colors. Musical improvisation in particular has been subject to certain strict laws and forms ever since medieval times in Europe. Similarly, the literary improvisations of professional improvisers have been form-bound and formula-bound as far back as we are able to trace them. In a way this strange fact—the interplay of a free flow of notes or words and strictly given forms—throws light on the inner dialectic of creativity, which can be observed as well at other, more conscious stages in the history of music, literature, and art.

Improvisations are carried out according to a given ritual pattern. What distinguishes them is not only the suddenness and speed of their invention but also the uninterrupted, never-ending flow.

An improviser—like a practiced speaker—never dries up. One note breeds another, one word another, one phrase calls forth another in a sort of endless chain reaction. The precondition for this is—let us repeat—that the performer possesses a practiced technique, which has become something of a second nature. Improvisation is only seemingly effortless.

The literature of musical history is full of accounts—from Landino to Bruckner—of the fascination exerted by the improvised work of art on a group of listeners. The feeling of being present at and experiencing a work *in statu nascendi* has undoubtedly contributed to the enthusiasm reflected in contemporary accounts. An intimate relationship arises between the improviser and his/her public; a chain of contact is established, with current flowing in both directions. The improviser affects the listeners, who affect the improviser through a sort of psychic feedback mechanism, which is well known from the theater.

The history of music contains well-known accounts of Bach, Mozart, Beethoven, and Liszt as improvisers. It was said of Johann Sebastian Bach that his improvisations on the organ, during which "everything sprang directly to life through his imagination," were more full of devotion, solemnity, and dignity than the compositions written down in musical notation.[2] We know of the infant prodigy Mozart that he already at age five improvised on given themes in every key. Beethoven was one of the best-known improvisers of his time, as a series of descriptions by contemporary and discriminating listeners testifies. An observation by Beethoven himself shows that he regarded improvisation as a type of psychic automatism: "Strictly speaking improvisation only takes place when one is not thinking of what one is playing."[3] Liszt was one of the most celebrated improvising pianists of his generation; one of his female listeners tells us that on the not infrequent occasions when he happened to strike a wrong note, he would save himself by a superior smile and an astonishingly witty musical turn, an instantaneous creative response of a simple or more complex nature. In this way even chance, a slip of the hand, or some technical mishap can lead the improviser to new achievements; a discordant note is dissolved or built into the theme through repetition or stress.

The musical ability to improvise has been valued very differently from one period to another. There were times when it was regarded as a danger to the genuine composer. At other times music teachers have understood that improvisation can stimulate original creation; in this respect Rousseau and Dalcroze were notable examples.

There are a number of striking similarities between musical and literary improvisation. Just as an audience could provide Mozart or Liszt with themes for improvisation, so professional literary improvisers were presented with subjects or themes. And just as musical improvisations were often executed in closed and given forms— Mozart frequently used the fugue, Beethoven the sonata or rondo —so professional literary improvisations were rendered in the traditional forms.

Best known are the professional literary improvisers of Italy and Germany of the eighteenth and nineteenth centuries.[4] They practiced their art in front of a listening audience, but were unwilling to compete with professional poets, unwilling to set down their ideas on paper. In the long list of improvisers from these two countries, there are only a few exceptions who simultaneously were poets using the written language as a medium. This, of course, is a crucial difference between the musical and literary traditions. Within the Western musical tradition the paths have not diverged in the same way as in literature—we have already noted a number of composers who alternately performed as improvisers in front of an audience and as composers at home. The history of music can equally point to numerous examples of compositions that are nothing more than the notational form of an improvisation; Bach's *Musikalisches Opfer* is the classic example. In the history of literature, on the other hand, it is probably necessary to go all the way back to renaissance poetics to find the demand, as in Scaliger, that a first-rate poet should also be able to extemporize. During the ensuing centuries, with the supremacy of classicist aesthetics, it became more and more unusual for one and the same poet to perform in both roles. Not until the advent of the romantic tradition do we find new examples of writers active in the fields of both improvisation and literary composition; Bellman, the Swedish eighteenth century poet, and Burns, Brentano, and for that matter, H. C. Andersen could all be named as signs that the two paths had converged again. The romantic era provides many examples of literary works that are, or are claimed to be, written manifestations of a spontaneous word flow.

In attempting to arrive at a picture of the professional improviser in action, the first thing to do is to turn to Italian documents of the eighteenth and early nineteenth centuries. We are not concerned here with the traditional Italian play, the *commedia dell'arte*, in which actors in set roles improvise their lines. It is more profitable to examine the solo performance of poets who, in front of an audience, extemporize narrative, lyrical, and dramatic pieces of considerable length on prearranged subjects. Most of the detailed accounts of such improvisational sessions come from travelers.

An early key witness is the French man of letters Charles de Brosses, who traveled in Italy during the years 1739 and 1740. In his account of his travels he provides the following picture of one of the most famous contemporary Italian improvisers in action: Bernardo Perfetti. Born late in the seventeenth century Perfetti died in 1747. De Brosses writes of him:

> The strangest spectacle that has been afforded us during our stay in Siena has been given us by signor Perfetti, a professional improviser. You know these poets who amuse themselves by composing on the spot [*sur-le-champ*] an impromptu poem on whatever subject you present them with. We gave Perfetti the Northern Lights as subject. He sat dreaming, with bowed head, for some eight minutes, while a clavichord played a muted prelude. Then he got up, quietly began to declaim stanza by stanza in ottava rime, still accompanied by the clavichord, which struck chords during his recital and continued to play a prelude so as not to leave empty intervals between the stanzas. To begin with the stanzas succeeded one another quite slowly. But gradually the poet's rapture increased and gradually as it became more violent, the accompaniment on the clavichord grew louder. Toward the end this remarkable man declaimed like a poet full of enthusiam [*comme un poète plein d'enthousiasme*]. The accompanist and the improviser left the concert with remarkable speed. Afterward Perfetti appeared to be exhausted; he has told us that he does not often like to make these attempts, which tire both body and soul. He is reckoned to be one of Italy's most skillful improvisers. His poem gave me great pleasure; its swift declamation struck me as mellifluous, full of thoughts and images.[5]

Following this account of his first impressions, de Brosses describes the contents of the poem and the impression it made. But at the end he voices a reservation. Perfetti, he tells us, had never wished to write down his poems, and the pieces that were stolen from him when he recited them had not lived up to their promise during the actual declamation.

This account is interesting from several standpoints, for instance, in the way it notes the ritual followed by the improviser. The interplay between music and literary invention is important; the accompanying clavichord music not only fills in the pauses but clearly also acts as a stimulant. Important, too, is the close relationship between improviser and public. The audience was magnetized by the performer's poetic frenzy, particularly in the thundering closing stages.

Another traveler, Tobias Smollett, tells us more about the form of improvisations in his *Travels through France and Italy*. He describes an improvisational session he attended during a visit to Florence in January 1765. This time the improviser was a Franciscan monk, who was accompanied by a violin player. Having been given his subject, writes Smollett, "he will, at a minute's warning, recite two or three hundred verses, well turned, and well adapted, and generally mingled with an elegant compliment to the company. The Italians are so fond of poetry, that many of them have the best part of Ariosto, Tasso and Petrarch by heart; and these are the great sources from which the improvisatori draw their rhymes, cadence, and turns of expression."[6]

An interesting and undoubtedly correct observation is that the meter, *ottava rima*, facilitated the incorporation of certain fixed elements and descriptive formulas into the improvised poems. The Italian *improvvisatori* did not start from scratch but carried on a rich, poetic tradition. The same has been observed of the actors in the *commedia dell'arte*; they were well versed in the best literature of their day.[7]

The aesthetic esteem in which the performances of these improvisers were held varied during the eighteenth century. The generations who had been brought up on the classicist ideal, with the prescriptions of Horace, Boileau, or Dryden in mind, tended to see the *improvvisatori* as no more than poetic acrobats. Voltaire's dis-

missive shrug of the shoulders in connection with the genre is typical of the age. "Improvisers can only achieve mediocre things," he
declares on one occasion, and on another: "the taste for improvisations is the seal of barbarity on Italians."[8] But there are also signs
of lively appreciation. The Italian dramatist Goldoni refers in his
memoirs to an occasion when he listened to the same improviser
that Charles de Brosses had heard, i.e., to Bernardo Perfetti. "The
poet sang stanzas in Pindar's manner for a quarter of an hour," he
writes, and adds that he had never heard anything more beautiful
or overwhelming.[9]

At the close of the century we find evidence of increased and
fulfilled expectations, there is a belief that improvisation is the
source of all true poetry. Gudmund Göran Adlerbeth, the Swedish
poet and politician, writes in his travel journal from Italy that "the
so-called *improvvisatori,*" compose extempore verses "with a taste
which at one and the same time demonstrates the fieriness of their
inventive faculty and the wealth of their language." He listened to
one of his era's most celebrated exponents of the art, whose professional name was Fortunata Fantastici. He had suggested to her
a mythological subject, the fable of Apollo and Daphne, and "without the least delay she launched into a song thereon, which lasted
very nearly half an hour, with an emotion and a fire which revealed
itself not only in thoughts and language but also in voice and face.
I had scarcely expected to see poetic rapture so vividly enacted."[10]

Alongside Adlerbeth's account we can place a corresponding
picture painted by the Dane Schack Staffeldt. In Florence in 1798
he heard the same Fortunata Fantastici, and in his memoirs, written in German, he describes an occasion when he saw her in action.
Like Adlerbeth, he was struck by the outer manifestation of her
poetic ecstacy: "While she improvised, her face showed all the signs
of rapture: her cheeks glowed, her breathing became quicker and
more audible (!), her eyes grew moist and shone, in every muscle
and fibre one could detect signs of excitement and exaltation.
When she had finished, I compared her poetry to a spring that
welled up spontaneously out of nature's hand, while art only presses up water through fountains."[11]

However highly the Italians themselves prized the *improvvisatori*, their fame and symbolic significance became if anything even

greater thanks to visitors from countries north of the Alps. For the latter the spectacle of improvisation meant more than the words themselves and the poetry—as foreigners they could hardly take upon themselves the role of literary critics of these verbally presented poetic works. The literary sightseers from the north saw what they wished to see and heard what they wished to hear. The myth of poetic inspiration became embodied before their very eyes in the person of the improviser, male or female.

There are many interesting testimonies from early nineteenth-century travelers. The Swedish poet Atterbom came with high hopes, which were partly disappointed. He has reservations about the increasingly narrow rules now customary in improvisations. He also has insight into the devices essential to improvisation, and he notes that its exponents always have on hand a few magnificent set pieces on storms, the sea, sunrises, and so on, to be presented whenever the opportunity arises. But he mentions with obvious interest an *improvvisatrice*, a seventeen-year-old girl, who had given her audience "a graphic idea of Pythia's appearance on her tripod."[12]

His compatriot Karl August Nicander made a similar association when he saw Rosa Taddei a few years later, and he wrote in his Italian reminiscences, "She was enchantment in her whole being, a sort of Pythia in Apollo's temple."[13] Nicander's companion, the German poet August von Platen, was equally enthusiastic. He confesses that this *improvvisatrice* afforded him the most delectable hours of his stay in Italy, and he adds a historical reflection, which also points back to antiquity: "This must be how the old rhapsodes sang their songs."[14]

August von Platen's associations are significant. Present-day researchers in folk poetry, who have examined the remains of the tradition of poetic improvisation which has survived a long time in Europe—particularly in Yugoslavia—have come to the conclusion that the Homeric rhapsodes, when delivering their recitations, must have used a method very much resembling that of latter-day *improvvisatori*. The Homer scholar Milman Parry showed, with the aid of much comparative material, what it is that technically speaking distinguishes the oral epic. His belief—supported by Alfred Lord in the book *The Singer of Tales* (1960)—is that every recitation of a poem of some length, in times before the tradition of written material, always constituted a sort of improvisation. An orally performing poet could enlarge or shorten his/her poem, embellish or simplify it, according to the time, the place, and the audience. Milman Parry demonstrated that the Homeric poems are built, to a much greater extent than had previously been observed, on thematic and syntactic formulas, which the poets used as bricks. Parry contends that the huge quantity of stereotypes in the Homeric poems proves that they, in the form in which we now read them, still are close to oral epic. This confirmed the assumption of an earlier Homer scholar, Martin Persson Nilsson, who had said of the art of the Homeric rhapsodes, "It was not the poem as such, but the art of poetry, which they had learnt."[15] Exactly the same is true of improvising poets and actors in all countries and ages. For let us recapitulate that an improvisation does not arise in a vacuum. It presupposes both a technique and a tradition.

2

On the basis of the phenomenon of improvisation, the myth of the *improvvisatore* as a sort of charmed Aladdin figure arose in the late eighteenth century. Traces of it can be found in many countries and over a very long period.

In a play he wrote for a small circle of friends in 1790, a *divertissement* called *The Birthday*, King Gustaf III amused himself by portraying people well known in Stockholm. He lets the poet and songwriter Carl Michael Bellman appear under the name *il signor improvvisatore*. It is easy to see the origin of the designation. The play *The Birthday* was written several years after Gustaf III's Italian journey, during which he probably had the opportunity of getting to know the Italian art of improvisation. And Gudmund Göran Adlerbeth, whose description of an *improvvisatrice* in action was quoted above, traveled in the king's suite and wrote his journal by royal command.

It was not incorrect to compare Bellman to the Italian *improvvisatori*, for we know that he fulfilled the functions of extemporizing poet during festive social occasions and of painstaking artist with quill pen and manuscript. His powers of improvisation are amply borne out. Carl Christopher Gjörwell, a contemporary Swedish aesthetician, speaks of "his airy gift for composing and singing verses in a twinkling," and Thomas Thorild calls him a *lyricus extemporalis*. Atterbom, two generations later, describes him as "this improviser who grew up in cold Sweden as by a miracle, like a plant from the paradise of the South." Literary scholars have lately rediscovered Bellman the improviser; the many recurring formulas in early drinking songs and *Epistles* have been assumed to point to improvised preliminary stages of his written texts.[16]

From the world of reality the *improvvisatori* stepped into the world of fiction. This first occurred in early nineteenth-century novels of artistic life, in some of which the *improvvisatore* and *improvvisatrice* become key figures. At the same time the phenomenon of improvisation affords writers an opportunity to air aesthetic and psychological reflections on the act of poetic creation, its conditions and development.

The first writer to present the new type of artist was Madame de Staël, in her novel *Corinne ou l'Italie* (1807). The book and the descriptions it contains are based on her visit to Italy a couple of years earlier.

Even before her journey she had touched on the theme of improvisation and improvisers in her book *De la littérature considerée dans ses rapports avec les institutions sociales*. But when she mentioned in this work Italian poets who "manufacture verses as swiftly as they speak,"[17] she was critical. She explained that the existence of such poets had been taken as proof of the particular amenability of the Italian language for poetry, and she maintained that the reverse is true. The flexibility and wealth of rhymes of the Italian language is a danger and an obstacle to a poet with more deliberate artistic ambitions.

She looks differently at improvisation in her novel. In it the central character, the Italian *improvvisatrice* Corinne, is drawn as an incarnation of the romantic ideal of the poet in touch with the spontaneous powers of nature. Madame de Staël's changed outlook is primarily due to her direct experiences in Italy. She heard an *improvvisatore* for the first time in Bologna, and she describes the impression it made on her in a letter to her friend Vincenzo Monti.

In Rome she listened to a young and beautiful *improvvisatrice*, Isabella Pellegrini. In Florence she watched two more sessions of improvisation, one of which was given by the same Fortunata Fantastici who had captivated Adlerbeth and Schack Staffeldt.

Contemporary readers of Madame de Staël's novel connected the name Corinne with that of Corilla Olympica, one of the most celebrated of eighteenth-century *improvvisatrici*. In a note to the 1807 edition of her novel Madame de Staël tells her readers not to confuse the Corinne of her novel with the Italian poetess Corilla, "improvisatrice italienne dont tout le monde a entendu parler."[18] There was of course no question of identity—in spite of the similarity of their names—between Corinne and the historical Corilla Olympica, who furthermore was dead before Madame de Staël's Italian visit. Yet it is difficult to overlook entirely certain similarities in the lives of the historical and the fictional character. Corilla Olympica's greatest triumph occurred when she was crowned with laurels on the Capitol. Corinne of the novel receives the same accolade. The historical Corilla Olympica improvised a song on the theme *Le lodi di Roma* at the celebrations on the Capitol. Corinne's improvisation in Madame de Staël's novel has a similar theme: *La gloire et le bonheur de l'Italie*.

Even more important than the two lyrical improvisations, which Madame de Staël places in Corinne's mouth and expresses in rhythmic and rhetorical prose, are the reflections on the writing of poetry and poetic creativity. Here the influence of German romantic aesthetics becomes crystal clear; it was not for nothing that Madame de Staël had August Wilhelm Schlegel, one of the propagandists of German romanticism, with her on her Italian journey.

Now, not only was the novel's Corinne possessed of the gift of improvisation, she also wrote poems by hand. On one occasion she is asked which part of her production she values most highly. Is it the works that are *"ouvrages de la reflexion"* or those that are the fruits of *"l'inspiration instantanée"*? Without hesitation she accords the prize to the improvisations. I feel, she declares, that I, in the state in which they are produced, experience *"un enthousiasme surnaturel."* I feel, she continues, as though I was not speaking myself but that a divine voice spoke through me: *"ce qui parle en moi vaut mieux que moi-même."*[19] At the end of the book—and in order to increase the glory of the divine Corinne—a second-rate *improvisatore*, conventional in his choice of subjects and exaggerated in his demeanor, is introduced. Nothing could be more painful to Oswald, once Corinne's adorer and now returned to Italy, than to see her art thus travestied, parodied, and rendered ridiculous. We are told of Corinne that she was *"un miracle de la nature."* Of the wretched *improvisatore* we are told that he with his empty gestures and movements resembled a wound-up clockwork mechanism, which could not be turned off before a certain time.[20]

For herself, Madame de Staël never claimed competence in the art of improvisation. Yet it goes without saying that she had projected something of herself into her portrait of the Italian poetess, for though Madame de Staël was no *improvisatrice*, she was certainly a conversationalist of genius, demonstrating the ability to turn a swift phrase, rich in inventiveness. It is significant that when Corinne of the novel wishes to describe improvisation, she compares it to a lively conversation; I would say, she explains, that improvisation for me is "comme une conversation animée."[21]

A number of the basic aesthetic beliefs of the romantic era are embodied in the novel and in the figure of Corinne. All the features stressed in Madame de Staël's account as being particularly characteristic of improvisation—i.e., the sudden impulses, the spontaneous flow, the enthusiasm, and at the same time lack of self-consciousness of the performer—appear in many romantic and later accounts of a related phenomenon: that of inspiration.

Madame de Staël's novel was read for many years as the apotheosis of the dream about Italy and improvisation. Scandinavian nineteenth-century romantics read it; H. C. Andersen read it; it stood on the shelves of Swedish manor house libraries, where Selma Lagerlöf found it. It is the book that in *Gösta Berlings saga*—the story of the conflict between the improvised existence of the cavaliers and the demands of workaday life—is thrown into the mouth of hungry wolves during a wild sleigh ride.

3

The book that turned the concept of the Italian *improvisatore* into something of a romantic archetype for the Scandinavian public was H. C. Andersen's novel *The Improviser*. While he was working on the novel he wrote to his friend Henriette Hanck: "I hope my book is not a Staël-Holsteinian Corinne, a crazy mixture of a 'Guide' and a love story."[22]

Like Madame de Staël's novel, only more so, H. C. Andersen's book is based on its author's life. Antonio, Andersen's central character, discovers his gift for improvisation as a child. He continues to train himself in this art until he switches to the profession of writer—toward the end of the book—with the written language as his chief medium. H. C. Andersen himself had also sung, improvised, and told stories ever since his childhood in Odense. In the memoirs known as *Levnedsbog*, he tells us how people used to visit the tobacco factory in his hometown to hear him sing. Yet— he adds—"the silliest thing was that I didn't really know any songs, but I *improvised* both text and melody, both of them very strange and ponderous. 'He must go on the stage,' they all said."[23] H. C. Andersen did indeed go on the stage, and during this period he sought to get in touch with Oehlenschläger. The earliest proof of this contact is a poem, dated October 1821, sent by Andersen to the established poet and provided with a small apologetic dedication, as follows:

> *Improvvisatori*
> is this poem of mine,
> scarcely to the liking
> of the Sacred Sisters Nine.[24]

Both the words from his autobiography quoted above and the poem to Oehlenschläger were written before the novel *The Improviser* and constitute early proof of Andersen's interest in improvisations.

He was twenty-eight when he came to Italy in 1833. His experiences in Rome can be followed practically day by day in his *Roman Diaries* published in our time. He was introduced to Rome by friends in the Scandinavian artists' colony, one of whom was the sculptor Thorvaldsen. Andersen never mentions any Italian improviser by name in his diary, but one day he notes that he had listened to "a blind improviser."[25] In his novel, written in Rome, he mentions signor Sgricci, with the added remark, "an improviser famous in our day."[26] Sgricci, whose speciality it was to improvise one-man dramas, was indeed well known in Europe then. He had been listened to by Atterbom, August von Platen, and Lamartine, among others, during their visits to Rome, and he sat for Thorvaldsen, who did a bust of him.

Danish scholars have traditionally associated the title of H. C. Andersen's novel *The Improviser* with a remark made by the critic J. L. Heiberg in a letter to Andersen's patron, Collin senior, who passed it on to Andersen in Rome. In a diary entry for 16 November 1833, Andersen writes: "I received a criticism by Heiberg of my two vaudevilles. I am *but an improviser*."[27] A week later, 27 November, he notes in the same diary: "Started work this evening on my novella *The Improviser*." The fact that Andersen took the word "improviser" as the title of his book has generally been seen as an ironic acceptance of or riposte to Heiberg's criticism. It is not unlikely that Heiberg's words fastened like a barb in the sensitive Andersen; he was to entitle a later novel *Only a Fiddler (Kun en spillemand)*, with distinct emphasis on the word "only." But clearly he had had a real interest in improvisation long before this, as the above quotations indicate. In his Roman environment, where song recitals and the declamation of poetry were common occurrences, the phenomenon and spectacle of improvisation captured his imagination once more. The myth of improvisation, the view of the *improvvisatore* as a natural poet, was familiar to him from literature, possibly through Schack Staffeldt, certainly through Madame de Staël.

H. C. Andersen introduces into his novel some fictive improvisations, just as Madame de Staël had done in *Corinne*. Or rather, both transcribe and translate the pretended improvisations, which must be assumed to have been originally in verse, into billowing prose. For the first improvisation he delivers in Andersen's novel, the young Antonio is given his theme by the young woman who has awakened his love. The theme of the improvisation—typical also of the author of the novel—is immortality. On another occasion we are told how Antonio performs as a professional *improvvisatore* in a Naples theater, where he follows the custom of his colleagues and assumes a stage name, Cenci. The subjects he is given by the audience resemble those we know from accounts of authentic improvisations, for instance, *Fata morgana*, Tasso at the court of Ferrara, and the death of Sappho.

"I struck some chords and my thoughts turned into speech, my speech into rippling verse"—in this way Antonio describes one of his improvisations.[28] The interesting thing from the historical or genetic standpoint is that these supposed improvisations of Antonio's, in the words of the Danish scholar Paul Rubow, "already are half-stories *(Eventyr)*." And Rubow continues, "H. C. Andersen went on for the rest of his life to write in this genre, but reinforced it with strict architecture, solid form."[29] He attaches particular importance to Antonio's improvisation on *Fata morgana*, elements of which are repeated in the stories *The Wild Swans* and *Under the Elder Tree*. Another feature of Antonio's improvisations might be reminiscent of the later stories: the transposing of Andersen's childhood memories and other experiences to the symbolic world of fiction. "It was you I saw in every poem,"[30] affirmed Santa, one of the main female characters in the book, as she listened to Antonio's improvisations in Naples. Her words provide a key resembling the one used by the scholar Hans Brix when he unlocked the secrets of Andersen's *Tales*.

Similarities of motifs, style, and technique between the fictive improvisations in the early novel and the later stories do not in themselves, of course, tell us anything about Andersen's method of writing his stories. But the question can and has been asked: to what extent was Andersen himself an improviser in his role as storyteller?

In Edvard Collin's valuable account of H. C. Andersen as storyteller, we read the following:

> In many of the circles he visited daily, there were small children, whom he addressed himself to; he told them stories that he partly *made up on the spot* [italicized here], partly borrowed from well-known tales: but whether he was telling one of his own or repeating another one, his way of telling it was so entirely personal and vivid that it enchanted the children. . . . The flow of words was uninterrupted, richly embellished by turns of phrase familiar to the children, and by suitable gestures. He invested even the driest of sentences with life; he did not say: "The children got into the carriage and then drove off," but "Then they got up into the carriage, goodbye Father, goodbye Mother. The whip cracked,

swish, swosh, and away they went, gee-up, get a move on." Those who
later have only heard him *read* his stories can only picture very faintly
the extraordinary vivacity of his storytelling surrounded by children.[31]

Many features in Collin's portrait of the storyteller in action recur in descriptions of genuine literary—or musical—improvisations:
the instantaneous invention ("made up on the spot"), the spontaneous welling up of material ("the flow of words was uninterrupted"), and the unique effect on the original audience, which a reading aloud from the written or printed page could not rival.

However, even though H. C. Andersen donned the guise of the
improvvisatore both in the novel and in real life, he was in fact an
artist who worked with ever-increasing conscientiousness at his
desk. This was demonstrated by, above all, Topsøe Jensen, the
greatest Andersen scholar of our time, through his examination of
Andersen's diaries and manuscripts. *From an Author's Workshop
(Fra en digters værksted)* (1962-63) and *The Author at Work
(Digteren ved arbejdet)* (1966) are two typical titles from his
studies of Andersen at his writing desk. By no means were all of
Andersen's stories improvisations, in the sense that they were first
told verbally; many of them were developed over a year or a decade, as demonstrated by extant documents.

In the commentary H. C. Andersen included in the 1863 edition
of his *Adventures and Tales (Eventyr og historier),* he provides
some information about how the stories came to be written. About
the actual contents of the stories, he writes that as a rule they
arose "instantaneously, in the way a familiar melody or song can
do." About one story, and one story only, *The Islands of Vænoe
and Glænoe*, he mentions that it originated directly from a festive
improvisation among adults, or in his words: "in an improvised
speech at the dinner-table at Holsteinborg."[32]

In H. C. Andersen's letters from later years there are not infrequent references to improvisations in verse; the index to his published correspondence provides numerous examples. He describes
a cruise he took with the royal family in an 1844 letter to Jonas
Collin. "Onboard, the day before yesterday, we spoke of improvisation, and I said to the Queen that I could do this quite well, for
instance at Bregentveed and wherever I felt at ease and at home,

whereupon she replied, 'I hope you feel at ease and at home with us.' "[33] Evidently he did come to feel at home there: both his diary and letters tell of a number of occasions when he acted as an *improvvisatore cortegiano*, reciting impromptu poems in the royal circle. On one occasion after an improvised toast in verse, he was told: "You cannot have composed that at this very moment, how could you have made it up straight away?" Andersen felt rather offended by this suspicion: "He believed I went about with my impromptues written down beforehand."[34] It was clearly H. C. Andersen's ambition to be able—when necessary—metaphorically speaking to produce verse out of his hat at a moment's notice.

He already had this gift as a child, and he practiced the art throughout his life. This ability gave him a feeling of kinship with the Roman *improvvisatori* and led him to choose one of them as the main character of his first novel. But it is obvious that he in his novel—like Madame de Staël in hers—reinterpreted the art of improvisation in a romantic light. Antonio is the romantic natural genius incarnate. When he on one occasion expounds his view of poetic creation, he formulates something of a romantic aesthetics and is reminded of the Platonic idea of recollection: "I often think that it is memories, lullabyes from another world, which awaken in my soul, and which I have to repeat."[35]

The problems of the imagination and creativity, which absorbed H. C. Andersen while he was writing *The Improviser,* continued to engage his interest throughout his life. The contrast between spontaneity and reflection, which in the novel is represented by the conflict between the natural genius Antonio and the crotchety versifier Habbas Dabba, recurs in Andersen's *Tales,* i.e., in *The Nightingale.* But although he favors the myth of spontaneous artistic creation, he is not ignorant of the importance of the writing desk and application. It is possible to read the introduction to the story *Under the Elder Tree* as an allegory of creativity in its improvising phase. In the same way the story of Psyche, with its interiors from a sculptor's studio, can be read as a hymn to artistic work. The writer who, in both fiction and real life, loved to pose as the improviser was in fact well aware of the labor of creation and the dialectic of creative life.

4

The myth of the *improvvisatore* did not die with Madame de Staël's or H. C. Andersen's generation. Traces of it can be found in many European literatures, not only in French and Scandinavian literature but also in English, German, and—as the German literary scholar Weintraub demonstrated—very markedly in Russian literature. Richard Wagner, on what might well be called the last day of the romantic era, succeeded in giving the myth a definitive musical form, and *Die Meistersinger von Nürnberg* has been called the Song of Songs of the art of improvisation.[36] In his opera Wagner intertwined the musical and the poetic elements of improvisation. Walther von Stolzing, the victorious master singer, is familiar with the traditional musical forms of the guilds of singers. But he boldly breaks loose from them and creates a new form which to the musical notions of the master singers is extremely daring. Wagner succeeded in expressing this break with tradition, this musical innovation. For not only is Walther an improviser, he is also an innovator.

The contrast on which the opera is built is basically the same type of conflict that appears in so many novels of artistic life written by the romantics. On one side stands a creative artist, whose powers are closely allied to nature and the soul of the people—here represented primarily by Walther von Stolzing himself. On the other side stands a mechanically producing craftsman. Wagner gives him a name that has become attached to the type. He is a *Besserwisser* and is called Beckmesser.

It is important to draw a dividing line between improvisation as an aesthetic phenomenon, and the myth of improvisation and the *improvvisatore*. The romantic myth of improvisation can be said to have arisen as the result of a brilliant misunderstanding.

As a historical phenomenon the art of improvisation—in both its literary and musical manifestations—was exceedingly dependent on formal elements. Benedetto Croce characterized profesional literary improvisation quite excellently as a "rhetorical and theatrical form of spontaneity."[37] He might have added: a deliberately provoked form of spontaneity. Professional literary *improvvisatori*, as we have got to know them, were tied not only by traditional and rhetorical forms but also by ideas given from outside, by suggested subjects presented to them on very short notice. This does not mean that the improvisations—of fortunately gifted individuals—could not and did not on occasion reach a high artistic level.

Not only did the *improvvisatori* and *improvvisatrici* master to perfection the art of speech, they also controlled their movements and gestures like genuine actors. When romantic visitors, safely arrived in the land of their dreams, witnessed the Italian art of improvisation, they were tempted into believing that they were seeing poetic fervor personified. In the words of Adlerbeth, "I had scarcely expected to see poetic rapture so vividly enacted."[38] The myth of improvisation—the poetic Aladdin myth—received added impetus when the romantic belief in genius or the exceptional being met Italian reality. The predominantly imitative art of improvisation was seen as an expression of spontaneous and creative originality.

In recent socioliterary studies it has been customary to interpret the aesthetic of genius and originality as theoretical justification for the new literary productive forces—ranged against an older, feudal, rule-bound aesthetic under pressure because of the current competitive situation in the marketing of books.[39]

Irrespective of how we interpret the background, "improvisation" and "to improvise" became terms of high esteem with writers of the romantic nineteenth century. Lamartine is a good example. In Italy he had seen, heard, and admired Signore Sgricci, mentioned above and well known throughout Europe as Roman *improvvisatore*. Lamartine used the word "improvisation" several times in the titles of his poems. *Improvisation sur le bateau à vapeur du Rhone* is one of them, *Improvisation à Saint Gaudens* another; a third, *Improvisé à la Grande Chartreuse*, can be found in his *Nouvelles meditations*. In a note to this latter poem he adds, *"C'est une inspiration complète."* The concepts improvisation and inspiration have become synonymous.

Many remarks by Lamartine indicate that he regarded, or interpreted, the writing of poetry as a spontaneous act. "To create is delightful, but to correct, alter, cover pages with ink, that is tedious"; as he wrote in a letter to Aymon de Virieu: *"c'est l'oeuvre des maçons et non pas des artistes."* In another letter he explained that he was incapable of working with a file (*"incapable du pénible travail de la lime"*), another lunge at Horatian rules.[40] That

Lamartine's poetic manuscripts by no means always bear out his contentions is typical of the repeated contradictions found in the romantics who cherished the myth of improvisation and inspiration.

Samuel Taylor Coleridge is one of the English-speaking poets who associated themselves with the phenomenon or myth of improvisation. One of his lesser-known poems has the Italian title *Improvvisatore*. It consists of an introductory prose dialogue and a lyrical poem, the latter spoken by an improviser. The poem hardly demonstrates any particular interest in the art of improvisation; the *improvvisatore* is treated with some condescension. But Coleridge himself has gone down in the history of aesthetics in the role, among others, of poet of spontaneous inspiration. One of his most famous poems—if we are to believe his own account—is nothing more or less than a dream improvisation. The poem in question is *Kubla Khan*.

Coleridge
and His Dream Poem

*Mein Freund, das grad' ist Dichters Werk,
das er sein Träumen deut' und merk'.*

Wagner
Die Meistersänger von Nürnberg

Shelley expresses a belief common to the whole romantic generation of poets when he writes in *A Defence of Poetry*: "I appeal to
the greatest poets of the present day, whether it is not an error to
assert that the finest passages of poetry are produced by labour
and study."[1]

Coleridge's *Kubla Khan* is a good example of a poem that took
shape without any feeling of conscious effort by the poet. For according to Coleridge's well-known prefatory remarks, the poem
was "as it were given to him," and in the history of aesthetics it
has come to represent an ideal example of a spontaneous poem,
written without intellectual control or calculation. Kenneth Burke
described it as "the great surrealistic masterpiece," written more
than a hundred years before the dream improvisations of the
surrealists.[2]

Kubla Khan was first published in a small volume that contained
three poems by Coleridge, and the book's title consisted of the
titles of the poems: *Christabel, Kubla Khan, A Vision, The Pains
of Sleep*. The year was 1816, heyday of English romanticism. On
its own title page inside the volume *Kubla Khan* has the extended
title *Kubla Khan or a Vision in a Dream* as well as the explanatory

subtitle *Of the Fragment of Kubla Khan*. It is clear that Coleridge from the very first publication of the poem was keen to underline that it is a dream vision and a fragment, not a completed poem.

The poem is first mentioned in 1800. Everything points to its having been written two or three years earlier. Coleridge himself dates it to 1797. So it had evidently been in existence for over fifteen years before publication—in itself a most unusual feature considering Coleridge's publication habits, and one that calls for an explanation.

The poem opens on an Oriental note:

> In Xanadu did Kubla Khan
> A stately pleasure-dome decree:
> Where Alph, the sacred river, ran
> Through caverns measureless to man
> Down to a sunless sea.
> So twice five miles of fertile ground
> With walls and towers were girdled round:
> And here were gardens bright with sinuous rills,
> Where blossomed many an incense-bearing tree,
> And here were forests ancient as the hills,
> Enfolding sunny spots of greenery.

The first edition of 1816 is prefaced by the following remarks (the "poet of great and deserved celebrity" being Lord Byron):

> The following fragment is here published at the request of a poet of great and deserved celebrity, and as far as the Author's own opinions are concerned, rather as a psychological curiosity, than on the ground of any supposed *poetic* merits.
>
> In the summer of the year 1797, the Author, then in ill health, had retired to a lonely farmhouse between Porlock and Linton, on the Exmoor confines of Somerset and Devonshire. In consequence of a slight indisposition, an anodyne had been prescribed, from the effects of which he fell asleep in his chair at the moment that he was reading the following sentence, or words of the same substance, in "Purchas's Pilgrimage": "Here the Khan Kubla commanded a palace to be built, and a stately garden thereunto. And thus ten miles of fertile ground were inclosed with a wall." The Author continued for about three hours in a

profound sleep, at least of the external senses, during which time he has the most vivid confidence, that he could not have composed less than from two to three hundred lines; if that indeed can be called composition in which all the images rose up before him as *things*, with a parallel production of the correspondent expressions, without any sensation or consciousness of effort. On awaking he appeared to himself to have a distinct recollection of the whole, and taking his pen, ink, and paper, instantly and eagerly wrote down the lines that are here preserved. At this moment he was unfortunately called out by a person on business from Porlock, and detained by him above an hour, and on his return to his room, found to his no small surprise and mortification, that though he still retained some vague and dim recollection of the general purpose of the vision, yet, with the exception of some eight or ten scattered lines and images, all the rest had passed away like the images on the surface of a stream into which a stone has been cast, but, alas! without the after restoration of the latter:

> Then all the charm
> Is broken—all that phantom-world so fair
> Vanishes, and a thousand circlets spread,
> And each mis-shape the other. Stay awhile,
> Poor youth! who scarcely dar'st lift up thine eyes—
> The stream will soon renew its smoothness, soon
> The visions will return! And lo, he stays,
> And soon the fragments dim of lovely forms
> Come trembling back, unite, and now once more
> The pool becomes a mirror.

Yet from the still surviving recollections in his mind, the Author has frequently purposed to finish for himself what had been originally, as it were, given to him. Σαμερον αδιον ασω: but the to-morrow is yet to come.

   As a contrast to this vision, I have annexed a fragment of a very different character, describing with equal fidelity the dream of pain and disease.

The account given in this preface was all that was known of the poem's genesis until a manuscript was discovered in 1934. This belonged to a private collection, was first published in the *Times Literary Supplement* the same year, and has since been purchased by the British Museum, where it is now preserved between sheets of glass as a valuable rarity. This manuscript—in which the form of the poem in a few places departs somewhat from the previously known version—contains the following note: "This fragment, with a good deal more, not recoverable, composed in a sort of Reverie brought on by two grains of Opium, taken to check a dysentery at a Farm House between Porlock and Linton, a quarter of a mile from Culbone Church in the fall of the year 1797."

The preface to the 1816 edition and the note in the manuscript differ in some not unimportant respects. This presents us with a well-known methodological problem: we have two documents about the same events, one of which (the manuscript version) appears to be much closer in time to these events than does the other.

The first question to be answered is, what is the date of the manuscript? English scholars have sought to establish this by first examining the watermark of the paper. The same watermark is in a Coleridge letter of 1796. External criteria therefore point with some probability to a manuscript dating from the late eighteenth century. No one has, on the other hand, dared either to claim or to deny that this manuscript is the original; nor, strange to tell, has any close investigation of Coleridge's handwriting and the changes it underwent been conducted in order to shed light on the manuscript.

The variations, as compared with the published text of 1816, are few but significant. "Kubla" is still spelled "Cubla"—the same spelling as in Purchase's old travel account, which Coleridge himself points to as a poetic source. The mountain is called "Mount Amara"— a name in *Paradise Lost*; this has been changed to "Amora" in the manuscript, and to "Abora" in the printed version. The original association with Milton is not uninteresting; like Milton, Coleridge in his poem describes a Paradise lost and a Paradise regained. We also know from other sources that Milton's works occupied a prominent place in Coleridge's thoughts at this time.

Since the manuscript was written much earlier than the published preface, we have reason to note closely the small divergences of information offered about the poem's origins. The manuscript describes the poet's condition at the conception of the poem as "a sort of Reverie," whereas the second, later, and longer version speaks of "a profound sleep" as being, so to speak, the womb of the poem. The preface to the 1816 edition is much more elaborate, cast in narrative form and with dramatic tension. The man from

Porlock makes his first fateful entrance in 1816—and has since then become in England the prototype of commonplace man, the Philistine or scholar who clumsily barges in and destroys a web of dreams and misunderstands or interrupts the genius engaged in creative work.

Modern English Coleridge researchers—represented by Elisabeth Schneider, for instance, in her book *Coleridge, Opium, and Kubla Khan* (1953)—show increasing skepticism about Coleridge's account as it appears in the preface to the 1816 edition, a skepticism supported by a number of arguments. Coleridge used to record his nocturnal dreams in his notebooks. On many occasions he would wake up and write down an isolated sentence recalled from a dream. It has therefore seemed strange that there is no trace in the notebooks, which he kept with pedantic thoroughness, of the dream reputed to underlie *Kubla Khan*. Skeptical scholars have taken this as an indication that the account from 1816 is fictional. Doubters have also observed the fact that nowhere, neither in Coleridge's own writings nor in those of his circle of friends, do we find any mention of the preternatural origins of the poem until 1816. On numerous occasions Coleridge discussed both dreams and poems with his friends, but as far as we can tell from accounts of these conversations, *Kubla Khan* was never mentioned as an example of a poem composed in sleep. At least two of Coleridge's contemporaries came to express doubts about the veracity of the preface. One of them was Robert Southey, who insinuated that Coleridge had only *dreamed* that he wrote the poem in a dream! The other was Charles Lamb, whose cautious words about the poem—"what he *calls* a vision, '*Kubla Khan*' "—have led people to believe he had doubts about the poem's dreamlike or visionary origin.[3]

Elisabeth Schneider pointed to another dream that Coleridge confided to his notebooks, which has certain similarities with his remarks about *Kubla Khan*. In 1800 Coleridge wrote that he experienced the whole of Milton's *Paradise Lost* in a dream: "I have had a continued Dream representing visually and audibly all Milton's Paradise lost."[4] This new example of Coleridge's vivid dreams is interesting in several respects. A dream of this kind must have appeared to the dreamer as a representational and word sequence of very considerable length. Now it is a fact that opium dreams

often entail a transformed sense of time; the dreamer may feel
that she/he has lived through an endlessly long stretch of time and
events. So Elisabeth Schneider asks herself whether it is not this
dream, or the recollection of it, which found its way into the narrative of the *Kubla Khan* preface. Conversely, it would be possible,
assuming one believed Coleridge's account, to argue that the one
type of dream experience if anything strengthens the likelihood of
the other.

In fact Coleridge on a couple of occasions—in letters, not pub-
licly—does write that he *has* dreamed poems. In an 1803 letter to
Thomas Wedgewood, he quotes four lines, which he says he composed in his sleep while dreaming he was dying. He reports the exact time and place of the occurrence: the previous Tuesday night
at the Black Bull, Edinburgh. The lines constitute an epitaph written in the popular comic vein.[5] The other example resembles this
experience, and not even the greatest skepticism toward romantic
mythology can on principle rule out the possibility that an imaginative master of words is capable of continuing poetic exercises in
his/her sleep; indeed this has demonstrably been true of poets
other than Coleridge. That Coleridge, when recounting the above
short dream poems, does not simultaneously relate them to or associate them with the genesis of *Kubla Khan* can scarcely, as Elisabeth Schneider suggests, be something for which to reproach him.
One might instead conceivably draw the conclusion that his silence
was due to the fact that the *Kubla Khan* experience was so powerful and strange that he kept it to himself for a long time.

Considerably more weight attaches to another argument that
has been adduced, namely, that a poem of four or five lines can
conceivably be verbalized automatically in a dream but that a
composition of such considerable length—over fifty lines—and
with such a stable structure and intricate rhyme scheme as *Kubla
Khan* can scarcely be entirely the product of a spontaneous dream
improvisation.

A decisive question, which it should be possible to answer, is of
course whether the poem, in its present form, departs from the
rest of Coleridge's poems. Does it stand apart by virtue of its associative play, its visual or eidetic qualities, its images and imagery,
and hence more powerfully than Coleridge's other poems remind

one of dreams: Opinions on this are divided, according to respective critics' view of the poem's genesis. John Livingston Lowes, whose book *The Road to Xanadu* (1927) appeared *before* the manuscript was discovered, trusts Coleridge's account in the 1816 preface of how the poem arose in a dream. He persuades himself and us to believe that the poem has typical dream characteristics. Elisabeth Schneider, on the other hand, who has been most critical in her assessment of Coleridge's account, says that she has never had the impression that *Kubla Khan* was composed in any other way than were the rest of Coleridge's poems.

J. L. Lowes has done more intensive research on the prehistory and origins of the poem than anyone else. With the aid of Coleridge's reference to Purchas's *Pilgrimage* and by exploiting all the information in the poet's diaries about his reading, he managed to identify most of the material in the poem. He was able to trace the natural descriptions in the poem back almost word for word to travel journals and travel stories read by Coleridge. The description of the landscape, "the pleasure dome," the oriental names (sometimes slightly altered), the Abyssinian girl—all are mosaic pieces from Coleridge's reading that have subsequently been merged into the poem. For Lowes, the result of his minutely detailed study confirms that the poem arose in a dream. The dream creates from scattered memory fragments—in the same way that Coleridge believed the imagination does.

Lowes's research has undeniably shed light on how Coleridge's lyrical imagination functioned. But it cannot, of course, confirm the conclusion that the poem is a spontaneous dream product. This deduction of Lowes's is already invalidated by the fact that he, by dint of his knowledge of Coleridge's reading of travel accounts, has found the very same amalgam of shreds of memory in *The Ancient Mariner*. Coleridge originally subtitled *The Ancient Mariner* with the same term he used in the note to the *Kubla Khan* manuscript, i.e., *A Reverie*. But a reverie is simply a daydream. One might venture to assert that the metaphors and imagery in *The Ancient Mariner* follow certain dreamlike laws of association too. But no one, not even Coleridge himself, has ever claimed that it was produced spontaneously in a dream.

Elisabeth Schneider is one of those who refuse to concede that there is much truth in the 1816 preface. Instead of regarding it as an autobiographical document, she thinks of it as a literary narrative, more or less freely invented. Regarding the poem *Kubla Khan* itself, she believes that this grammatically well-structured mass of words, with its consistent rhyme scheme, scarcely differs in any important respect from Coleridge's other poetry. At the same time she admits that the poem might very well have originated in a daydream, in a state of "idle half-sleep," and that it need not be built on any deliberately executed plan. This would explain the air of improvisation that the poem conveys, apparently to her as well.[6]

If we wish to look a little behind both preface and poem, it is worth recalling the relationship of dream and literature, which romantic philosophers and authors discovered. Coleridge himself speaks in a famous passage of how imagination also functions in our dreams as "the true inward creatrix."[7] In a letter from the later part of his life he declares that dreams had more and more become "the substance of my life." He had plans for a work about dreams, visions, and magic, in which he would seek to explain how our thoughts, "in states of morbid slumber," can become dramatically and poetically creative.[8] If we read ideas of this sort into the preface, we find that it undoubtedly contains a core of truth—in any event for poets of Coleridge's type.

Coleridge was far from being the only one in his generation who held such views on dreams and poetry. The connection between literature and dreams was often stressed in the German romantic tradition, which he knew better than any of his English contemporaries. Jean Paul spoke of the spontaneous and autonomous poetry to be found in dreams: "Der Traum is unwillkürliche Dichtkunst."[9] Like Coleridge, he kept a close account of his dreams in his diary. And a romantic of a somewhat later generation, Friedrich Hebbel, voiced the most radical formulation of the proximity of poetry to dreams when he wrote that his idea that dreams and poetry are *identical* has been confirmed more and more.

A modern scholar, Albert Béguin, who in his book *L'âme romantique et le rêve* examined early nineteenth-century attitudes toward dreams, made a detailed comparison of the dreams noted down by Jean Paul in his notebooks and the dreams that frequently appear in his literary works. In no single instance did he find any direct or striking correspondences between the real and the literary dreams. Jean Paul clearly recast and stylized the dreams he used in his novels. On the other hand, Jean Paul—and quite certainly Coleridge—must have studied with particular psychological attention the ways dreams shape their material and the way the dreamer associates. He used the word *"nachgeträumt"* about one of his literary works, in which he undoubtedly tried to reproduce the way a dream presents its substance. It should be added that Jean Paul was in the habit of listening to music or using artificial stimulants to achieve a productive state of reverie. The parallel with Coleridge and his account of the mild state of opium stupor is self-evident.[10]

Jean Bosquet, the scholar who most recently examined the connection between the romatic poets and dreams, provides an important additional insight: the element of absurdity and incoherence that we often associate with dreams is quite lacking in dreams in romantic literature. Dreams in the works of Jean Paul, Tieck, and Novalis are not disconnected; on the contrary, they are linguistically well articulated and their chronologies are straightforward. The same observation, writes Bosquet, applies to Coleridge's *Kubla Khan* and Keats's *Endymion*.[11]

That Coleridge's poem observes the logic of poetry rather than the alogical structure of a dream cannot in itself, however, be regarded as indicating that his point of departure was *not* a dream. The fact is that the romantic poets always worked within the bounds of their particular aesthetic conventions and ideals; reproducing the absurdity of a dream or its absurd elements was not an aesthetic possibility for them. It devolved upon a much later generation to break these bounds.

The romantic writers' view of the creative forces at work in dreams goes back to ancient beliefs in oracles and temple sleep, but at the same time it anticipates the discoveries of depth psychology. Freud and later psychoanalysts attribute to the imagination a function related to that of dreams—both poetry and dreams are held to provide contact with subconscious layers of the personality. It is to these deep layers that contemporary creativity psychologists trace the creative forces.

Psychoanalytically orientated scholars who have dealt with dreams and literature are conscious of both the nearness and the distance between dream fantasies and creative literature. This is true of both Freud himself and of Wilhelm Stekel, author of the book *Die Träume der Dichter* (1912). The latter emphasizes that dreams and imaginative literature are related but not identical phenomena. Many of Stekel's most illuminating examples are taken from Hebbel, the late-romantic German writer already referred to, whose diaries bear witness to his strong interest in his own dreams. In them Hebbel describes poems he dreamed he had written, which seemed—while he was dreaming—both remarkable and wonderful. But on waking he found them to be quite worthless. It would seem, writes Hebbel, as though one weighed and measured with different systems in dreams and in real life. For Hebbel, dream poems insofar as he was able to recollect them, proved disappointing. Occasionally a poem was entirely obliterated from his memory when he awoke, something Stekel attributes to censorship by Hebbel's conscious mind.

Stekel also interviewed contemporary writers, one of whom, Clara Blüthgen, told him that her dreams often did preliminary work for her (*"mir häufig die Vorarbeit geleistet"*). This only confirms, observes Stekel, the existence of the subconscious, which he says he never doubted. Nor, for that matter, did Coleridge, who was one of those writers who intuitively understood and openly discussed the interplay of consciousness and the subconscious mind. Indeed he was one of the first—if not the first—to introduce the word "unconsciousness" into English literary criticism, with the same sense that nowadays attaches to the term "the subconscious."

The possibility and value of dream composition has also been discussed in relation to music. There is a well-known story that Berlioz—twice—heard a whole new symphony in a dream. However, he never wrote them down, which he explained by saying that he feared the expense of performing them would have ruined him. Needless to say, the story is impossible to verify, and it has been received with fitting skepticism.

Early in this century F.v. Hausegger interviewed a number of composers about dream work. Most of them spoke of a similarity between the dream state and the creative state, but v. Hausegger heard nothing about valuable thoughts or inspiration arising in dreams or about compositions executed in dreams. On the other hand, it appeared that for composers—as well as for writers and other "creative" persons—the moments immediately after waking, and sometimes also immediately before falling asleep, were fruitful for creative ideas.[12] This is reminiscent of Coleridge's account that he wrote down *Kubla Kahn* immediately upon waking from his slumber or state of reverie.

The interviews conducted in the 1930s by the musicologist Julius Bahle, mentioned in Chapter 1, in which he asked questions about creativity in dreams, elicited an entirely negative response. H. Neal describes his dream experiences as follows: "In the first instance in the dream you feel quite intoxicated by the value and beauty of the idea. But if you examine it by the light of day, its value decreases more and more, particularly when it is set down on paper, and after a short while you come to regard the dream creation as worthless, trivial or simply a reminiscence."[13] The last point is of considerable interest. The same composer describes how he once was captivated by a dream improvisation and wrote it down that morning. His enthusiasm for the musical dream theme continued unabated—until he discovered its close resemblance to a theme from *Carmen*, whereupon it immediately became worthless to him. We should note that for a *writer* of Coleridge's type, the fact that a dream contained reminiscences from other literature would not be fatal in the same way that it would be for a composer. As Lowes demonstrated, the poem *Kubla Kahn* can be regarded as a pattern, created out of new combinations of fragments, some of them verbatim, from Oriental travel stories.

Another well-known, somewhat older story from the annals of musical history is often quoted in connection with dream composition: Tartini's account of the origin of *The Devil's Sonata*. Tartini says that one night he dreamed he was bargaining with the Devil for his soul. He got the idea of giving the Devil his violin, in order to see what he could make of it. "Great was my astonishment," continues Tartini, "when I heard him play with exquisite accomplishment a sonata of such untold beauty, that it exceeded my wildest dreams." Upon waking, Tartini seized his violin and tried to reproduce what he had heard: "In vain. The piece I then composed was admittedly the best I have written, but how inferior it was to the sonata I heard in my dream!"[14]

These examples of the experiences of dream-conscious writers and composers point to the fact that a direct transposition of words and musical notes from the language of dreams to that of real life seldom seems to produce artistically satisfactory results. For when the process of memory has been successful, the result has most frequently been artistically disappointing. Only when the memory process has been unsuccessful does the dream composition appear to retain the aesthetic value it had in the dream. Perhaps this can be explained in the following way: the demands made on an artist —demands dictated by tradition and technical skill—are seldom realized by dreams, which are essentially irresponsible. When a poet like Coleridge claimed to have written a longish poem in a dream, he *may* have been rationalizing (or possibly have been subjected to a *déjà-vu* phenomenon). That short poems or verses can, word for word, arise directly in a dream is, on the other hand, not inconceivable and is not denied here. Many poets, among them Swinburne, have had such an experience; the first three stanzas of his poem *A Vision of Spring in Winter* were, by his own account, given him "during actual sleep."

Needless to say, we should not deny the possibility of individual differences in the dream lives of various creative artists, arising out of different psychic dispositions. For instance, it is symptomatic that Berlioz, who has just provided us with an example of a composer who claimed to have dreamed a whole symphony, belongs to the category that historians of music call "the purest inspirational type." It was he who said that most composers are simply *"Schreiber eines musikalischen Kobolds, den sie in sich tragen."*[15] In this respect H. Neal, referred to above, is his direct opposite, for Neal explained that in his opinion fantasies never produce ready-made compositions but only raw material, harmony sequences, melodies, which are often forgotten but which can reappear on some later occasion.[16]

An important aspect of Coleridge's description of the origin of *Kubla Khan* remains to be discussed. Both in the note to the manuscript of the 1790s and in the longer narrative of the 1816 preface, he mentions a two-gram dose of opium which he had taken shortly before the poem arose in his consciousness.

Many books have been written on the subject of the opium habits

of the English romantics and the effect of opium on the imagination and creative powers. One of the most recent is Alethea Hayter's
informative and critical investigation, entitled *Opium and the Romantic Imagination* (1968). The poets Crabbe, Coleridge, and de
Quincey (author of *The Memoirs of an Opium-Eater*) are the chief
characters in her book, but she also touches upon the opium habits
of such writers as Poe and Baudelaire.

Like many of his contemporaries, Coleridge started to use opium
as a medicine, in the form in which, dissolved in alcohol, it was to
be bought in apothecaries' shops under the name Laudanum. He
had not yet, during the 1790s, become what he was to become
later—a slave to opium. During the initial period, sometimes called
the opium-eater's "honeymoon," the substance often produces
euphoria, a paradisal feeling of bliss; in time, the artificial paradise
is transformed into an artificial hell. On many occasions Coleridge
described the effect of opium upon his state of mind. In a letter
to his brother George in March 1798, he speaks of the "divine repose" he experienced as an effect of taking opium. He describes
his feeling of joy in a series of landscape images: "Laudanum gave
me repose, not sleep; but you, I believe, know how divine that repose is, what a spot of enchantment, a green spot of fountain and
flowers and trees in the very heart of a waste of sands."[17] This letter, quoted by Lowes in *The Road to Xanadu*, is an admirable
parallel and prose commentary to *Kubla Khan*, written under the
influence of opium at about the same time.

One of Coleridge's literary contemporaries provides us with a
story that in many respects resembles his preface to *Kubla Khan*.
The actress and writer Perdita Robinson was Coleridge's close
friend around the turn of the eighteenth century. Furthermore,
she was the first person positively known to have been aware of
the existence of the poem *Kubla Khan*; as early as October 1800
she refers to it in a poem of her own. In the memoirs published
shortly after her death in the early nineteenth century, there is a
description of how she composed her poem *The Maniac*. This took
place during a visit to Bath in 1791. Her daughter, who recounts
the episode, regards it as an example of the unbelievable ease with
which her mother could compose poetry. One night, so her daughter tells us, when she had had more pain than usual, she took nearly

eight drops of opium on her doctor's advice. When she had slept some hours, she woke, called her daughter, and asked her to take a pen and write down what she dictated. Miss Robinson, who assumed that this wish arose out of the condition produced by the opium, tried—vainly—to dissuade her. Mrs. Robinson's inspiration was not to be denied, and she recited from beginning to end the pleasing poem *The Maniac*, much faster than it could be taken down on paper. She lay, while she dictated it, with closed eyes and spoke as though asleep. Here we have another of the wondrous tales of the English romantic era, about a poem composed with improvisational speed and confidence. The resemblance to Coleridge's account is self-evident, although it was not claimed that Perdita Robinson literally, word for word, had dreamed her poem but simply that she dictated it as though in a trance.

How much credence are we to lend to this account? A period of ten years had elapsed between the reported events and the daughter's account; in the meantime, the incident might have grown and become magnified, memories might have become displaced. Elisabeth Schneider concluded that Perdita Robinson's story underlay Coleridge's preface to *Kubla Khan* and served as a paradigm. But it could of course have been the other way round: Coleridge's verbal account to her of how his poem was written could have encouraged Perdita Robinson to recollect—or fabricate—a similar experience. It is also conceivable that both accounts—Perdita Robinson's as well as Coleridge's—arose independently of each other and that both contain some truth.

If we are to believe the accounts collected by medical researchers, sensory experiences are greatly intensified in the euphoric state produced by opium; abstract ideas are transformed into images and powers of association are increased, as is the flow of words in conversation. As against this it is a vexed question whether opium and similar stimulants are directly conducive to artistic creativity. The majority of nineteenth-century writers were convinced that they were. Present-day opinion is considerably more skeptical. But the question whether various artificial stimulants are able to enhance creativity has continued to interest writers and psychologists in this age of psychedelic poetry. Those who believe that it does, resort to various explanatory models, for instance, that the artistically gifted individual achieves more direct contact with the creative resources of the subconscious with the aid of drugs acting on the central nervous system. The removal of repressions and the weakening of the censorship mechanism of the conscious mind are seen as positive stimulants to creativity.

The belief, held by many nineteenth-century writers, that opium affects artistic creativity is connected with the belief that opium stimulates dream activity. This is another idea with which modern medical experts disagree. Opium does not produce intensive dreams in people who do not normally have vivid dreams. Opium dreams have more or less disappeared from modern medical literature. Many so-called opium dreams, particularly in the early stages of habituation, have been found to be daydreams. But the daydreaming subject has less power or ability than normal to control and lead the direction of the dream, which seems to have a certain autonomous character. This is how Alethea Hayter presents the case in her chapter on dreams, and it fits in well with Coleridge's "state of reverie."

Modern scholarship is very skeptical about the opium dreams described by de Quincey and regards them as pure literary fictions in some respects. In any case, it is obvious that the thought that an opium dream should necessarily evoke Oriental scenery and associations is a compound product of the exoticism and dream cult of romanticism. Coleridge's account gives an entirely adequate explanation, which has never been doubted, of the Oriental aspects of *Kubla Khan*. Immediately before falling into his state of reverie and subsequently writing his poem, he had been reading Purchas's Oriental travel description, in which Kubla Khan figured.

The many and circuitous arguments about how Coleridge's poem was composed cannot lead to any definite knowledge but to certain probable conclusions. It is conceivable and likely that Coleridge never succeeded in finishing the poem he had in mind. We have his word that the poem remained a fragment, which might explain the ten-year delay in publishing it. Many critics have pointed to the abrupt break in the poem, the gap after the thirty-sixth line. They suggest that his preface to the 1816 edition may have functioned as an excuse for the fact that the poem was never completed or rounded off. On the other hand, the poem is in all probability no

pure dream product. In company with many contemporary scholars, we can doubt that the poem, in its highly structured form—
and in spite of the gap or break—arose word for word as it now
stands on paper. But we have no reason to doubt that Coleridge
himself experienced it as a spontaneous poetic product, a lyrical
shooting star. The poem presumably originated in a reverie induced
by opium, "without any sensation or consciousness of effort," a
flowering of the imagination "as it were, given to him." In this respect it is by no means a unique phenomenon. The transition from
the inner stream of words of the silent creative act to the writing
down of the poem on paper took place with the speed of improvisation. The extant manuscript cannot be adduced as proof of such
a creative process; nor can it be used to prove the opposite. The
manuscript presents us with a completed poem, which does not allow us to follow the process that Baudelaire, another poet who
took opium, called the labor whereby a reverie becomes a work of
art: *"le travail par lequel une rêverie devient une oeuvre d'art."*[18]
Interpretations of *Kubla Khan* have to some degree been based on
views held about the poem's origin. A psychoanalytical *Traumdeu-
tung* has been natural for those who regard the poem as a dream
product. H. S. and C. D. Bliss attempted to interpret its images
and symbols with the help of a Freudian dream key in the psychoanalytical journal *American Imago*. Maud Bodkin, on the other
hand, who works in accordance with Jung's depth psychology,
found in the poem a number of archetypes, for instance, heaven/hell,
whereby Mount Abora and the pleasure dome represent the archetype of heaven, and the caverns measureless to man represent
archetypical hell.[19] Other commentators, such as Kenneth Burke,
have noted the poem's connection with an opium reverie and have
seen in it a symbolic description of the opium stupor itself, whereby the state of being "high" is expressed by the mountainous landscape and Mount Abora, and negative aspects and frightening moments of opium intoxication are expressed by rivers—like snakes—
meandering with a mazy motion.

Those scholars, on the other hand, who see in *Kubla Khan* a
product deliberately shaped by the poet's artistic consciousness—
and this is particularly true of Elisabeth Schneider and Marshall
Suther in his *Visions of Xanadu* (1965)—have been at pains to

demonstrate the poem's composition, its structure or architecture, its well-balanced contrasts and parallellisms, its linguistically and rhythmically well-built form. The extreme of this school of thought is represented by Marshall Suther, who even maintains that the poem has no break in the middle and is not composed of two joined fragments but follows an inner, consistent, unbroken compositional line.[20]

There are over ten different interpretations of the poem's symbolic code. However, many scholars are agreed on at least *one* reading. The poem, or rather a part of it, should—also—be seen as a description of the process of poetic creativity. *Kubla Khan* includes a poem about poetry, about poetic enthusiasm and vision. A central portion speaks of the visionary experience in much the same words that Plato uses in the dialogue *Ion*, well known in England thanks to Shelley's translation. But it also speaks of the absent vision, of how it refuses to appear at command. The emphasis lies on the word "Could":

> A damsel with a dulcimer
> In a vision once I saw
>
> . . . .
>
> Could I revive within me
> Her sympathy and song
> To such a deep delight t'would win me
> That with music loud and long,
> I would build that dome in air,
> That sunny dome! those caves of ice.
> And all who heard should see them there
> And all should cry, Beware! Beware!
> His flashing eyes, his floating hair!
> Weave a circle round him thrice
> And close your eyes with holy dread
> For he on honey-dew hath fed
> And drunk the milk of Paradise.

The fact that *Kubla Khan* is also a poem about the creative state, "a diagram of the creative imagination,"[21] has undoubtedly contributed to the role it has been assigned in subsequent aesthetic discussions. Even though Coleridge with becoming modesty reduces its significance to that of "a psychological curiosity," it has not played so unassuming a role in the aesthetic debate of the nineteenth and twentieth centuries. As we already heard, Kenneth Burke refers to it as "the great surrealist Masterpiece."

The surrealists of the 1920s elevated the idea of the creative act as an unconscious dream state into aesthetic dogma and poetic practice. In the first surrealist manifesto André Breton declared that surrealism rested on a belief in a higher degree of reality in certain—previously denied or ignored—forms of association, on a belief in *"la toute-puissance du rêve."* In the manifesto he also tells an anecdote about the poet Saint-Pol-Roux, who before going to bed at night hung a notice on his front door, consisting of the following portentous words: LE POÈTE TRAVAILLE. The same legend could—if we are to believe Coleridge—have been hung on the front door of the lonely farmhouse between Linton and Porlock, where Coleridge was inspired to write *Kubla Khan.*

But dreams have also had their detractors in modern aesthetics. Paul Valéry is the best known of them. We can round off this chapter by stating three of his observations, three final assertions dismissing the power of spontaneous dream inspiration. Valéry writes in *Variétés* that "the authentic state of an authentic poet is what separates him most from the dream state." In one of his *Pièces sur l'art* he proclaims that "one must always be afraid of committing the modern mistake of confusing dreams and poetry." Finally, he points out in the introduction to the French translation of Martin Lamm's book on Swedenborg that "a dream is a hypothesis, since we never ever can get to know it, except through a memory, which in itself is necessarily a construction."[22]

E. A. Poe and
the Aesthetics of Work

Any damn fool can be spontaneous.

Ezra Pound
Quoted in *Writers at Work*

1

Poe's poem *The Raven* was first published in 1845 in an American periodical. No author name appeared under it, simply the pseudonym Quarles. It was soon reprinted in other periodicals, now under the author's own name. In March 1846 in Graham's Magazine, Poe published his famous essay on how he wrote his poem, under the title *The Philosophy of Composition*.[1]

Looking at Poe's essay in its historical context, it becomes clear that, consciously or unconsciously, his statement is diametrically opposed to Coleridge's preface to *Kubla Khan*, written a couple of decades earlier. That Coleridge really was in Poe's thoughts while he was writing his *poem* can be considered a reasonably well-proved fact.[2]

In his analysis of the poem's genesis, Poe says nothing about how long he actually spent writing *The Raven*. Opinions on the length of this time period vary. According to a Mrs. Weiss, who cites Poe himself as her source, the poem lay unfinished in his writing-table drawer for more than ten years, while he worked on it from time to time.[3] According to another report, which also cites Poe as its source, the poem was written within the space of one day![4] Whether Poe himself in fact communicated these mystifying and contradictory data about his poem is, naturally, impossible to verify. What we know with a fair degree of certainty is that the poem already existed in some form in 1842; Poe spoke of its existence to several people during this and the following year; when he came to New York in 1844 he read it aloud to his hostess.[5] He continued working on it and altering it even after its first publication. This is well known, for instance, through Poe's correspondence with Augustus Shea: a letter of February 1845 to the latter contains a new version of the eleventh verse, with an underlined alliteration. And Poe continued to make minor alterations in his poem in subsequent editions. It is, however, impossible to follow the manuscript history of the poem; an extant manuscript, recently published in facsimile, does not appear to offer anything of interest.[6]

Poe himself, like his contemporaries, had a very high opinion of his poem: "The Raven has had a great run," he writes in a letter of May 1845,[7] and on another occasion he says that this poem, compared with his other poetic works, will be regarded as a diamond of purest water, more sparkling than all the others.[8]

It was therefore scarcely fortuitous that he chose this poem to illustrate his aesthetic tract *The Philosophy of Composition*. "I select *The Raven* as most generally known," he explains in the essay.[9] This motivation is not unimportant; he chose it because it was the best known of his poems and not because the way it was written was unique or different in principle from that of his other poems. "It is my design to render it manifest that no one point in its composition is referrible either to accident or intuition—that the work proceeded, step by step, to its completion with the precision and rigid consequence of a mathematical problem."[10]

Early on in the essay Poe makes a sort of apology for his undertaking: "I have often thought how interesting a magazine paper might be written by any author who would—that is to say, who could—detail, step by step, the processes by which any one of his compositions attained its ultimate point of completion. Why such a paper has never been given to the world, I am much at a loss to say—but, perhaps, the authorial vanity has had more to do with the omission than any one other cause."[11]

Then follows Poe's explanation of the nimbus that until then attached to the whole problem of creation, typical of a poet living during the final phase of the romantic era:

> Most writers—poets in especial—prefer having it understood that they compose by a species of fine frenzy—an ecstatic intuition—and would positively shudder at letting the public take a peep behind the scenes, at the elaborate and vacillating crudities of thought—at the true purposes seized only at the last moment—at the innumerable glimpses of idea that arrived not at the maturity of full view—at the fully matured fancies discarded in despair as unmanageable—at the cautious selections and rejections—at the painful erasures and interpolations—in a word, at the wheels and pinions—the tackle for scene-shifting—the step-ladders and demon-traps—the cock's feathers, the red paint and the black patches, which, in ninety-nine cases out of the hundred, constitute the properties of the literary *histrio*.[12]

After this passage, with some of its imagery from the world and workshop of the theater, Poe goes on to note his distinctive mark as an artist, his power of introspection into his creativity. "I am aware," he writes,

> that the case is by no means common, in which an author is at all in condition to retrace the steps by which his conclusions have been attained. In general, suggestions, having arisen pell-mell, are pursued and forgotten in a similar manner.
>
> For my own part, I have neither sympathy with the repugnance alluded to, nor, at any time, the least difficulty in recalling to mind the progressive steps of any of my compositions; and, since the interest of an analysis, or reconstruction, such as I have considered a *desideratum*, is quite independent of any real or fancied interest in the thing analyzed, it will not be regarded as a breach of decorum on my part to show the *modus operandi* by which some one of my works was put together.[13]

Now follows the justification, already referred to, for choosing *The Raven* as the object of analysis. "Let us," says Poe, "dismiss, as irrelevant to the poem, *per se*, the circumstance—or say the necessity—which, in the first place, gave rise to the intention of composing *a* poem that should suit at once the popular and the critical taste. We commence, then, with this intention."[14]

Poe's initial consideration concerned the length of the poem. It should be neither too long nor too short—and here Poe repeats thoughts he develops elsewhere, for instance, in *The Poetic Principle*. It should not be so long that it cannot be read at one sitting, nor so short that it disappears in a breath. Poe decided to write a poem of about one hundred lines. In fact it amounted to one hundred and eight lines.

The next consideration concerned the choice of impression or effect to be conveyed. "Beauty," declares Poe, "is the sole legitimate province of the poem."[15] For contemplation of beauty provides a pleasure that is at once the most intense, the most elevating, and the most pure. A rule applying to all art is that effects should spring from direct causes—that objects should be attained through means best adapted for their attainment. So if beauty is the atmosphere and essence of the poem, the next question is, how should it manifest itself so that it achieves the greatest effect, what would be the *tone* of its highest manifestation? "All experience," Poe claims, "has shown that this tone is one of *sadness*."[16] In its highest manifestation beauty always brings the sensitive soul to tears—and so melancholy, according to Poe, is the most legitimate of poetical tones.

Now that the length, province, and tone of the poem had been established, Poe next cast around for some "artistic piquancy which might serve me as a key-note in the construction of the poem—some pivot upon which the whole structure might turn."[17] After much deliberation about all the usual artistic effects, he decided that no technique had been so universally used as that of the *refrain*. However, uniform repetition is monotonous, and Poe decided to vary and enhance the effect by retaining the monotone repetition of sound but varying the thought behind the repetition, i.e., he decided to achieve constant new effects by varying the meaning of the refrain.

The next consideration concerned the nature of the refrain. Since it was to be repeated so often, it had to be short. For it would have been insurmountably difficult to devise a lengthy sentence capable of serving as a refrain and of being varied. So he chose a single word.

Now the character of the word had to be decided on. If the poem was to be made of stanzas—as a refrain indicates—the refrain should form the close of each stanza. Such a close has to be sonorous and emphatic. Hence the choice of long *o* as the most sonorous vowel, in connection with *r* as "the most producible" consonant.

Now that the sound had been determined, a word had to be found that embodied this sound-combination and that at the same time conveyed the melancholy tone Poe had decided on. The first word that then occurred to him was "nevermore." Next a pretext had to be found for the continuous use of this one word. It was difficult to envisage a human being with so limited a vocabulary; whereupon Poe hit upon the idea of a nonreasoning creature capable of speech. First he thought of a parrot, which was swiftly superseded by a raven; ravens can also be taught to speak, and a raven would undoubtedly be far more in harmony with the intended tone of the poem.

Poe continues:

> I had now gone so far as the conception of a Raven—the bird of ill omen —monotonously repeating the one word, "Nevermore," at the conclusion of each stanza, in a poem of melancholy tone, and in length about one hundred lines. Now, never losing sight of the object *supremeness*, or perfection, at all points, I asked myself—"Of all melancholy topics, what, according to the *universal* understanding of mankind, is the *most* melancholy?" Death—was the obvious reply. "And when," I said, "is this most melancholy of topics most poetical?" From what I have already explained at some length, the answer, here also, is obvious— "When it most closely allies itself to *Beauty*: the death, then of a beautiful woman is, unquestionably, the most poetical topic in the world— and equally is it beyond doubt that the lips best suited for such a topic are those of a bereaved lover."[18]

Now these two ideas had to be combined: a lover mourning the death of his beloved and a raven endlessly repeating the word "Nevermore." The only possible way of combining these two elements was to let the raven speak the word in reply to the lover's questions. "And here it was," writes Poe,

> that I saw at once the opportunity afforded for the effect on which I had been depending—that is to say, the effect of the *variation of application*. I saw that I could make the first query propounded by the lover . . . a commonplace one—the second less so—the third less, and so on—until . . . the lover . . . is at length excited to superstition, and wildly propounds queries of a far different character . . . propounds them half in superstition and half in that species of despair which de-

lights in self-torture—propounds them not altogether because he believes in the prophetic or demoniac character of the bird . . . but because he experiences a frenzied pleasure in so modeling his questions as to receive from the *expected* "Nevermore" the most delicious because the most intolerable sorrow.[19]

And this is where the poem was begun, at its close. Poe put pen to paper and wrote the stanza:

> "Prophet," said I, "thing of evil! prophet still if bird or
>   devil!
> By that heaven that bends above us—by that God we both
>   adore.
> Tell this soul with sorrow laden, if within the distant Aidenn,
> It shall clasp a sainted maiden whom the angels name
>   Lenore—
> Clasp a rare and radiant maiden whom the angels name
>   Lenore."
>
>   Quoth the raven "Nevermore"

Earlier in his essay Poe had propounded the belief that all real works of art should be commenced at the end and then executed backward. Every intrigue should be worked out with its climax in mind. In this instance Poe justifies beginning at the end by saying that only in this way could he vary and graduate the earlier questions, which the lover had to pose, and plan the rhythm, meter, length, and general arrangement of the stanza so that none of the foregoing ones would surpass it in rhythmical effect. "Had I been able," he writes, "in the subsequent composition, to construct more vigorous stanzas, I should, without scruple, have purposely enfeebled them, so as not to interfere with the climacteric effect."[20]

Poe goes on to deal with versification. Here, too, his objective was originality. But originality, he stresses, is not to be attained by impulse or intuition but has to be "elaborately sought." Poe does not claim originality in either rhythm or meter—he uses familiar feet and lines. But although these had all been used before, their combination into stanza form had never before been attempted, with the short end line, new rhyme effects (partly internal), and alliteration.

The stanza having been found, he now had to find a way of bringing together the lover and the raven. A forest or fields would have
seemed natural, but he remarks that "a close *circumscription of
space* is absolutely necessary to the effect of insulated incident:—it
has the force of a frame to a picture."[21] It should, therefore, be a
room. When the *locale* was settled, a way had to be found of introducing the bird, and letting him fly in through the window was
self-evident. The idea of letting the man in the room first imagine
that the bird against the shutter is a tapping on the door was due
to a desire to increase the reader's curiosity, a desire to achieve an
incidental effect when the lover opens the door only to find everything dark outside and thus be led to half-fancy that it was perhaps
the spirit of his dead mistress. Poe made it a stormy night for two
reasons: first, to explain why the raven sought shelter; second, to
achieve a contrast against the serenity of the room. In addition, he
let the raven settle on a bust of Pallas for the effect of contrast between the marble and the plumage, and he chose this particular
bust not only because it was in keeping with the scholarship of the
lover but also because the word itself—"Pallas" was sonorous.

Poe next explains that he availed himself of the contrast between
fantastic, near—ludicrous effects in the middle part of the poem
and the increasing seriousness that follows. Finally he speaks of
the need for complexity and suggestiveness—"some under-current,
however indefinite, of meaning"[22] —which he satisfied by adding
two concluding stanzas to the original "last" stanza, so that the
bird finally becomes emblematic, a symbol of *Mournful and Never-
ending Remembrance.*

2

Poe's account of the writing of *The Raven,* like Coleridge's corresponding account of how he wrote *Kubla Khan,* gives rise to the
question: to what extent is it trustworthy? The question was
asked soon enough by Mallarmé, who had read Poe's *Philosophy of
Composition* in Baudelaire's translation. "Que penser de l'article, tra-
duit par Baudelaire sous le titre de *Genèse d'un poème* sauf que c'est

un pur jeu intellectuel," he wrote in the introduction to a volume of his own translations of poems—including *Le Corbeau* by Poe. At the same time he translates part of a letter from a Suzan Achard Wirds, which had recently been published in a Poe biography. "En discutant du *Corbeau* (écrit Mme Suzan Achard Wirds à M. William Gill) M. Poe m'assura que la relation par lui publiée de la méthode de composition de cette oeuvre n'avait rien d'authentique; et qu'il n'avait pas compté qu'on lui accordât ce caractère. L'idée lui vint, suggérée par les commentaires et les investigations des critiques, que le poème aurait peut-être ainsi composé."[23] However, this disclosure—the truth of which, needless to say, is also open to doubt—in no way shook Mallarmé. It has never been believed by those poets and aestheticians, like Mallarmé himself, Valéry, the young Swedish author Pär Lagerkvist, and Gottfried Benn, who have recognized their own experiences of the processes of poetic composition in Poe's philosophy of writing.

To modify the more provocative aspects of Poe's essay, Mallarmé resorted to an interesting argument in the introduction to his translation volume. He suggests that had Poe lived in a country with theatrical traditions and a living theater, he, with his *facultés d'architecte et de musicien*, might have devoted himself to the theater as a dramatist. And—says Mallarmé—in the realm of the drama the various acts and scenes are always structured with highly conscious skill and artistry. Poe's innovation was that he transposed the methods of the dramatist and theatrical producer to a new genre. The play of chance has to be banned from the modern work of art or else occur only as a pretence, a sham.

3

The fact that Poe actually had the theater in mind is substantiated by the imagery in his aesthetic tract. He speaks in the essay of taking a peep behind the scenes at "the wheels and pinions—the tackle for scene-shifting—the step-ladders and demon-traps—the cock's feathers, the red paint and the black patches." He compares the author, however, more to "the literary *histrio*," i.e., actor, than to the dramatist.

Now it is well known that there are two divergent theories about the psychology of actors. On the one hand, there is the idea that actors wholeheartedly and artlessly throw themselves into their parts with every fiber of their beings and every emotion they can muster. On the other hand, the notion exists that actors on stage are emotionally cool, calculating their effect on the audience without for a moment being involved in the feelings they are portraying. The latter view, known as Diderot's paradox, supposes that the perfect actor is master of all forms of emotional expression, without feeling any sorrow, anger, or joy when performing; she/he acts solely with a view to producing an effect on the public. So Poe's idea of the author as literary histrio could be seen as an extension of Diderot's philosophy of acting, for he regards the writer not as the victim of his/her emotions but as a deliberately calculating role-creator striving to achieve certain definite effects. Poe draws a sharp dividing line between the poet and the poet's experience, "the intoxication of the heart," on the one hand, and the poem she/he writes, on the other. A view propounded more recently by T. S. Eliot is his distinction between "the man who suffers" and "the poet who creates."

Music was another form that fascinated Poe and from which he took terminology and images. He touches on points of contact between music and poetry in *The Poetic Principle* (1850) and finds this chiefly on the rhythmic level. In another connection he speaks, in an essay of 1839, of "that merely mathematical recognition of equality which seems to be the root of all Beauty."[24] The very title of the essay in which he describes how he wrote *The Raven* contains the term *composition*, most often associated with music.

It is an interesting and indisputable fact that composers often, and without any reservations, have commented on the technical means whereby they have sought to achieve a certain aesthetic effect. Valéry—in many ways an admirer and follower of Poe's philosophy—writes, in *Fragments des mémoires d'un poème*, about the conscious artistry of composers: "No one has presumably ever dreamed of reproaching a composer with the comment that the many years he has spent studying harmony and orchestration would weaken the power of his particular genius. Why should one deprive the poet of the same advantage, why should he not be allowed to work with the same degree of technical deliberation and technical calculation?"[25]

In connection with this, it might be instructive to quote what Carl Maria von Weber, an elderly musical contemporary of Poe's, had to say about his strategy when composing the music for his opera *Der Freischütz*. Weber referred to a point in the libretto at which Max speaks the words *"Mich umgarnen finstere Mächte."* These words, said Weber, indicated the underlying mood the opera should have.

> As often as possible I must remind the audience, by means of tone and melody, of these "dark powers." I have long deliberated and considered what the right central tone [*Hauptklang*] can be for this fearful thing. It must of course be a dark, somber tone, that is to say the deepest regions of the strings and wind instruments, particularly the lowest notes of the clarinets, which seem to me particularly suited to represent what is terrifying, in addition the plaintive sound of bassoons, the deepest notes of horns, the muffled whirls or solitary muted beat of kettle-drums.[26]

These early deliberations of Weber's took place during an abstract and preparatory phase of composition, before tone and melody sequences had crystallized in his mind. In the same way—and this is the interesting point of resemblance—Poe's thoughts were on an abstract-schematic level and largely preceded verbalization. It should be remarked that Weber's example is far from isolated in musical history; Bahle provides several contemporary parallels and could undoubtedly provide examples from the past as well. It is difficult to say whether Poe himself received inspiration for his analysis of the art of composition from actual composers, but it is well known that he was familiar with the deeply musical German romantic writer E. T. A. Hoffman. As confirmation of how well Poe formulated experiences shared by creative musicians, we could choose two remarks out of several pertinent ones by composers of the late nineteenth century. In an essay entitled *Music and Edgar Allan Poe*, M. G. Evans points out that both Debussy and Ravel recognized their own compositional methods in those described by Poe. Maurice Ravel went so far as to cite *The Philosophy of Composition* as norm and pattern for compositional activity.[27]

4

Poe's method is by no means as rare in the annals of literary aesthetics as has at times been suggested. Admittedly his *Philosophy of Composition* possesses undeniable originality because it was diametrically opposed to what was then the majority view on literary composition. But in fact romantic aesthetic theory already included the idea of poetry as a mathematical or architectural construction—perhaps as an inheritance from an older, rhetorical tradition. Friedrich W. Schlegel, who distinguished between two types of writer, the synthetic and the analytical, wrote in one of his *Kritische Fragmente* in *Lyceum*: "The analytical writer observes his reader, what he is like; after this examination he does his calculation, prepares his instruments in order to achieve the desired effect on him."[28]

If we look behind romantic aesthetics, we find even more striking parallels to Poe's compositional experiences and rules. During the lengthy period when a classicist aesthetic reigned supreme and when the writing of poetry was regarded as an art to be learned, the rhetorical handbooks contained close counterparts to Poe's account of how a poem is composed with the aid of reflection and planning.

Windfuhr's book *Barocke Bildlichkeit*[29] contains a detailed description by the German seventeenth-century writer of a poetic handbook, one Reimmann, in which he relates the procedures he observed when composing a dirge on a student.

I was to write a *Carmen funebre* on a virtuous theological student. And since he had been plucked away in the flower of his youth, the image of a glass pleased me best and more than other inventions, and I ascertained about this (material), partly through meditation, partly also through reading (*per lectionem*), the following facts:
1. When the glass is heated up and melts, it takes on the most beautiful shapes.
2. It neither withers nor rusts.
3. It can be ground in the most intricate ways.
4. In addition it can be painted and gilded.
5. It is transparent and as free from blemishes inwardly as outwardly.
6. It can be placed in a fire from 3 to 4 days, and the longer it there re-

mains, the cleaner and more unblemished it becomes.
7. It is fragile and can easily be broken.
8. The glass must be blown, if anything proper is to come of it.[30]

Reimmann first summarizes in an abstract and logical way the various qualities of glass, which could be used as points of comparison in a poem. He then goes on to write:

> After this I addressed myself to the poem's disposition, and dealt with it as follows. I kept the three parts—that is to say, three according to poetic convention—Praise, Sorrow and Comfort (*laudem, luctum* and *solatium*), always in mind. And since first I had occasion to praise his character, his readiness to learn, his piety, knowledge, patience and sincerity, second I had to mourn his premature decease, and third I had to propound his blessed state, I sketched out the following plan based on each of my images above.[31]

Now follows a detailed plan for every one of the poem's projected eight stanzas. Six of them are to embrace *laus*, i.e., praise of the deceased; the seventh to embrace *luctus*, sorrow over his death, the eighth *solatium*, comfort for the bereaved. Already in the first stanza the image of *Du warest wie ein Glas* is introduced, with a reference to number 8 on the list of attributes of glass provided above. The second stanza, which in accordance with the plan is to speak of his character (*naturam*), refers back to image number 1; the next stanza about his readiness to learn refers back to number 3; the fourth stanza about his piety refers back to number 4; the fifth stanza about his patience refers back to number 6; the sixth stanza about his sincerity refers back to number 5. Now comes the stanza that is to lament his death under the title *"Deine Qualiteten sind verschwunden,"* which naturally ties in with number 7, the fragility of glass; and finally the closing stanza bringing comfort in the thought that neither your body nor your soul have been subjected to suffering, which refers back, with amplification—i.e., just as the glass is not devoured by worms or rust—to number 2. The outline is now established and is succeeded by the working out of form and detail. In the next paragraph, introduced by the words *"Endlich geriet mir die Elaboration also,"* stanza upon stanza of the poem follows in a kind of alexandrine *ottava rima*, with a shortened final line. The image of glass, seen from the various aspects indicated in the list of attributes, plays a part in each stanza.

There are, of course, differences between Poe's poetic method and that represented by Reimmann in his *Poesis germanorum*. Set next to Poe's more sophisticated arguments, Reimmann's exposition appears as the work of a guileless craftsman or rule-of-thumb carpenter. But the similarities are also striking. The two poets stand on either side of the great divide represented by romanticism and its philosophy of inspiration. Reimmann's compositional beliefs are ultimately based on classical rhetoric, which always strove for effect and had as its prime objective the influencing of the reader. In this respect Poe is a conscious or unconscious heir to the classical rhetorical tradition, for he continually operates with the desired effect as his lodestar. Both Reimmann and Poe work methodically, logically, discursively. In this connection it is of less importance that Reimmann works from a given outline sketch to be filled in, whereas Poe—offspring of the romantic age—aims for a more original product, innovative both in verse form and in language. The essential similarity resides in their method of work, the successive and progressive deliberations, the rational decisions, the manufacturing aspects—for Reimmann does not use words like "create" or "discover" either: his words are *"machen"* and *"Elaboration."* At the same time it must be admitted that Reimmann excludes from his account of the compositional process any mention of tradition, the common poetic pool, given forms. For him, these were self-evident.

5

In his book on the structure of modern poetry, Hugo Friedrich adumbrated Poe's remarks on the literary creative process in the following way: Poe reverses what was taken as the natural order of the creative procedure. Where others were in the habit of seeing the poem's "form" as an end product, Poe sees it as the starting point. He sees a poem's "content" as a secondary result, whereas it used to be regarded as the starting point.[32] Initially there is a tone that makes itself felt, and in order to express it, the poet searches for suitable sounds in the language, sounds which approximate it.

But the sounds are tied to words, and the words are grouped into themes, from which some sort of meaningful coherence finally emerges. Ultimately poetry can be said to arise out of language impulses, out of the creative power of language itself.[33]

Interpreted in this way, Poe's aesthetic philosophy becomes a stepping-stone to poetic modernism, and he soon won disciples and adepts in France. As mentioned, one of the first was Baudelaire, who translated not only a number of Poe's weird stories but also the poem whose French title was *Le Corbeau*, as well as the essay *La Genèse d'un poème*. In the *Notes nouvelles* with which he prefaced his translation of thirteen of Poe's *Tales of Mystery and Imagination*, he wrote that people who believed in inspiration would find in Poe's theories blasphemy and profanity. He himself had arrived at an aesthetic conviction that basically corresponded to Poe's.

Baudelaire repeats Poe's words almost verbatim when he writes that sensitivity of the heart is not an advantage at the moment of poetic creation. He who wishes to write poetry must work according to a plan, build up the poem architecturally, and make use of impulses inherent in the language. It is customary to point to the fact that Baudelaire arranged the first edition of *Les fleurs du mal* (1857) according to a strictly geometric pattern as an example of a mathematical principle of composition; the collection contained one hundred poems, divided into five groups of twenty. He abandoned this numerological principle in subsequent editions. Nevertheless, in his posthumously published essays *Curiosités esthétiques* (1868) and *L'Art romantique* (1868) he reverts to a discussion of theoretical principles in line with Poe's views on planned order and deliberate choices. He does not necessarily for this reason regard Poe solely as an exponent of a rationalistic aesthetic.

In France Stéphane Mallarmé is representative of those who have followed Poe's compositional principles even more strictly. In a well-known letter to Henry Cazalis (12 January 1864) he describes in detail how he applied Poe's principles when composing his poem *L'Azur*. Poe taught him to exclude chance (*le hasard*) from the act of composition and led him to calculate the semantic, syntactic, and euphonic element of every word he included in his poem. And he writes to Cazalis that the farther he proceeds, the more faithful he will remain to the ideas his great master Edgar Poe had bequeathed to him.[34]

Paul Valéry subsequently carried on the double tradition from Poe and Mallarmé. He writes to Pierre Louÿs in 1890 that his ideal poet would never abandon himself to the vagaries of inspiration—*aux hasards des inspirations*—and would never write a poem during a single feverish night. *"Je n'aime pas Musset,"* he adds.[35] Valéry several times followed Poe's example and analyzed the writing of his own poems. How close he came to his master can be seen, for instance, in the passage in *Tel Quel* that illustrates his poetic practice:

> I seek a word (says the poet) a word which is
> feminine,
> has two syllables,
> contains p or f,
> ends in a mute vowel,
> is synonymous with the word *brisure*
> which is not a learned or unusual word.
> Six conditions—at the very least!

With his customary intellectual precision, Valéry sees his poetic problem in mathematical terms. It must be solvable, just as a crossword puzzle is solvable. The Valéry scholar Hytier amused himself by trying to discover *which* word Valéry had in mind, and he suggested *"rupture,"* which appears in the poem *Grenades: "Cette lumineuse rupture."*[36]

The poets who, following in Poe's footsteps, declare their skepticism about romantic inspirational aesthetics and spontaneity regard poetic composition as a selective process of choosing and rejecting words. Mallarmé and Valéry did so, as we have seen, and so did Mayakovsky in his essay *How to Make Verse* (1926). Much of this essay consists of an account of how he wrote the poem *To Sergei Yesenin*, and there can be no doubt that he had in mind Poe's analysis of the composition of *The Raven*, using it as both model and contrast. Although Mayakovsky's basic view of poetry and its functions is radically different from Poe's, he reiterates some of the latter's experiences with word seeking and composition. He declares in one of the ten theses concluding the essay that poetry is an "industry"; during earlier epochs "craft" would have been the word. He warns both himself and others against too easy poetic solutions. He declares that all the poems he had written straight off, with great enthusiasm, and which had initially seemed satisfactory to him, had by the following day appeared flat and one-sided.[37] This conviction is shared by both Mallarmé and Valéry— enthusiasm is not the poet's ideal state.

Let us choose Gottfried Benn as the last of the exponents of an aesthetic of work, following on from Poe.[38] In his well-known lecture *Probleme der Lyrik* (1951), Benn rejects, as Poe, Valéry, and Mayakovsky had done before him, the romantic notion of the inspired creative poet. What happens when a poem is produced is not that a young man stands and looks at a sunset, he says. Poems seldom if ever arise; they are made (*wird gemacht*). Benn uses an example from his own poetic experience, in which two decades elapsed between his completion of the first and second (final) stanza respectively of a poem of his, *Welle der Nacht* from the collection *Statische Gedichte*.

Yet in his ideas on composition Gottfried Benn has been influenced by such different men as Poe and Nietzsche, and his presentation of his theories involves considerable contradictions. Although he stresses the need for technical skill and perfection of form, he does not deny the more mysterious wellsprings of creativity. He speaks, as does Nietzsche, of the Dionysian element, of familiarity with intoxication and the underworld of dreams. At this point the intellectual schema of Poe's *Philosophy of Composition* is definitively cracked wide open.

Very early on, commentators criticized the provocatively intellectualistic stance of Poe's essay and the fact that his account of the creative process dispensed with the role of the subconscious.[39] Marie Bonaparte, a psychoanalyst with literary interests, has done extensive research into Poe's life and work. She sees in his theory of the entirely deliberate, mathematically planned composition a retrospective rationalization employed for a special reason: because Poe desperately needed to convince himself and others that no hidden, random, subterranean powers threatened his creativity and his life. In fact he was, at the time of writing *A Philosophy of Composition*, experiencing a productivity crisis and a period of severe decline, of alcoholism, opium addiction, and threatening mental illness. If we accept Marie Bonaparte's basic premise, we should note that all the poets mentioned above as sharing his poetic philosophy had personalities with strong inner conflicts and with tensions between their rational self and irrational depths. For them, Poe's theories could have had the additional advantage of supporting their productive efforts in the face of threatening chaos and unproductiveness.[40]

The fact that Poe's pronouncements on poetic composition evoked such a response must, however, largely be due to their deliberate one-sidedness. Poe drew the attention of his contemporaries and succeeding generations to factors in the process of literary creativity that had been exluded from the well-nigh stereotyped romantic concept of inspirational writing. He voiced his objections to this romantic concept when he said that there is no greater mistake than surmising that true originality is a question of impulse or inspiration. Original creativity is the same thing as combining with care, patience, and intelligence. On the other hand, this does not mean Poe believed that anyone could become a poet. The poet, with his/her special gifts, thirst for "supernal beauty," power of "invention" and "imagination," was for Poe a chosen individual and an exception. In this respect he shared the aesthetic beliefs of the romantics.[41]

Finally we can ask ourselves how it came about that Poe, in his American environment, was the first person to draw attention to the problem of deliberate poetic effects and the significance of application and work. He himself lived as a rather poorly adjusted Bohemian in a society going through a period of expansion and growth; his isolation in this environment has often been stressed. Yet his innovative ideas and discoveries in the field of aesthetics may be linked to his surroundings. Two hypothetical connections are worth considering. One concerns his belief in effect, the other his doctrine of work.

Poe regarded poetry not—primarily—as a means for poetic "self-expression" but as a means of achieving an effect on the *reader*. As background, we should recall not only the classical rhetorical tradition and Poe's well-known interest in the effects of hypnotism but also a peculiarly American phenomenon. In America, the land of newspaper advertisements and the young advertising industry, the persuasive power of words had been both noted and exploited. Like the writer of advertisements, Poe consciously strove to make an impression with his words. His guiding principle was *effect*.

Furthermore, the United States with its widespread puritan morals was a country that did not look down on work: the self-made man served as its ideal. It was perhaps easier within the framework of such a society than elsewhere to find support for the notion of the poet as a worker among other workers—albeit in the field of words. The philosophy of Bohemian artistry and the myth of divine inspiration, with its concomitant view of literature as the product of inspiration rather than labor, was ill-suited to a country of immigrant enterprise and huge achievements based on hard work. As Goldmann would put it, there was a "homology" between the aesthetic philosophy of work and the structure of American society at the time.

Whatever the true inwardness may be of Poe's relationship to his age and environment, the fact remains that his idea of the writer as an engineer in words was to prove long-lived. Generations of poets have repeated and verified his philosophy of composition. But at the same time they have also provided it with natural and essential complements. Nor did Poe banish the idea of inspiration. Baudelaire was well aware of this when he wrote in his preface to *La Genèse d'un poème* that Poe had genius and *"plus d'inspiration que qui que ce soit,"* if by inspiration one means the energy, the intellectual enthusiasm, and the ability to keep one's mental faculties awake. He also loved work more than anyone else, writes Baudelaire; he often repeated—being himself entirely original—that originality is something one can learn (*chose d'apprentissage*).

The influence exerted by Poe's aesthetic theories on the continent, particularly within the French poetic tradition, began early and lasted a long time. But Poe also aroused vehement opposition, particularly among the surrealists. André Breton was to speak slightingly in the second surrealist manifesto of "the police methods of the intellect." And he continued: "Let us, in passing, spit on Edgar Poe"—*'Crachons, en passant, sur Edgar Poe.'*[42]

Paul Valéry
and *Le Cimetière marin*

\

Inventer, ce n'est que se comprendre.

Paul Valéry
Oeuvres, vol. II

1

The French literary historian Gustave Cohen gave a celebrated lecture at the Sorbonne in the early 1930s, arranged as an *explication de texte* or close reading of Paul Valéry's *Le Cimetière marin*. Valéry himself was present in the audience. When Cohen's *Essai d'explication du Cimetière marin* was published in 1933, Valéry wrote a commentary entitled *Au sujet du Cimetière marin*, later republished in the third collection of his *Variétés*. In the early 1950s L. J. Austin gained access to Valéry's manuscripts and examined what they reveal about the poem's genesis in a couple of articles published in French periodicals. In 1954 Austin published a facsimile edition of the manuscripts of this poem, with an introduction summarizing his research.[1]

So we find ourselves in an unusually privileged position. We have access to authorial comments on the poem, by a poet with rare powers of self-analysis and exceptional insight into the laws of poetry. We also have a gramophone recording of Valéry himself reading a number of stanzas from the poem. Finally we possess a genetic analysis by a highly qualified scholar, who has been in a position to survey the entire extant manuscript resources.

In his essay *Au sujet du Cimetière marin* Valéry casts his mind back over the history of the poem and tells us that its completion was in fact more a product of chance than of design. The role of "the man from Porlock" was played by Valéry's friend Jacques Rivière, who came one evening to visit Valéry and found him engrossed in the poem, reworking it, cutting, substituting, interpolating. "He refused," writes Valéry, "to leave me until he had the poem in his hand, and when he had read it, he took it away with him."[2] No one, adds Valéry quizzically, can be as firm as the editor of a literary magazine. (Rivière was the editor of *La Nouvelle revue française*.)

The point Valéry illustrates—and wishes to illustrate—with this anecdote constitutes a foundation stone of his aesthetic, namely, that a literary work of art is strictly speaking never finished. It can be handed over—to a fire or to the public—but this act of consignment always has something fortuitous about it, as does abandoning a train of thought out of tiredness, or annoyance, or because some external event forces one to. There was a time when people criticized Valéry for publishing different versions of the same poem, even contradictory versions. He always had arguments in his defense, and he openly urged his poetic contemporaries to do what composers working with musical material do, i.e., produce and leave for posterity a wealth of variation on a given theme. W. H. Auden and the Swedish poet Gunnar Ekelöf (1907-70) both followed this advice.

According to Valéry's dictum (admittedly contradicted by other pronouncements of his), just as a poem never is completely finished, so it has no clear beginning either. Behind the first word set down on paper there can be both wordless stages and a row of impulses and tentative variations, which it would be meaningless to try to trace to a "first beginning."

Austin pointed out that as early as 1890 Valéry speaks of a poem—a sonnet entitled *Cimetière*—in a letter. Valéry himself considered the poem so insignificant that he refused to submit it to Mallarmé for an opinion. For many years there was no trace of the poem, and Austin could justifiably speculate whether it was perhaps a first version of *Le Cimetière marin*. The sonnet came to light during the 1950s, however, and proved to have no connection with *Le Cimetière marin*; Austin writes in the introduction to the facsimile edition that it cannot be regarded as a preliminary stage of the latter poem, since there is no resemblance between them in either underlying idea or theme.

Valéry himself said that the idea for *Le Cimetière marin* first presented itself to him as an empty, rhythmic schema, which for a time obsessed him. It appears that this schema preceded the words, which only subsequently, in the shape of syllables, word elements, and whole words, filled in the blanks. We might at this point recall what Valéry said in another connection about the process of articulation: "to put one's thoughts into words is to step out of one's inner disorder and step into a homogeneous world."[3]

In the beginning was rhythm. This is an interesting and by no means entirely uncommon initial phase of a poem's inception, as has been confirmed by the notebooks and manuscripts of a number of writers. Shelley's notebooks, which have been so carefully studied by Neville Rogers, contain a number of examples indicating that an initial musical-rhythmic impulse preceded articulation. In the margin of the manuscript of the *Ode to Naples*, Shelley marks the beats of the stanza form *before* writing the poem. Before the poem *O world! O Life! O time!* he employs another system and writes "na ná na ná na ná," and before *The Beauty Hangs about Thee* he establishes the stanza form by means of meaningless syllables.[4]

Parallels from the world of music are even more significant. When Beethoven sketched out his seventh symphony on paper, it was not musical ideas but a rhythmic pattern that emerged. The melody arose out of the rhythm, and the rhythmic idea was so obsessive that it took over practically all the melodic impulses that passed through his mind—so that the scherzo for instance, which later was rewritten in $3/4$ time, originally had a heavy, dactylic beat.[5]

Regarding the inception of *Le Cimetière marin*, Valéry tells us that the phase of rhythmic delibertation was quite long and that it was the subject of clear, conscious reflection. The rhythm sounding in his head was decasyllabic. He devoted considerable thought to this particular rhythm, rarely used in modern poetry. He describes in mythical language how a "demon of generalization, perhaps a demon of the mystique of numbers,"[6] gave him the idea of raising the number ten to the dignity of twelve. The rhythm was then given concrete form in a special stanza of six lines, which led to the idea of a composition based on a certain number of stanzas, reciprocally determined by a number of tones and functions. Valéry's account of the process is reminiscent in several ways of the intellectual problem solving demonstrated by Poe in his *Philosophy of Composition*. But although Poe's essay may have provided Valéry with a model—as several scholars have suggested—there is no reason to deny the truth or likelihood of his own account. For Valéry was never given to mystification. In his recollection ten years later, this is how he thought the composition had taken place.

Valéry spoke at length elsewhere about an original rhythmic impulse. In *La création artistique* he tells again of being possessed by a rhythm, which *"s'imposait à moi, avec une sorte d'exigence."* And he continues:

> It seemed as though it wanted to achieve a bodily form, reach the perfection of existence. But it could not approach any closer to my consciousness without borrowing some speakable elements, syllables, words, and these words and syllables were without any doubt at this point of their inception determined by their musical value and musical attraction.[7]

A rhythm that desires the bodily form of words, this is how Valéry with well-nigh biblical association describes the process of poetic creation. Valéry stresses that at this early stage—*état enfantin*—form and material, rhythm and words are scarcely distinguishable. After these interwoven states comes, according to Valéry in *La création artistique*, a third, no less important stage. Instead of the syllables or the tentatively adopted words, a whole line takes shape in Valéry's mind. And it is fully developed from the start, impossible to alter or change: *"comme impossible à modifier, comme l'effet d'une necessité."*

Valéry does not refer to any single line as the point of crystallization or beginning of *Le Cimetière marin*. For a considerable time he keeps his account on an abstract plane, as Poe did. Parallels and contrasts between stanzas were required, and to satisfy this condition, says Valéry, the poem had to become a monologue in which the simplest and at the same time most constant elements of his emotional and intellectual life were developed, interwoven, and contrasted—themes which had absorbed him already in adolescence and which were associated with the sea and the light over a particular spot on the Mediterranean coast. This was the churchyard in the little harbor town of Sète, between Marseille and Perpignan. All this led his thoughts in the direction of death. The lines of the stanzas were to be dense and strictly rhythmical; he was moving toward a monologue simultanesously as personal and as universal as it was in his power to make it. The form of line and stanza that he had chosen had possibilities that favored certain of the poem's "movements" and "allowed certain changes of tone, called forth a certain style." "*Le Cimetière marin* had been planned. A great deal of work remained," writes Valéry.[8]

Up to this point the deliberations and decisions Valéry recounts— admittedly with the dislocation entailed by a distance of ten years and his own aesthetic convictions—are those in the stage preceding that of the written word or manuscript. Yet his account, like Poe's, has been questioned. Hytier, the leading specialist on Valéry's critical writing, objects to that part of his creative myth which maintains that a work is produced as a result of considerations of pure form, more and more consciously reflective. The plan for a poem, Hytier points out, is not the same thing as the poem itself. Seduced by constant comparisons with the work of architects and engineers, Valéry forgets that a poem is *"bien plus organique que mécanique."* Just as the "subject" of *The Raven*—desolation and the beautiful woman's death—was the fruit of not only Poe's intellectual considerations but also his own experiences, so the "subject" of Valéry's poem is deeply rooted in his most personal experiences.[9]

2

The "great deal of work [that] remained" after the first abstract planning of the poem can in large measure be followed in the manuscript series that Austin had access to and that now is published in a facsimile edition. For no other poem by Valéry are there so many background documents available, even though *La Jeune Parque* and *Narcisse* have an interesting manuscript history. Valéry's poetic manuscripts certainly seem to corroborate much in his aesthetic theory—his ideas on poetic creativity as a process governed by reflection and calculation. As impulses and ideas occurred—and often were written down on sheets of paper spread out like a fan—they were swiftly subjected to his critical judgment. Austin points out that the documents reveal how spontaneity and critical faculty go hand in hand.

The extant manuscript material comprises three main stages. At every stage we find a number of stanzas in sequence. An important question is, however, what existed *before* the fairly advanced manuscript stages which Austin acquaints us with?

Valéry's method of work appears to have been to note down on small scraps of paper fragmentary lines or verses, which he later elaborated. Most of this preliminary material has been lost, but not all of it. Among the manuscript pages to another poem, *La Jeune Parque*, Austin found a sheet that more closely resembled an original outline than did any of the other manuscripts. It contained only one stanza of *Le Cimetière marin*, the one that was to become the twenty-first, apostrophizing the philosopher Zenon, plus three lines of what became the final stanza, beginning *"Le vent se lève . . ."*

Did Valéry really start writing the poem from the end? Austin dismisses the notion without considering that this is exactly the procedure that Poe recommended to poets and which he claims to have adopted himself when composing *The Raven*. Scholars believe that Yeats began some of his poems at the end, basing their conclusion on manuscript series. Strictly speaking, nothing about a poem's inception should be ruled out, and we can by no means exclude the possibility that Valéry, too, started his poem at the end, with *le dénouement*.

In its present form *Le Cimetière marin* consists of one hundred and four lines, divided into twenty-four stanzas, with every stanza having six decasyllabic lines. In the first stage that Austin demonstrates for us, the poem had *seven* stanzas, in the second stage it had *ten*; and in the third stage it once had *twenty-three*. Each of these three main versions has a wealth of variants on the manuscript pages; the two first versions also contain a rough outline for new stanzas which were not completed and added to the poem as a whole until later. Austin believes that there are likely to have been more stages between the ones we now know of.

We know roughly when and for how long Valéry worked on his poem. He indicated in conversation that he had written some of the stanzas while working on *La Jeune Parque*, and the manuscript page containing two stanzas of *Le Cimetière marin* that was found among the manuscript material of *La Jeune Parque* appears to confirm this dating. *La Jeune Parque* was written in 1915 and 1916, and published the following year. The first *dated* draft of *Le Cimetière marin*—the seven-stanza one—contains the note *"fin octobre— nov 17"* in Valéry's handwriting, the title *Mare Nostrum* (the old name of the Mediterranean), and in brackets under these words— and added later—*"dans le vieux Cimetière de C . . ."*[10]

For all intents and purposes, five of the seven stanzas in the seven-stanza version already have a definitive form, whereas the remaining two (numbers two and three) are covered with corrections and alternative suggestions. From what is known of Valéry's work habits, it has been concluded that the five stanzas represent a preliminary whole. The remarkable thing is that this poem of five stanzas, later expanded to seven, describes exactly the same curve as the completed poem of twenty-four stanzas. In short, this manuscript could be said to provide a small-scale version of the final poem. The first stanza of the early seven-stanza poem—*"Ce toit tranquille où marchent des colombes"*—is also the first stanza in the final version, just as the last verse—*"Le vent se lève, il faut tenter de vivre"*—is the same in both versions. The middle stanzas (numbers four and five) of the early version also occupy a central position in the final version. In the compressed first version of the poem, the stanza *"Zénon: Cruel Zénon: Zénon d'Elée!"* with its philosophical argument is the penultimate one, whereas it is number twenty-one in the final version.

Because of its contrastive arrangement, the polarity between the first and last stanzas, the poem proceeds from a state of immobility to one of movement. Initially there is calm over the golden sea in the glowing midday heat. But soon the wind gets up, the violent wind which shakes the oak and lifts the wave to a breaker in the next stanza. We must assume that the final lines of the poem stood as an antithesis from an early planning stage, with their insistent imperatives:

> *Rompez, vagues: Rompez d'eaux réjouies*
> *Ce toit tranquille où picoraient des focs.*

The lines of the seven-stanza manuscript are already very well elaborated. Commenting on the definitive nature of the seven-stanza version, James Lawler quotes Valéry's recommendation in a notebook from 1917: "When you engage in a poetic work, first find a part which you raise to the highest attainable beauty, so that it can serve you as impulse and condition for completing all the others which would not wish to be inferior to it."[11]

Two points are worth commenting on before we leave this initial, seven-stanza stage of the poem. First, Valéry apparently commenced work on it while he was engaged in writing other poems; he tells us that nearly all the poems in *Charmes* were written *simultanément.* This situation is not unusual, and we can find many parallels in the notebooks of other poets. Ideas and impulses tend to well up on all sides during a productive period. This is of course also true of musicians, and Beethoven wrote a letter of 29 June 1800: *"So wie ich jetzt schreibe, mache ich oft drei, vier Sachen zugleich."*[12] Second, although the manuscript indicates many alternative choices, Valéry appears to have had a vision of the whole poem before him from an early stage—however, we cannot say exactly *how* early. An intuitive total picture of this sort is referred to by many poets and musicians. Carl Maria von Weber affirms that *"Das Ganze muss ganz gedacht sein."*[13] Even though Valéry never expressed himself so categorically, it seems clear that in *Le Cimetière marin* the whole preceded the parts, that is, a plan of the whole directed the further development of the poem.

The next stage in the composition of *Le Cimetière marin* is demonstrated by a ten-stanza manuscript. The opening, middle, and final stanzas of the seven-stanza version are retained, only very slightly altered. But the poem is longer because insertions were made both before and after the stanzas about space and the dead. The sequence of the stanzas remains unaltered. There is no change in the geometrical pattern; each verse occupies its rightful place, like the segments of stained glass in a gothic cathedral. In the margin of this manuscript, which we will call ms B, we can see how six new stanzas were added, all but the last dedicated to one of the themes of the poem: the churchyard and the dead. Concurrently with this expansion, the original title was altered and now stands as *Le Cimetière marin*. *Mare nostrum* is retained only as subtitle or motto.

This version of the poem, ms B, exists in both handwritten manuscript and typescript. Presumably written at about the same time is a sort of index in which Valéry, using only initial words, sketched out a projected poem of twenty-eight stanzas. The final manuscript, the third complete one—i.e., version C—has, as we know, twenty-three stanzas. The published version has twenty-four.

In his aesthetic speculations Valéry repeatedly stressed that emptiness and want are creative factors. "*Le vide crée*," he writes in a paragraph in *Tel quel*.[14] He says the same thing with different words in his well-known *Lettre sur Mallarmé: "c'est le Discontinuum, qui bouche les troux."*[15]

If we pursue Valéry's train of thought, we can conclude that it must have been exactly this experience of emptiness and discontinuity between the stanzas which impelled him on from the first version of his poem to the last. *Transition* is an important concept in his philosophy, and what the new stanzas represent are precisely transitions or bridges between the poem's beginning, middle, and end.

In the manuscript containing the poem of twenty-three stanzas, some of these are still fragmentary. Lines and elements from two of the already completed stanzas were later contracted into one single stanza—the eighth which appears to be the last to receive its final form. On a couple of pages the reverse side and margin carry outlines of coming stanzas, i.e., numbers two and four of the version printed in *La nouvelle revue française*. Four of the new stanzas in ms C deal with the sea, thereby redressing the balance between the twin themes of the sea and the churchyard.

It is perhaps surprising that the arrangement of the twenty-three stanzas of ms C seems arbitrary or capricious. At this stage Valéry was probably more concerned with individual stanzas than with the poem as a logical-compositional whole—its basic features had been established early on. The poem's first ten stanzas apparently were in a certain internal state of flux, for not content with the sequence of stanzas in the manuscript that Jacques Rivière took from him for *La nouvelle revue française*, Valéry rearranged the first nine stanzas when he later published the poem in his *Oeuvres*. Several of these were written last; the end of the poem took shape earlier than its beginning.

From seven to twenty-four stanzas in a number of clearly discernible stages—this is the pattern of the poem's development. However, throughout its "growth" or "construction"—and Valéry at various times used both types of metaphor—its underlying character remains the same. The additional stanzas and interpolations develop, reiterate, contrast, and enrich themes, which are expressed or hinted at from the start. The size of the poem increases by a sort of reproduction by division, to quote Lawler's phrase.[16] But as we noted several times already, the beginning, middle, and end have existed as foundation stones from the beginning: the first three stanzas with their evocation of the sea, the middle stanzas that contrast the peace of the dead with the anxiety of the living, and the end stanzas that set Zenon's paradox, with its denial of the possibility of movement, against the final stanza, with its acceptance of movement, the element of life and wind. Austin writes in his analysis of the poem that it, like a flower, in its final form reveals that which existed in bud and seed.

It would be meaningless to comment line for line in English on the successive transformations of the poem, particularly since Austin followed the changes so sensitively, laboriously, and illuminatingly. This much we can safely say—Valéry considered no stanza sacrosanct in its entirety from the beginning. On the other hand, many single lines found their right form from the start and were never altered. We already had occasion to note Valéry's distinction between two sorts of poetic line: *"les vers donnés"* and *"les vers calculés."* He applied the first term to those fortunate impulses which have a sort of poetic incontestability and which cannot be improved upon, whether they arise by chance, grace, or genius—he uses all three terms as explanations. The others, *les vers calculés,* are not "received" but "made"; the poet manufactures them by copying the model of the "received" lines, in order, if possible, to outshine them.[17]

3

In the manuscript text of individual stanzas we can sometimes find concrete evidence of how Valéry set about finding the right line, or *le mot propre*. He spreads out a whole sheaf of words, or variants, to choose between. We already find an example of this in the inception—or manufacture—of the first stanza. In ms A (the seven-stanza poem), the third and fourth lines of the first stanza run as follows:

> *L'or maritime y compose de feux*
> *La mer, la mer: toujours recommencée . . .*

"L'or maritime" in Valéry's language means the sun on the sea or the sunlit sea. In the following manuscript, ms B, he notes in the margin *"le milieu du jour,"* then *"Et l'or sublime,"* *"Un songe d'or,"* and *"Le pur solstice."* Finally the definitively chosen word *"Midi"* is introduced, but with a row of varied attributes. He tries out no less than five different adjectives: *"sublime," "le pur," "le même," "le morne,"* and *"le calme"*; and makes a provisional choice of *"Midi le pur,"* which is written into the text. He does not find a new adjective until he writes ms C; there the line finally is given the form admired by so many French commentators:

> *Midi le juste y compose de feux.*

In lines of this type—which surely belong to the category *vers calculés*—Valéry is guided by both semantic and phonological considerations. Traces of phonetic considerations can be seen when he writes the letter *s* in the margin of the third stanza. This letter is already well represented in the first three lines:

> *Stable trésor, temple, simple à Minerve*
> *Masse de calme, et visible réverse!*
> *Entre les pins, oeil qui gardes en toi . . .*

Valéry evidently found the first word of the third line unsatisfactory. He first tries the alliteration *Parmi les pins* but rejects it in favor of an expression with a dominant *s* sound: Eau *sorcilleuse*.[18]

What poetic manuscripts reveal—when they have something to reveal—is how calculated lines are put together: we see the poet as a composer who tries first one and then another sequence of notes, first one and then another chord. But what we never can observe—with the same certainty—are the *vers donnés*. We may think that we recognize them by virtue of their poetic givenness, a feeling of inevitability. However, even when a line of this kind stands unaltered in the manuscript from the very beginning, it can of course nevertheless be a product of lengthy calculations and considerations in the poet's mind. We might guess that a line like *"La mer, la mer! toujours recommencée"* belonged to the category *"vers donnés"*—and the manuscripts do not contradict the assumption. We might also guess, without referring to the manuscripts, that the beginning of the final stanza, with its air of rightness and poetic inevitability, had arisen spontaneously in the poet's mind:

> *Le vent se lève . . . il faut tenter de vivre!*
> *L'air immense ouvre et referme mon livre,—*

But our poetic intuition has deceived us. A draft of the first three lines in ms A, immediately after the stanza on Zenon, shows us that the second—*but not the first*—line was set down ready-made. The first line originally read *"Il faut tenter c'est vivre,"* and it was not until later that Valéry, who had circled the words, wrote in *"de vivre"* and gave the line the perfection that now appears self-evident. Faithful to his declared principle, Valéry strove to make the "manufactured" lines as good as the spontaneously received ones, or even to outdo them.

It is a fact that Valéry several times voiced his distrust of the spontaneously given, the first impulse. "The spontaneous, however excellent it might be, never seemed to me to be my own to a sufficiently high degree," he once said.[19] But he also spoke of the flashes of genius—*éclairs de genie*—and verbal illuminations that the poet immediately recognizes as *not* being fleeting illusions. They dictate to the poet all of a sudden a certain combination of words "as though this group of words possessed an unknown inner power, one might even say an unknown will, to exist."[20]

We must bear these and similar pronouncements in mind when looking in detail at the manuscripts of *Le Cimetière marin*, which in so remarkable a fashion lead us into the creative process. Jean Pommier, who gave his inaugural lecture at Collège de France on the subject of *Paul Valéry et la création littéraire*, scattered all the above quotations in his lecture and applied to Valéry what the latter had said about Baudelaire and Poe: "It is an exceptional circumstance to find a critical intelligence allied to poetic ability."[21]

If we were to believe that the consciously willed and totally determined creative act underlying *Le Cimetière marin* is generally valid or paradigmatic in Valéry's poetry, we would be making a mistake, however. As we saw above, part of *La Jeune Parque* was written at the same time as *Le Cimetière marin*. Although the manuscripts of the latter poem indicate that the architect at all times had a firm basic design, the manuscripts of *La Jeune Parque* reveal a much more fluctuating process, with samples of many different poetic methods. In *La Jeune Parque* on which he worked for a long time, Valéry tried a purely musical pattern and started by noting down a musical-rhythmic schema, to which he then set words—and this is reminiscent of an early stage of *Le Cimetière marin*. But in addition he tried other methods, through free association. In the margin of the manuscript he gives himself advice, for instance: *"essayer par les mots juxtaposés à partir des idées," "peindre par fonctions,"* and again *"ici au lieu de peindre mêlé peindre séparé."* What Valéry's exhortations reveal, and what scholars have sought in the manuscripts, is a series of different semantic principles, successively tried out.[22] In general terms, it can be said of Valéry's creative work that he looks for resistance in language, in the traditional rules of prosody, or in the temporary rules he sets up for himself.

Le Cimetière marin, which we have been considering here, is a poem about contrasts, about the sea and a churchyard, about life and death, about mobility and immobility. It is a poem about life's great polarities but also about the polarities within the human soul. In his book *Valéry et la tentation de l'Absolu* (1964), Alfred Schmitz, one of the most recent in a long line of interpreters of the poem, chose the word *"reflection"* as rubric for stanzas one to eighteen. For the five last stanzas he chose as rubric a word from

Bergson's conceptual arsenal: "*Élan vital.*" And he elaborated with the words: "the triumph of the creative will." The earth is associated with symbolic qualities like rest, immobility, the heavy, meditative element of the human spirit. The sea, wind, and movement are in *Le Cimetière marin* directly linked to inspiration, to what is unconscious and creative: "la vie inconsciente et créatrice."[23] In this way something of the dialectic of creativity can ultimately be seen in the poem, too.

The Writing of Ibsen's *Brand*

J'invente, donc je suis.

Paul Valéry
Oeuvres, vol. II

1

In 1888 the Norwegian writer Henrik Jaeger published a book about Henrik Ibsen, in some ways an authorized biography. Jaeger had been in touch with Ibsen, who had provided him with the autobiographical notes contained in the book. It is therefore likely that Ibsen himself is responsible for an interesting factual note about the play *Brand*: "Ibsen originally started the work as a narrative poem."[1] This is the earliest official statement that a "narrative *Brand*" had existed.

The next time Ibsen's narrative *Brand* is mentioned is in reminiscences by Lorentz Dietrichson—republished in *Times Past (Svundne Tider)*. Dietrichson recalls the period when he and Ibsen both lived in Rome: "I remember well, that shortly before my departure from Rome in the spring of 1865, he read aloud a song from a narrative poem."[2] The song contained a description of a celebration of 17 May (Independence Day) in the Norwegian countryside. Later on, it occurred to Dietrichson that the song did not appear to have any connection with the play *Brand* but that the *motif* reappears in Ibsen's play *The League of Youth (De unges forbund)*, completed four years later.

Some earlier, additional information is found in Ibsen's letters.

In a letter written in September 1864, he mentions that he is working on a major narrative poem. The next mention comes in a letter to Bjørnson exactly a year later: "I have now chucked overboard what I have tormented myself with for a whole year without getting anywhere." In the same letter Ibsen announces that he has started writing *Brand* as a drama.[3]

Ibsen deposited his uncompleted narrative *Brand*, with some other papers and books, with the Scandinavian Society in Rome. He did this in 1868, on leaving for Germany. Ten years later he returned to Rome but was unable to find the manuscript, which appeared to have vanished from the face of the earth. In the 1890s a Danish bibliophile living in Rome had the good fortune to come across some Ibsen material, including the manuscript of *Peer Gynt* and the lost manuscript of the narrative *Brand*, in a secondhand bookshop. After the Danish collector's death both manuscripts were acquired by the Royal Library in Copenhagen, and shortly after Ibsen's death they were published in 1907 in a carefully prepared edition by Karl Larsen.

The publication of Ibsen's narrative *Brand* became a literary sensation of the first order, which was eagerly discussed and commented upon by literary scholars. It was remarkable enough in itself that a lost Ibsen work had reappeared and been published without its author's sanction. In addition, there were questions about the form of the poem, which demanded an answer. The poem, clearly unfinished, consisted of a prologue and four songs. The prologue existed in two metrically unalike versions. One was regularly iambic, the other had a freer rhythm, more reminiscent of a folk song and familiar to us from *The Feast at Solhoug (Gildet på Solhaug)* and *Peer Gynt*. The publication of the poem soon touched off a debate on the relationship between these two versions: namely, which version was written first?

Discussion centered on the first song, entitled *To the Guilty Accessories,* in which Ibsen gives vent to his indignation over the betrayal of Scandinavian political ideals in 1864. As a Scandinavist, he had been a passionate supporter of Norwegian and Swedish intervention against Germany on behalf of threatened Denmark. "I wrote the poem '*A Brother in Need.*' Which needless to say had no effect," he writes in a *Chronological Confession*, and continues: "I then went into exile. When I reached Copenhagen, Dybbøl fell. In Berlin I saw Kaiser Wilhelm march in with trophies and booty. *It was during those days that Brand began to grow like a fetus within me.*"[4]

Karl Larsen, who published the narrative *Brand*, was convinced that Ibsen first wrote the metrically freer version, which he then transposed into a regular iambic meter. Having examined the manuscripts and arguments, Hans Brix, an eminent Danish literary historian, came to the opposite conclusion; he believed that Ibsen started writing the poem in regular "academic iambs" but tired of them after a while and changed to a freer form with varying meters. In his opinion Ibsen undertook the recasting with considerable energy and not inconsiderable success—the first line of the freer version, "My folk, my *poor* country in the North," already gives a more suggestive opening than the iambic "My folk, my country *fair*, my Northern home."

Halvdan Koht, Norwegian historian and editor of Ibsen's posthumously published works, argued along the same lines and broadened them with parallels from Ibsen's other works. He was able to demonstrate that Ibsen—for *Peer Gynt*—first wrote a scene or part of a scene in prose and then recast it in regular iambs, after which he wrote the final version in a freer meter. Koht believed that Ibsen followed the same procedure with the narrative *Brand*. A detailed scrutiny of alterations from version to version shows that Ibsen achieved more concrete words and vivid expressions in the freer version: "playful flight" becomes "fluttering flight"; "the rain falls heavily" becomes "the rain pours down violently"; "stillness" becomes "calm weather." Koht compared the development of this poem with Ibsen's manner of reworking other poems that exist in several published versions with an indisputable chronology.[5] It appears that Ibsen's alterations in these poems always tend toward a more concrete wording, a more expressive phrase. A number of additional arguments have been adduced in favor of the view that is now generally accepted: that Ibsen began writing his narrative *Brand* in regular iambic verse, the same meter that Paludan Müller used for *Adam Homo*.

In two essays published in *Det ny aarhundrede* (1907-8), Hans Brix examined the order in which the various songs in the poem were written. He showed that Ibsen probably wrote the prologue *To the Guilty Accessories* before writing the song *Over the High Mountain*, with its expository scenes. He believed that Ibsen then interpolated between the prologue and *Over the High Mountain* a new song, entitled *From the Time of Ripening*, in which the background to Brand's character is sketched. The final two songs, *The Paths to the Church* and *At the Church*, are assumed to have been written in sequence, the last one giving the impression of being unfinished.

In the song *Over the High Mountain*, which originally was to lead into the action, we meet the main characters. At first, they were called Koll, Axel, and Dagmar. The name Dagmar is changed to Agnes at an early stage in the manuscript, but Koll does not become Brand until later. This last name change constitutes *one* important moment in the work's history, for the name has significance for character and characterization. Koll is an Old Norse name, associated with cold and winter—one side of Brand. In the hymn he sings as he walks across the mountain, he does not pray only for pain: "Lord, make me rich in pain/shy of each tempting pleasure!" but also for coldness of the senses: "Teach me to walk through the land of the flesh/blind to the sun and summer." The earth appears to his eyes as a "winter's night."[6] Koll's opposite is Axel—later called Einar. For him life is a "summer life," and Agnes is his "lovely butterfly."[7] The contrast between the two men is strongly marked from the beginning. But Koll (Brand) has not yet found his identity, become the fiery prophet. He is searching for his task, his own self: "Say, where is he who *wills*, *believes* and *sees*, who *strikes* for that same goal for which he *burns*."[8] Thus speaks the priest who is to become, and be named, *Brand*, which in Norwegian means *fire*.

2

Ibsen explained how he came to abandon the narrative form in favor of the dramatic in a letter to Bjørnson, written in Aricia 12 September 1865. He first describes the worries brought on by the narrative work. He could not make any headway. And the reworking of the manuscript, which was never completed, provides us with concrete proof of his vain endeavors.

> Then one day I went into St. Peter's—I was in the center of Rome—and there I suddenly had a vision of a strong and clear form for what I had to say. I have now chucked overboard what I have tormented myself with for a whole year without getting anywhere, and in the middle of July I started on something fresh, which went ahead at a pace, which nothing else hitherto has ever done for me. . . . It is a dramatic poem, contemporary subject, serious contents. Five acts in rhyming verse (no *Love's Comedy*). 4th act will soon be ready and I feel that I can write the 5th in a week; I work in both morning and afternoon, which I have never been able to do. It is blessedly peaceful down here, no acquaintances, I read nothing but the Bible—it is powerful and strong.[9]

Although Ibsen had worked on his narrative poem *invita Minerva*, so to speak, he had now found release. The change of genre seems to have been a fact, as demonstrated by the incident in St. Peter's. From this moment the *play* begins to take shape, with a speed that astonished Ibsen himself. He experienced increased well-being at work, accompanied by a feeling of intense happiness and power. "I felt a crusading jubilation within me, I cannot think of a thing that I would have lacked courage to face," he wrote, and again: "I have a working capacity and power, fit to kill bears with."[10]

What proof can we find in the manuscript itself of this transformation or the route to the new form?

We cannot assume that we possess Ibsen's working papers in their entirety. The oldest extant manuscript of the narrative *Brand* in its regular, metrical form is probably itself a fair copy. Scholars agree that the consistently beautiful handwriting, perfectly shaped, hardly can be explained in any other way, even allowing for Ibsen's exceptional talent for versification. In spite of this, some parts of the manuscript look like first attempts at writing down the material. Frequently the rhymes, and occasionally the names, were changed during writing. It is likely that Ibsen, as was his wont, worked with sketches and outlines that were not continuous wholes but fragments. We know he employed a similar method in his *Verse Letter to fru Heiberg*, and there are direct parallels in the way he wrote his dramas.[11] So we must imagine that this earliest extant manuscript of the narrative *Brand* pieces together still earlier fragments and includes some new parts composed as Ibsen wrote the work down.

In among the manuscript pages of the narrative *Brand* there lay—and does so to this day—a torn-off sheet containing only four lines. It is a fragment without any direct connection with the body of the manuscript. The form of these lines is different from the rest of the narrative poem and represents a verbal exchange between two anonymous individuals. Naturally, scholars dealing with this material were quick to spot the fragment, which appears to represent the work at a metaphorical crossroad.

On the torn-off sheet we read the following:

> The First:
> See, she stares at him, intent
> As a scout in enemy camp.
> The Second:
> Now seeks to catch her friend's eye,
> In silence awaits a winning answer.

If we now turn to the *narrative* version of *Brand* to see where this exchange might find a home, we come upon the stanza that describes Agnes's first meeting with the stranger, *Brand*:

> The young girl stared at him intently,
> as one who scouts within an enemy camp.
> Then trustingly she sought her friend's eye
> and asked, in silence, for a winning answer.

We are witnesses to Agnes's contradictory emotions, faced with the disturbing stranger. She still hopes that Einar will be the winner in the verbal exchange between the two men. In the narrative *Brand* the action is *narrated*; first she stares at the stranger, then she seeks out Einar's eye. In the fragment the action has been *dramatized*; two anonymous spectators have been introduced, and it is their reactions—not those of the invisible narrator—that are presented to us. There are no verbs of speech; the dialogue follows directly after the colon.

If we look for a corresponding passage in the completed *play*, we seek in vain. No such exchange is included there. No outsider comments on Agnes's emotions as she watches Einar and Brand speak. On the other hand, Ibsen makes use of figures called "the First" and "the Second" in the second act of *Brand*, at the point when Brand and Agnes get into the boat.[12] *If*, as some scholars have supposed, this small fragment of dialogue was the first experiment, the first documentary sign of the recasting of the narrative in dramatic form, it was nevertheless not allowed to stand. However, the dramatic impulse did survive the first attempt at dramatic form. This confirms an observation made elsewhere, i.e., that the first product is not always worthy of survival. It can be dispensed with, once it has served its purpose.

But there is also another theory concerning the four-line fragment. When Karl Larsen published the narrative *Brand*, he believed it was a relic or fragment from a dramatic *Ur-Brand* or *Proto-Brand*. According to the theory, Ibsen started writing *Brand* as a play, gave up the idea and began to work on a narrative poem instead. When this was not successful either, he reverted to the dramatic form.

The only supporting evidence for the belief that this kind of transformation from drama to narrative to drama had taken place comes from a relatively late, verbal source. Lorentz Dietrichson claims that Ibsen said in Rome "that he had decided to change the dramatic form of the work he was engaged in, to a narrative poem"[13] and that he read a song from this narrative poem in the spring of 1865.

There is no statement by Ibsen himself to the effect that his original plan was to write a drama. But his authority underlies Henrik Jaeger's words that he originally—*oprindeligt*—started work on *Brand* as a narrative poem. Ibsen's statement to a Norwegian friend, J. B. Halvorsen, that some three or four pages of the narrative *Brand* had been written when he changed over to writing a play point in the same direction. Nothing in the letters can be construed as confirmation that the work had undergone the strange metamorphosis from play to narrative and then back again to play.

Conclusive proof that the small dramatic fragment was written at a late stage in the development of the narrative *Brand* is provided by the actual paper it is written on, which no one, oddly enough, seems to have examined. The four lines are written on a torn-off sheet of writing paper. Paper of the same type is found only *once* in the manuscript of the narrative *Brand*. On this sheet is a stanza from the song *Over the High Mountain.* (In Karl Larsen's edition, this is the second stanza on page 76.) But the stanza is an addition, which clearly was *glued onto* the manuscript at a later date. In addition, the four lines are written with the darker, Indian ink that is used only in the late, fair copies of the narrative poem.

Everything, therefore, seems to point to the fact that this little verbal exchange on a lonely sheet of paper really is a document from the first moment of the transformational process. "It is a specimen of the new approach echoing inside the writer," says the literary historian Just Bing in his short work *Henrik Ibsen's Brand*, and he continues: "It is but a passing chord, which was noted down on paper. But for this very reason it must be the strangest, the most intensely vivid document that the history of *our* literature has to offer."[14]

3

Åse Hiorth Lervik is the latest scholar to write about genre transformation, and she also comments on the four-line fragment in her book *Ibsen's verskunst i Brand* (1969). She notes that the metrical form of the fragment is different from that of the narrative poem. The narrative poem is written in broad, five-foot verse, the fragment in four-foot verse. So one can perceive that the transition to dramatic form and to four-foot verse takes place simultaneously; the play as a whole—just as these four lines—was written in four-foot verse.

One of the weaknesses in the narrative *Brand*, which Ibsen himself must have been aware of, was its wordiness, not only in the descriptive, but also in the narrative, sections. There is no trace of this in the play, which has a stricter control of language throughout. "The significance of the transition from one form to another has in this case shown itself both in the writer's productivity, and in the product's quality," notes Åse Hiorth Lervik. We have no means of telling, she continues, how much of this effect is due to the change from narrative to dramatic form and how much is due to the simultaneous transition from iambic five-foot stanzas to the shorter, four-foot, stichic, partly iambic and partly trochaic verse, with its varied rhyme scheme. Clearly the change of meter in itself demanded a stylistic reworking tending toward greater conciseness, which Åse Hiorth Lervik illustrates with telling parallel quotations from the narrative and dramatic versions respectively.[15]

In his thesis about Ibsen's verse, another Norwegian literary scholar, Hallvard Lie, once more raised the question, what actually happened inside Ibsen during his visit to St. Peter's? How could it have triggered the metamorphosis that *Brand* underwent?

Halvdan Koht had already touched on this in his Ibsen book. He suggests that the impression the mighty building made on Ibsen was what helped him find the new shape he needed for his work. This sort of symbolic transposition of an experience from one medium to another—from the stones of architecture to the architecture of words—is not unreasonable or unique. It is known as symbol equivalence.[16]

Hallvard Lie objected to Koht's reasoning by pointing out that even if the architecture had inspired Ibsen to give his work a stricter form, this would scarcely explain the change of genre from narrative to drama. The dome of St. Peter's and Michaelangelo's masterpiece may have made a tremendous impression on Ibsen, but this is not a sufficient explanation for the change in genre.[17]

Lie himself has another hypothesis. He imagines that Ibsen went into St. Peter's while a service was in progress and that he listened to a mass with Latin hymns. Church liturgy is the original source of all worldly drama—and Ibsen stood at the very source. It would be understandable, says Lie, if Ibsen, while listening to a requiem mass in which medieval Latin hymns of the type *Dies irae, dies illa* dominated with their four-beat stanzas, decided to change his unsuccessful narrative poem into a play. Lie believes there are signs that a religious experience preceded the literary mutation. He points to a changed inner stance in the work, as it turned from narrative to drama, a "theologizing." In the narrative version the conflict was still predominantly of a humanistic-ethical nature, whereas in the play Brand becomes a religious fanatic, striving toward the beyond.

Hallvard Lie's hypothesis is ingenious but extremely uncertain.

It is possible, however, to establish at what point Ibsen abandoned the descriptive narration in order to present his material by means of action. In his narrative poem he had reached a point corresponding to the beginning of the second act of the play—Brand's meeting with the villagers outside the church. He now had the task of explaining how Agnes had become Brand's wife. This he never did. The demands of narrative—as the Danish scholar Hans Brix once put it—sealed the poem's fate. Even in the play we do not learn how Brand won Agnes's hand. We are told that three years have elapsed between the second and third acts, and when the curtain rises Brand and Agnes are married and have a son. "It is as easy as that in a play," writes Hans Brix, "But here was an incredibly difficult task—that of presenting Brand as suitor." Brand could be all things except lover. So Ibsen solved the problem during the play's interval. He had not succeeded in solving the problems of his narrative poem by adopting a freer meter. Then came the day in St. Peter's, which in a very literal sense involved a moment of illumination. Whereupon Ibsen, in Brix's words, "turned the pyramid upside down and completed *Brand*".[18]

4

Ibsen himself evidently regarded the transformation from narrative poem to play as a leap and a literary mutation. But while working on the play he kept his narrative draft handy, and a number of expressions, images, and rhymes recur in the play. There is also, in fact, some fragmentary material from Ibsen's preliminary work on the *play*, and in two instances this draft material is closer to the narrative poem than to the final drama. It contains verbatim phrases from the poem—phrases that seem better adapted to a narrative than to a play. At a later stage Ibsen either excluded or altered them. We have to think of Ibsen's struggle with dramatic form as a process during which he deliberately abandoned narrative in favor of drama. This holds true for the first two acts. For all intents and purposes, from the third act on he worked independently of the earlier, narrative version, which had been discontinued at an early stage of the story line.

If we maintain that the play *Brand* arose by virtue of discontinuous action rather than as a result of organic growth, it is worth seeing how much—or how little—Ibsen carried over from narrative to play, in terms of scenes, *motifs*, and phraseology. Karl Larsen pointed out the important transpositions in his edition of the narrative poem. The only words that are repeated literally, or with minimal variation, are those constituting the exchange between Einar and Agnes: "Agnes, my lovely butterfly" and her reply "I am a butterfly small and pure." These passages could be transposed, since they already constituted a dialogue, and they added a touch of lyricism to the play, in much the same way that they had done in the poem. Other transposed elements—*motifs*, situations, verbal exchanges—were altered in accordance with the demands of the new genre and the shorter meter. As a character, Brand himself became more and more inexorable. Whereas he reasoned and reflected in the poem, his language in the play is like hammerblows; scarcely any of the dramatic phrases that have become well-known quotations can be found word for word in the poem.

One remark that *has* been transposed is made by Agnes after her first meeting with Brand; Einar tries to tempt her as the Viking Frithiof once tried to tempt Ingeborg in Esaias Tegnér's *Frithiofs saga*—with all the delights of the South, with laurel groves, lemons, and grapes, and Agnes replies by referring to something else: "But did you see how he grew while he was speaking!" These are the final words of the song *Over the High Mountain* in the poem. This highly charged remark appears in the corresponding part of the play but is interrupted and hence more striking:

> Agnes: (. . .) But tell me if you saw—
>
> Einar: What?
>
> Agnes: How he grew, while he was speaking!

"To be an author is, basically, to see," Ibsen used to say,[19] and this picture of Brand growing in stature through the inner power of his words is strikingly visual.

The narrative poem *Brand* was introduced by an admonitory sermon, in which Ibsen states his task as author: to sing a somber song for his country and his compatriots, perhaps his last. The central imagery of *To the Guilty Accessories* is represented by words like "death," "corpses," "sickness," "pestilent air"; in short—something was rotten in the state of Norway! The Norwegians were a people who lived on memories of the past, without heeding the call to action of the present. It is Ibsen's task to express the crime, pain, and remorse of his people. This is his reason for being an author, and this is why he has turned away from fraudulent daydreams and illusions. These have to be destroyed so that something better may take their place:

> That which is dead, cannot be lied alive,
>
> that which is dead, must in the darkness down,
>
> One task alone it has, which is to be
>
> itself the nourishment for new-sown seed.[20]

We can ask ourselves what happened to this prologue when the work was recast? It returns—reshaped—at the end of the play, in Brand's last long monologue in the fifth act. It has a shorter rhythm, a higher tempo, yet the images and anaphoric rhetoric are the same:

> the corpse cannot be lied alive,
>
> the corpse must in the darkness down,
>
> the corpse's task is but to be
>
> nourishment for new-sown seed.

Brand is a play in which monologues still occupy much space, possibly as remnants from the poetic version. The last powerful—and long—monologue contains not only elements from the first song but also many images and ideas from Brand's speech in the song *Over the Great Mountain*. But it is striking and significant that the original situation, Ibsen's indignation at a particular political event, the indignation that provided the incentive for the poem, is never directly expressed in the play. It was the booster rocket that fell off.

Untapped for the time being were other themes and material in the narrative poem, which later functioned as a reservoir of *motifs* and images for Ibsen's plays. The story of the boy who cut off the fingers of his right hand to avoid being called up, which reflected press notices from 1864, was later used in *Peer Gynt*. The description of the celebration of 17 May was to reappear in a different form in *The League of Youth*, written four years after Ibsen had rejected his narrative poem. But, of course, other material in the poem was never put to use, either in the play *Brand* or elsewhere. Both selection and rejection were part of the process we refer to as the genesis, or—as in this instance—the regeneration, of the work of art.

Henrik Ibsen was a conscious and methodical playwright. As a rule he started a play by writing a prose-outline, in which he noted acts and scenes. After this he worked out single scenes in detail, which functioned as buttresses to the final composition. We have no knowledge of a prose-outline for *Brand*, and it is possible that the poem provided a preliminary outline; but we do know that he worked out some individual scenes—a couple of which have been preserved in the final version. The play was finished within three months. Ibsen's flowing pen and versificatory talent scarcely failed him during this time.

5

Only in rare instances—and then only for works of art of limited scope—does the phenomenon of spontaneous inception take place during the space of a few minutes or hours. We have seen examples, and will see more, of lyric poems that have come into being by an unbroken, creative act, as it were ready-made. Literary works of greater scope, like musical ones, need time, often considerable periods of time, for their execution. "This execution is vital to such a degree that it is in fact through this that the artist's magnitude becomes apparent."[21] These words by Max Dessoir, German aesthetician of the old school, might have been coined expressly for Ibsen, for he, if anyone, was a man of labor and painstaking execution.

In his play *When We Dead Awaken* (1899) Ibsen chose a sculptor, Professor Rubeck, as the main figure. To the end of his days Rubeck wears himself out with lumps of clay and blocks of stone.[22] In a play written seven years earlier Ibsen chose Master Builder Solness as his representative. In his younger days he had selected the man working down in the pit, Bergmanden, the mining engineer:

> So he carries on blow by blow
> until sinking down weak and slow.

These two lines are from the first printed version of the poem *Bergmanden* (1851). Twelve years later Ibsen reformulated them, giving even greater prominence to the aesthetic of work, of which he was so outstanding an exponent.

> Hammer-blow and hammer-strife
> Until the last day of life.[23]

The flowing ease with which he wrote the play *Brand* was an exception in his authorial experience. It can be seen as a victory over his material—the resistant clay and stone of words.

Gösta Berlings saga
and Its Transformations

I have had an attack of poetic rapture, or whatever I should call it. It is a habit with me, long periods of stagnation and then in between a period of swift and easy production.

> Selma Lagerlöf
> Letter to her friend
> Henriette Coyet

1

Gösta Berlings saga, like Ibsen's *Brand*, was transformed a number of times. It was originally planned as a series of romances, then for a while projected as a play, and finally completed as a novel.

In the whole of Swedish literature there is scarcely any other work whose genesis has been more carefully investigated. It was well into the twentieth century before manuscripts covering its various stages became available. The Swedish literary scholar Helge Gullberg presented and analyzed this material in three careful studies.[1] Selma Lagerlöf herself provided information about how she wrote the book, partly in letters from the late 1880s and early 1890s (when she was actually writing it), partly in the detailed and stylized account in the piece *A Story about a Story* (written later than the book and published in 1902), and finally in some references in two essays (one on her friend Esselde [Sophie Adlersparre], the other on her literary models [*In the Steps of the Giant*]).

When Selma Lagerlöf gave the title *A Story about a Story* to her half-fictional account of how she wrote *Gösta Berlings saga*, she was both adopting and renewing a literary form in the same way that H. C. Andersen did when he called his autobiography *The Adventure of My Life*. In both instances the choice of authentic material

119

was dependent on the genre and style used. The fact that Lagerlöf stressed concrete and symbolic aspects of the course of events meant that she excluded the theoretical and intellectual factors that also played a part in the novel's inception. The Lagerlöf scholar Erland Lagerroth, who has pointed this out, believes that Selma Lagerlöf, by forcibly molding the genesis of *Gösta Berlings saga* into a story or tale, in some respects fell prey to her own genre. Her grappling with the aesthetic and theoretical problems of her first work is reduced to the categories of the folktale. She herself becomes the unthinking and uncomplicated child of nature of such tales, who sets out to find fortune and happiness and does so after various delays and complications.[2]

The decisive moment when it became clear to the budding authoress that she had to write "the story of the cavaliers of Värmland" was described by her in a much-quoted passage. She was twenty-two years old at the time and attending a college, the Lyceum for Girls in Stockholm, as a trainee teacher.

> Then something strange happened the same autumn, after she had lived a couple of months among gray streets and walls. One morning she came walking up Malmskillnadsgatan with a parcel of books under her arm. She had just attended a class in literature. It must have been about Bellman [the author of *Fredman's Epistles*] or Runeberg [the author of *Fänrik Stål's Tales*] because she walked along and thought about these two and about the characters that appeared in their works. She told herself that Runeberg's good-natured fighting men and Bellman's carefree carousers were the best material any writer could have to work with. And suddenly the idea occurred to her: The world in which you lived, far away in Värmland, was no less remarkable than the world of Fredman or Fänrik Stål. If you can only learn to deal with it, you have got every bit as good material to work with as these two.
>
> This is how she caught sight of her story for the first time. And at that same moment the ground began to sway under her feet. The whole street as far as the fire-station heaved up toward the sky and then sank down again, heaved and sank. She had to stand still a good while, before the street settled down again, and she gazed in surprise at the passersby, who walked along so calmly, unaware of the wonder that had taken place. At this moment the young girl decided that she would write the story of the cavaliers of Värmland, and she never ever let go of the thought. But many a long year was to pass before she was able to put it into effect.[3]

One cannot help asking what really happened that day in 1881, when Selma Lagerlöf saw the street swaying under her feet. She herself dates her "decision" to write a story about the Värmland traditions to this episode. Pierre Audiat, a scholar who has devoted himself to a study of what he calls the biography of the literary work, believes that the central impulse or *"l'idée génératrice"* behind a work almost invariably arises *"brusquement."*[4] We have, of course, no reason to doubt that Lagerlöf experienced her creative impulse almost in a religious sense, with strong physical symptoms. But what exactly did her revelation consist of? All she tells us is that she suddenly became conscious of the fact that she possessed material for a literary work that was every bit as good as Runeberg's and Bellman's material. There is not a word about how it was to be shaped, what the basic plan was to be, or who would be the leading character. There is something mysterious about this call to literary action, which indeed is reminiscent, in more than one respect, of Rousseau's account of what happened to him on the road to Dijon.

Lagerlöf stresses the long interval between her decision to write and the execution of this work. There is very little documentary evidence of the saga's development between 1881 and 1890, when a few of its chapters were sent in to a literary competition organized by the magazine *Idun*. In Lagerlöf's own words, the story first appeared to be "a whole host of stories, an entirely nebulous cloud of adventures, which passed back and forth like a swarm of lost bees one summer's day."[5] This description from *A Story about a Story* uses an image that relates directly to the closing lines of the finished novel *Gösta Berlings saga*, the lines about the bees and the beehive of reality.

Lagerlöf emphasizes that an important factor in the development of her story was choosing her main protagonist and his name. During a holiday from her teaching she sat talking to her father about the old days. He happened to mention that a friend from his youth was a man of exceptional charm: "This man brought happiness and gaiety with him, wherever he went. He could sing, compose music, improvise verses. . . . If he drank himself tipsy, he played and spoke even better than when he was sober, and when he fell in love with a woman, it was impossible for her to resist him.'''[6] Lagerlöf tells us that after this conversation she could see her hero better than before: "with that, more life and movement came into my story. One fine day my hero even got a name, and was called Gösta Berling!"[7]

We do not know exactly when this conversation with her father could have taken place, but at the latest it was in 1884, since he died in the summer of the following year. Nothing appears to have been written down yet. "On another occasion," she tells us in *A Story about a Story*," she spent the Christmas holidays at home. One evening they drove a long way to a Christmas party in a heavy snowstorm. The journey took longer than anyone could have imagined. The horse could only proceed step by step. She sat for several hours in the snowstorm and thought about her story. When they finally arrived she had thought out the first chapter. It was the one about Christmas Eve in the smithy. It was initially written in verse, since the original plan was for a cycle of romances like Runeberg's *Fänrik Ståls sägner*."[8] The chapters—or verse episodes—written after "Christmas Eve" were, she tells us, "The Story of the Ball at Borg" and the scene in "Svartsjö churchyard."

For a long time the only evidence of the romance cycle was Selma Lagerlöf's own account; then in 1958 part of the verse manuscript came to light. By examining the spelling in the manuscript— Selma Lagerlöf followed her Värmland compatriot Adolph Noreen's example of radical spelling for a short while—it has been possible to date it to the year 1887.

Helge Gullberg, who examined the manuscript in detail, believes that it represents a draft. He supposes that the lines not yet properly formed into verse and only loosely arranged were the first to be written.

> Gösta Berling came one day
> No one knows where the grave
> The old master of Säby gård
> Was sleeping in his grave
> But no precious
> You far-flung lake with steep shore.

Gullberg describes them as "rather disparate, tentative attempts, which have already been crossed out." Next come a few lines that prove Lagerlöf is trying out the four-foot trochaic meter, which she later adopted in the manuscript. As Gullberg points out, this verse scheme closely resembles that of poems like *Munter* in *Fänrik Ståls sägner*, and we recall that Selma Lagerlöf cited Runeberg's verse cycle as a direct model.[9]

The manuscript contains only *one* complete poem. Entitled "The Card Game in the Churchyard," it covers the same subject that later figured in the chapter about Svartsjö churchyard in the novel. There are three persons in the poem. One of them is Gösta Berling, who receives the epithet "poor genius," and the other two participants in the card game are Rustam and Captain Kristian Berg. The dead man is called "Hök." When the scene is transposed to a prose chapter, the actors' names are changed: from Gösta Berling to Colonel Beerencreutz; from Rustam to Ruster; and from Captain Kristian Berg to Major Anders Fuchs.

The poem about the card game in the churchyard demonstrates, with its clumsy wording, that poetry did not come naturally to Selma Lagerlöf. Among the other verse fragments is a short draft written in a *Nibelungen* meter, which opens:

> At Ekeby, home of the Colonel, they had a drinking bout
> The handsome Gösta Berling he sat there in company good.

Helge Gullberg rightly pointed out that the obvious model for these lines is found in Tegnér's romance "Frithiof Comes to King Ring," which also describes a drinking bout: "King Ring he sat in his high seat at Christmas and drank mead." In addition to Runeberg, Lagerlöf evidently turned to Tegnér when seeking a model for what presumably was her first attempt at shaping her story about the cavaliers from Värmland.[10]

The verse fragments and the experiment with the romance show how tied Lagerlöf was to a genre that had seemed natural to her ever since childhood but that clearly in the long run was inadequate for her talents and her aims. We do not know for how many chapters she wrote verse drafts, but we do know—from *A Story about a Story*—that she tried her hand at a dramatic version after the poetic one: "for a while her intention was that it [the story] should be written as a play. And Christmas Eve was reworked so as to constitute the first part of it."[11]

We have no reason to doubt Lagerlöf's account of the successive transformations of her story. Admittedly we have no knowledge— to date—of any dramatic manuscript to *Gösta Berlings saga*, but we know that at an early stage she wrote verse dramas for a toy theater. In 1891 she was still considering whether she should print some of these early attempts, for which she named Atterbom and Tegnér (two Swedish poets from the romantic period) and Shakespeare as models. In any event, they were not published until after her death, under the title *Dolls' Theatre (Dockteater).* [12]

Selma Lagerlöf had a certain early familiarity with dramatic literature. In 1876 she read Goethe's *Faust* in Victor Rydberg's Swedish translation, and it may be worth noting that in "Christmas Eve"—in the form in which we know it—the cavaliers' pact with Sintram is commonly regarded as being modeled on the episode of the pact with the devil in *Faust.* [13]

But whoever decided to write a drama, even a verse drama, after 1887 must have done so knowing of the renaissance in Norwegian drama, led by Ibsen. The frequent parallels drawn between plays by Ibsen, on the one hand, and scenes and figures in *Gösta Berlings saga*, on the other, gain new significance when one remembers that at an early stage *Gösta Berlings saga* had a direct link with the dramatic genre.

Fréderic Paulhan, in his time a well-known French psychologist who had studied creativity, called a chapter in his book *"Le développement de l'invention par transformation."* He notes that an original idea or plan can undergo one or more transformations, so that the end result is a work other than the one envisaged. A work that starts as a novel can for one reason or another be transformed into a play. The type of process discussed by Paulhan in terms of a hypothetical example is concretely illustrated by the genesis of *Gösta Berlings saga*, which is probably the best Swedish example of a literary work that was developed through a series of genre transformations.

Paulhan believes that a transformation of this kind is never total. Something of the original impulse and intention normally survives. He speculates that the reasons for this are as follows: it is because there is something unchanging and stable in the author's consciousness that the transformations take place. Ultimately, it is the persistent power of the emotions and ideas connected with the work's inception that determines the transformations and eliminates obstacles. The creative process continues its work at the cost of a revolution. After being reduced to ashes several times on a metaphorical manuscript pyre, the Phoenix arises anew.[14]

Selma Lagerlöf gave up her attempts to express her story in narrative verse, just as she then abandoned her attempted play. As she says herself in *A Story about a Story*: "But this attempt was not a success either, and now she finally decided to write the story as a novel. So the chapter [it is still "Christmas Eve"] was written down in prose and filled forty pages. The last time it was rewritten it occupied only nine pages."[15]

However, the fact that she had hit upon the prose genre did not finally liberate her creative power. Work on the chapters—or at that time, more accurately, the individual short stories—was slow. "A great deal of material had indeed been collected. But why was it so difficult for her to write it down? Why was she never visited by inspiration? Why did her pen move so slowly across the paper?"[16] She reminds herself that the period was that of the 1880s, "the best age for strictly realistic literature." The prose style she tried first was the one her contemporaries used. She tried to write her stories "about ghosts and wild love, about beautiful ladies and adventurous cavaliers" in "calm, realistic prose."[17] Once more she experienced a conflict between the demands of form and content.

On one occasion, however, "she wrote a few small chapters in another style. One of them was a scene from Svartsjö churchyard, the other concerned the old philosopher Uncle Eberhard and his atheistic pamphlets. She wrote them mostly for fun, and with many an Alas! and Alackaday! in well-nigh rhythmical prose. And she noticed that she was able to write in this way, that it brought inspiration."[18] It was a breakthrough for a lyrical impulse.

A factor apart from the literary context and experiments, to which Lagerlöf ascribes crucial significance, was the sale of her childhood home Mårbacka. She traveled home to see the place for the last time in the summer of 1889, and this, according to her retrospective diagnosis, was the factor that precipitated a new wave of inspiration. This is a salutary reminder that literary "creativity" is not after all an independent and isolated capacity, that verbal fantasy and imagination have their roots in deep levels of the personality.

A few weeks after the sale of Mårbacka, Lagerlöf returned to her home in Landskrona and sat down at her desk.

> She began to write, she did not exactly know how it would turn out, but she was not going to be afraid of strong words, exclamations, questions. Nor was she going to be afraid of expressing herself, with all her childishness and all her dreams. And after this her pen started to move almost of its own accord. This made her feel almost dizzy, she was beside herself with joy. See, this was really writing! Unfamiliar things and thoughts, or rather, things she had no idea she housed in her brain, crowded down on the paper. The pages were filled with a speed she had never dreamed of. What she otherwise would have needed months, even years, to work out was now completed in a few hours.[19]

This description of how her creative power was released is the actual climax of *A Story about a Story*. After that she tells us how the story was subsequently completed and published: the competition in *Idun* magazine, the effort to finish her manuscript within the alloted time, finally the prize and the happy period of creativity that followed, when she, freed from her schoolwork, was able to finish her novel. "It was the happiest time she had known."[20]

The advertising of a literary competition, and the chances of publication it offered a hitherto unknown writer, provide us with an occasion for noting in concrete terms the connection between society's economic productive forces on the one hand and author-productivity on the other. The play of economic forces lay behind the compulsory sale of Mårbacka, a sale which Selma Lagerlöf assures us liberated her impulse to write freely. Another factor in the play of economic forces was the actual competition—for it spurred her on to intense, creative work, which continued after fame and prize money had come her way. We glimpse here, in other words, an interaction between productive forces and productivity that is far clearer than that in any of the other examples we have discussed.

Lagerlöf's account of what might be called her psychological spring flood, the release of her creative power, is similar to many reports from the heyday of romanticism on. She describes the flow of inspiration, improvisational ease, and the sense of euphoria. We can scarcely be wrong if we surmise that this experience is reflected in one of the first published chapters of *Gösta Berlings saga*, and is projected onto Gösta Berling himself. The chapter about Gösta, the poet, gets its title from a quotation in *Faust*: "As long as man strives, he loses his way." In it, Gösta Berling, who normally did not have vivid dreams, one night "dreamed that he had written poetry."[21]

"He, whom people called 'the poet,' although he had hitherto been the innocent victim of this nickname, now got up in the middle of the night, and half awake and half asleep he began to write. It was a whole poem, which he found on his desk the following morning. He would never have believed himself capable of it. Now the ladies were to hear it." And then follows the supposedly dreamed poem of six stanzas.[22]

This is the same kind of description of trancelike inspiration that is Coleridge's account of how he wrote *Kubla Khan*, and it is tempting to see in it an objectivization of the sort of inspirational state Lagerlöf herself experienced during the late phase of her work on *Gösta Berling*. The romantic cult of inspiration and improvisation was not far distant in time. Lagerlöf was familiar with one of its main documents: Madame de Staël's *Corinne*, the novel about the divinely inspired *improvvisatrice*. It is probably no coincidence that it is this very book which is thrown to the wolves to keep them at bay during the nocturnal sleigh ride in the chapter "Gösta Berling, the Poet."

With a concreteness that belonged to the genre, Selma Lagerlöf was able in *A Story about a Story* to tell of the trauma resulting from the sale of her family home, as well as the way she recaptured that which had been lost by writing *Gösta Berlings saga*. But the sale of a house—however painful it can be—creates no new style. Much later, in her essay *In the Steps of the Giant*, she spoke in detail of a stylistic impulse that affected her at a decisive moment. "What I at that time called writing in my own personal way consisted in boldly following the dictates of my imagination, with Carlyle as my model.[23] We must not of course exaggerate the importance of a single stylistic impulse, and stylisticians have pointed out that other models could also have inspired her to stylistic innovations with exclamation marks, questions, and invocations. But Georg Brandes remarked on the similarity between Lagerlöf and Carlyle in his review of *Gösta Berling*, and the Swedish literary historian

Fredrik Böök examined in detail what she might have learned by reading Carlyle's *History of the French Revolution*, not only about style but also about composition and general effects.

2

We have tried, insofar as possible, to follow the various transformations of *Gösta Berlings saga*, from romance cycle, to drama, and finally to novel, with its unusual, passionate, and highly charged rhetorical style.

One question remains. To what extent is it possible to discern the early stages of its development in the completed novel? Or to express it in concrete terms: are there any traces of the romance cycle or the play in the finished work?

The fact that *Gösta Berlings saga* contains both dramatic and lyrical elements does not of course necessarily mean that they, like marked isotopes, can be traced to early stages of the work. But when one knows that an earlier—only fragmentarily extant—version of the novel comprised a series of independent romances, the similarities, noted by a number of scholars, between *Frithiofs saga* and *Fänrik Ståls sägner* on the one hand and *Gösta Berlings saga* on the other hand become of interest. "Because I started off as a poet, I have developed a love of detail, and I want every chapter of my novel to be rounded off like the various songs in, for instance, *Frithiofs saga*," Selma Lagerlöf wrote to her friend Helena Nyblom on 18 March 1891.[24] So it is neither impossible nor improbable that the correspondence Swedish scholars found between "the cyclic form" of Tegnér, Runeberg, and Lagerlöf can be traced to her original plans for a romance cycle.

If one starts with the hypothesis—admittedly unproved—that literary influences make themselves most easily felt *within* a genre, i.e., from poetry to poetry and from drama to drama, then other similarities with Runeberg and Tegnér, with Goethe's *Faust* and Ibsen, become significant in terms of the genesis of *Gösta Berling*. Whatever opinion one may have about the possibility of proving influence and loans in literary work, it can hardly be denied that the comparative approach gains particular significance and applicability in a work that, like *Gösta Berlings saga*, underwent a series of genre transformations and passed from lyrical romance cycle to dramatic outline to prose draft in a naturalist style, which finally turned into the remarkable combination of the lyrical, the dramatic, and the narrative.

But whatever elements may have been absorbed from earlier stages, the fact remains that the big breakthrough came late and involved a total reshaping and rethinking of the work. We need only place the fumbling, almost comically awkward lyrical fragments next to one of the novel's chapters to see how different they are. The novel demonstrates, in both major and minor ways, an entirely new constructive ability. "I must tell you in confidence, dear Tante, that my powers of composition are as great as my imagination. How could I otherwise succeed in letting every chapter be a whole, but also the whole book a coherent work. I challenge anyone to repeat it."[25] These words, addressed to Sophie Adlersparre, her feminist authoress friend, show not only self-confidence but also self-knowledge. The constitutive compositional elements of *Gösta Berling saga*, in the form in which we now know it, i.e., the presentation of the action as a coherent whole invested with moral significance, the rhythmic seasonal pattern that provides a background to the cataclysmic upheaval, the revolt against order, and the final return to order—none of this could have existed in the versions preceding the final prose version. In fact, Lagerlöf worked on the composition and structuring of the whole right up to the end. Vivi Edström, one of the last scholars who examined the printer's manuscript of the novel, demonstrated that several important elements, which heighten the impact of the action, were added at the last moment.

3

Not only is Selma Lagerlöf's interest in the conditions of creativity and creative life reflected in *A Story about a Story* and a host of letters written around 1890, but it stayed with her throughout her life.

Her aesthetic creed combines belief in inspiration with confidence in hard work. Already in *A Story about a Story* she speaks as much about toil as about the creative flow. "Not many of the chapters were written in a single sweep like that," she says, after having described the sudden breakthrough; "most of them needed a lot of hard work."[26] In fact, *A Story about a Story* is an account, no less, of a prolonged creative process, delayed by many obstacles, starting from the day when she as a young twenty-two-year-old "decided that she would write the story of the cavaliers of Värmland," up to the point when she carried this out at age thirty.

An interesting insight into Lagerlöf's work habits during a somewhat later period is provided by the drafts and manuscript to *The Coachman (Körkarlen)*, which she allowed her personal friend and secretary Valborg Olander to publish in 1914 under the title *A Look inside the Workshop (En blick i verkstaden)*. The introduction is unsigned but is assumed to be by Lagerlöf herself. In it we read that not only the writer at the outset of his career, but also "the mature artist-author, often has to work out in concrete terms, like a sculptor, one draft after another, until he can see clearly which one most nearly reflects his intentions and measures up to the demands of true artistry."[27] Lagerlöf here demonstrates a side of her nature that contrasts with the legend surrounding her as an author—which she helped build up—a legend that she is a storyteller with a naive imagination and a spontaneous narrative gift. As an author she also had a highly professional approach, which included reflection, conscious calculation, and artistic craftsmanship.

The introduction to *A Look inside the Workshop* also contains the following observation:

> It is a widespread belief among the general public that an author, as soon as he has chosen his subject and sketched out a plan for the development of the action, only needs to let his pen run on, in order for the pages to be filled day by day, and for his book to be ready within the appointed time.
>
> There are without doubt writers who are capable of producing stories out of a hat in this way, but that this should be the rule for authors requiring artistry of themselves can scarcely be imagined by anyone with the least idea about literature.[28]

To demonstrate her method of work, she then presents many variants of the same scene—which is the description of the three men in the churchyard at the beginning of her novel *The Coachman*. She works in short spurts. First she writes a few words, phrases, then sentences, then a whole paragraph—after which she pauses. She crosses this out and tries a second time, but again is unsatisfied. She rewrites the whole passage a third or fourth time. We can see the method not only in *The Coachman* but also from the prose manuscript of *Gösta Berlings saga*.

"Most of these attempts," she writes about the drafts for the scene in *The Coachman*," were developed for four or five pages. After the author had finally settled on a plan and form for the first chapter, the remainder were written in quick succession."[29]

In *The Coachman* and in *Gösta Berlings saga*, "plan and form"— the solutions to problems of composition and style—were arrived at simultaneously. Referring to the long genesis of her first novel, Lagerlöf stresses what a long time a novelist may have to grapple with his subject. An apt comment on this is found in her well-known and oft-quoted lines in a letter to Helena Nyblom on 25 May 1891: "My struggle with the language is indescribably wearisome, it is only when I am very worked up that I can write easily, without having to correct and alter every sentence."[30]

Another common experience for Lagerlöf was the long "incuba-tion period"; in exceptional cases an idea could lie hidden and concealed for more than thirty years. She offered one of her stor-ies entitled *The Man (Karln)*, which was based on a ghost story she had heard from an aunt, to a Christmas journal in 1892. It was turned down.[31] More than thirty years later she used the same story, artistically reworked, in *The Ring of the Löwenskölds*. Another element in *The Man*, the monastery legend of the abbot who lets his monks read their Christmas Eve mass in the monastery garden for the benefit of the animals and birds, was taken out of that con-text many years later and included in *The Legend of the Christmas Roses*, published in 1905.[32] Here, too, there was an incubation period of over a decade.

4

We noted above that one of Selma Lagerlöf's stories was based on a story that had been told to her. It is characteristic of her creative reactions and methods that she had a so-called listening narrative technique.[33] While writing, she often listened to an inner voice, which she identified with that of her paternal grandmother or aunt. Her habit of feeling her way in a Värmland accent before deciding on a definitive form of wording is part of the same phenomenon. The use of the Värmland dialect must surely have been an attempt to return to the role of listener, a regression to the storytelling environment of her childhood.[34]

Lagerlöf often referred to her paternal grandmother in her works, as in this early stanza, quoted by Elin Wägner in her Lagerlöf biography:

My old grandmother who is dead and gone

Will sit beside me and tell stories

And when my memory starts to fail anon

I'll choose nor thoughts nor words, the glory is

That's done by grandmother who is dead and gone.[35]

It is interesting to note traces of the same inspirational technique at a very early stage of the romance cycle on the Gösta Berling theme. Among the early verse drafts, which can be dated thanks to the radical spelling, there is a longer poem that might even have been intended as a sort of prologue to the projected romance cycle. It will suffice to quote the opening strophe:

Granny we will sit very still

Dearest Granny tell us do

Of how long since you fared so ill

Though you were sweet and graceful too

Tell us how you took good care

Of the manor house so great

Tell us of the black dog there

Which stood on guard at the entrance gate.[36]

Placing her story in the mouth of another narrator was to become a sevice much used by Selma Lagerlöf, and it may in some way have been connected with the technique of inspirational listening referred to above.

It is an interesting fact that she used this technique—listening to an inner, speaking voice and then projecting the inner voice onto another character—until she was quite old. Particularly when her creativity dried up, she would have recourse to this technique by means of almost magical formulas. During the first world war, feeling in deep depression that nothing was going right for her, she burst out:

> Dear God, help Selma Lagerlöf!
> Christ Jesus, come and help me, tell me what
> I am to write.
> I am sitting and listening for God's voice.

and again:

> I am like a blank sheet of paper
> I am the unwritten page on which God himself
> writes down his thoughts.[37]

A projected sequel to her novel *Anna Svärd* shows us the same attitude of listening. It is said of a Miss Salvius, governess to the Löwensköld girls: "It is she who writes inside me, who wants it to be like this, for she is so remarkably old-fashioned. . . . She lets me sit here longing, straining to make a new attempt." Nils Afzelius, Selma Lagerlöf's bibliographer, who quotes the passage, remarks that "in the draft she [Miss Salvius] becomes no more or less than Selma Lagerlöf's genius, which dictates to her from subconscious material, which slowly and reluctantly wells up within her."[38]

Lagerlöf several times stressed the feeling of depersonalization that accompanies inspiration, as in this letter to Helena Nyblom, where she is speaking of the recently completed *Gösta Berlings saga*: "When I succeed in writing something I like, I feel as though I were only a spokesman for somebody else."[39] This letter from early in her authorial career can be compared with something she wrote late in life to a friend with theosophical interests: "I am sure I would have become a theosophist or spiritualist a long time ago, if I had had any experiences or acquaintanceship with Higher Worlds, but the only thing I have experienced with complete certainty is the poetic intuition which has fallen upon me with such power and strength that I simply dare not believe that it came from within myself." "It has seemed to me," she continues in the same letter, "that it was something which came from the unconscious depths of my soul."[40]

In a study of Selma Lagerlöf's artistic awareness, the Swedish literary scholar Sigvard Lindqvist pointed out that the experience of what she herself called "inspiration" or "intuition," which at first struck her as mysterious, later became psychologically credible when she became familiar with contemporary theories about the subconscious.[41] In a letter to the Danish philosopher Höffding in 1897, she thanks him for the insights she gained through reading his *Psychology*; in Höffding's work, as in that of many contemporary psychologists, the concepts of the subconscious and the unconscious played an important part. She wrote that Höffding's ideas "illuminated a great many things for me, which I had noted in myself, particularly with regard to writing, inspiration, and so on, things which I had not previously been able to see in their proper context and explain in a natural way. Above all it struck me as wonderful that my brain could function without my knowing about it, and that it at times could produce masses of ideas which I had not consciously thought out."[42]

Sigvard Lindqvist, who quotes this letter, also points out that already in the 1890s Lagerlöf uses imagery in her letters that presents the various levels of consciousness in spatial categories. This often occurs in her fictional work as well; in a short story from 1894 she speaks of thoughts rising up "to the threshold of consciousness," and in *A Manor House Story* from the end of the same decade, she writes of something "which lay so far beneath consciousness that human intelligence could not reach it."[43]

Sigvard Lindqvist puts it neatly when he says that Selma Lagerlöf "consciously makes use of the subconscious."[44] For her, not only is inspiration a precondition for being able to create with ease, it also becomes something of a retrospective criterion of value. She is convinced that what she has written with ease is also the best, and she exhorts her theosophical friend: "Read, for instance, the pages about Lady Sorrow in *A Manor House Story*; this is one of those complete inspirations. I wrote it down without knowing what I would find on the following page."[45]

Next to this sort of testimony about her happiness "when my brain has finally done its work" and she could write "with a great rush"[46] of spontaneous creativity, there are her numerous statements about a completely contrary work process. "In general I write slowly, seeking both words and thoughts,"[47] she wrote to Helena Nyblom. Her close friend Sophie Elkan says in a letter: "Those who know the way Selma writes, also know that she has enormous difficulties in finding the right style, and that in the beginning it is more than uneven, and that it is only her faithful, endless work which turns it into what it is."[48] Her drafts amply bear this out; "they are full of alterations, crossings out, repetitions," writes Nils Afzelius, who has studied her manuscripts more thoroughly than anyone else.[49]

5

Selma Lagerlöf was exceptionally conscious of the dialectics of creativity, of the connection between the moment of inspiration and methodical work. For her, inspiration was no supernatural gift; she looked for natural, psychological explanations for it, not authority from above. In a letter to Henriette Coyet, written in the 1930s and summing up a lifetime of authorship, she wrote: "Although I do not belong to the chosen few, I do have the capacity of receiving impulses from my subconscious, things which one quite clearly cannot think out, but which are a gift from *the inner workshop*. When in this state, I feel so happy and feel as though I were a particularly gifted and exceptional person, but those periods never last long and then I feel like the poorest and least talented author in the world. Whole years can go by, during which I write on sheer routine. I have the knack, after all, but I feel quite clearly that this is not the right way." And she confirms in this same letter that "effortless production is for her a promise or a criterion of the fact that what she had written would be living literature."[50]

Scholars who have penetrated Selma Lagerlöf's world have discovered that underlying her books are certain patterns of polarity and contrasting themes. The outstanding Swedish literary historian Olle Holmberg likens the constant tension in her imaginative world to the release of pent-up waters when the ice melts in the spring.[51] Vivi Edström carries this observation a step further when she writes: "With her it is always basically a question of how life can be rescued from everything that threatens to choke it or freeze it to death"; and she continues "Maybe it is the most deeply personal side of the writer which expresses itself in this basic pattern, thereby giving a degree of constancy to her production as a whole."[52]

What we have here is a theme expressed in many different dimensions, on many different planes—ethical, psychological, aesthetic. Without wishing to simplify or reduce the problem, we can note that Lagerlöf experienced it in her literary labors as well. She does not feel happy and relieved until she has overcome stagnation, resistance, and inhibitions. This is the "melting of the ice" she herself described in *A Story about a Story*, and it recurs time and again in her subsequent creative life.

Periodicity and the Stages of Literary Creativity

Der Schaffende muss warten lernen.

Max Dessoir
*Beiträge zur allgemeinen
Kunstwissenschaft*

1

The two preceding chapters on Ibsen's *Brand* and Lagerlöf's *Gösta Berlings saga* were chiefly intended to illustrate works that underwent a genre transformation. In addition, they threw light on one typical aspect of the creative life of these two writers: they showed them suddenly experiencing an inner release of creative power and its attendant happiness after periods of literary sterility. Such an experience is far from unique. Many creative individuals are subject to periodicity, a rhythmic alternation between phases of nonproductivity and productivity. Gottfrid Keller wrote in his diary of his contemporary Hebbel, a playwright and poet: "Sometimes he got nowhere with a work for months or years. On the other hand his productive phase was like a veritable springflood [*eine wahre Springflut*]."[1] The image calls to mind a cosmic rhythm.

It would be interesting to examine more closely the relationship between an author's production curve and his/her biological rhythm, i.e., the curve of human development and aging. Which, for instance, have been the most favorable ages for the productivity of lyric poets—apart, that is, from early youth? We know little about this. Literary history contains numerous examples of lyrical talents that were extinguished after brilliant youthful starts. But no general rule can be based on this observation, for there are also instances of poets who maintained their lyrical creativity decade after decade. The eighty-year-old Goethe provides a famous example of renewed lyrical inspiration with his *Marienbader-elegie*. And two twentieth-century poets, Bo Bergman and Anders Österling, are extreme examples of poets productive after age ninety. But whether a writer has a lifelong or temporally limited productivity span, it is normally possible to observe a certain periodicity in his/her creative work, an alternation of ebb and flow.

Writers are often tied to a special—diurnal—rhythm in their work habits. What the early hours of morning meant for writers like August Strindberg or Knut Hamsun is as well known as what the midnight oil meant for Balzac or Zola. Particularly prose writers have found it possible to set up a disciplined routine enabling them to work with clockworklike punctuality and regularity.

Some novelists—possibly more of the *productive* than the *creative* type—are also able to work under conditions of installment delivery or to regularly submit their manuscripts to their publishers annually or biennially. Naturally they are motivated by material, economic incentives. So their productive power—whether to the improvement or detriment of the artistic results—has been controlled by society's economic forces.

Lyrical poets, on the other hand, have only rarely been able to depend on their writing to make a living. The psychological prerequisites for the creative labors of poets are different from those for novelists. "Tie me to my chair!"—the advice given by present-day Swedish novelist Ivar Lo-Johansson[2] —would be rather inappropriate for poets, since poetry can hardly be produced by the same effort of will that underlies much narrative or dramatic literature. Shelley knew this when he wrote in *A Defence of Poetry*, "A man cannot say: 'I *will* compose poetry.' "

The above does not of course imply that prose writers are independent of the periodicity of creative life; Selma Lagerlöf's situation, which we recently looked at, is in no way exceptional. Nor does it imply that a poet is a helpless shuttlecock tossed about by inner emotional rhythms. On the contrary, only by dint of extended, intensive, and methodical practice can a poet achieve the technical skills that at the decisive moments enable him/her to become a creative writer.

T. S. Eliot illuminated this aspect of the poet's work habits in his essay on Ezra Pound. He points out that the life of a poet can be said to move along two lines. One line consists of conscious, perpetual effort to develop his/her medium—language—artistically. Ezra Pound and many others did this by working on translations and experimenting with words. The other line consists of the human experiences the poet accumulates and absorbs day by day and year by year. By the term experience Eliot means everything the poet has read, thought, and experienced. Occasionally, says Eliot, the two lines converge at a high level, and this is when poetic masterpieces are created. An accumulated store of experience has crystallized and becomes material for art, and years of practice with language and technique have prepared the poet's expressive faculty. The occasions on which the lines approach each other and coincide represent what we may call the creative periods. When the lines diverge, no works of importance are produced, perhaps even no works at all. These periods are the truly or apparently unproductive phases in a poet's life.[3]

The psychologist Kretschmer has considered the biological aspects of the periodicity of creative work. In his view, only endogenous, hormonal factors control the rhythm of creative life. "The Periodicity of Emotional Life" is the title of a chapter in his book *Geniale Menschen*, and in it he writes:

> No type of spiritual, and in particular highly gifted, productivity continues smoothly and uniformly throughout life. On the contrary, there is often in the spiritual lives of people of consequence a characteristic wave-motion, a coming and going, a flaring up of passionate emotion, a weakening and subsidence. There are periods when a gifted person, seized by a sudden ecstacy, as an artist is overcome by a wealth of images and notes, as a scientist by the most amazing discoveries and intuitions, and he works feverishly both day and night, for weeks and months on end, until he has given expression to them, whereupon he relapses, perhaps for a lengthy period, into inactivity, poverty of ideas and sterility. This periodic wave is often a very characteristic feature of exceptional and spiritual productivity, as opposed to the normal person's reproductive work which draws its nourishment from tradition and habit and proceeds uniformly from one day to the next.[4]

Kretschmer chooses two giants of German literature, Goethe

and Hölderlin, as examples. During Goethe's more than eighty
years of life we can see periods of high productivity interspersed
with sterile intervals. Kretschmer adopts the view of an earlier German psychiatrist, Möbius, who tried to establish a biological seven-
year-rhythm in Goethe's life. Even though this strictly mathematical rhythm has been rejected by modern scholars, the fact remains
that Goethe's productivity was rhythmic up to a point. Goethe
himself spoke of the "renewed puberty" of highly gifted people,
thereby hinting at a biological aspect to the rhythm of creativity.

Hölderlin's fate as man and writer, Kretschmer's other important example, differed widely from that of Goethe. His youth up
to age thirty constituted his creative period, marked by an ecstatic
and highly charged vitality. During the remainder of his life, until
his death at age seventy-three, Hölderlin existed in a state of extinguished vitality and creative power. Kretschmer diagnosed it as
a schizophrenic psychosis. Hölderlin turned away from the outside
world in an almost complete isolation. From the later period of his
life there remain only a few isolated poems and fragments. The
most immediately applicable explanation of this process is without
doubt the psychiatric one. Recently, however, the literary scholar
Bertaux and the playwright Peter Weiss have seen Hölderlin's in-
capsulated withdrawal and silence as a phenomenon provoked from
outside, as the disappointed revolutionary dreamer's paradoxical
way of reacting to the reactionary political climate of his day. The
various models proposed as explanations do at least indicate the
difficulties of trying to give an unequivocal explanation of the
rhythm and periodicity of a creative mind.

Some concrete examples from the lives of three twentieth-century poets and a composer will provide us with additional material
on the rhythmic course often observed in creative life. The poets
are Paul Valéry, Rainer Maria Rilke, and Gunnar Ekelöf; the composer is Hugo Wolff.

2

During his early youth Valéry wrote poems in the tradition of
Baudelaire and the symbolists. He was only eighteen when he pub-

lished his first poem in a French magazine in 1889. He soon came into personal contact with the leading writers of the day, among them Pierre Louÿs and André Gide. In the years around 1890 he wrote and published some thirty poems in various French publications, including *La conque*.

In 1892 he experienced a crisis that led to the more or less complete discontinuation of his poetic activities. A period of silence, which lasted nearly twenty years, ensued. This crisis has been compared to inner upheavals of the type well known from the psychology of religious conversion. But Valéry's transformation had no religious dimension. He describes it in *Lettre sur Mallarmé* as *"une étrange et profonde transformation intellectuelle."* He presents the fact that he abandoned poetry as one act in a purely intellectual drama.

In a letter to Thibaudet he describes the spell cast on him by the writings of Edgar Allan Poe at that time, the ecstatic lucidity (the *"délire de la lucidité"*) that Poe's ideas evoked. "As a result of reading Poe, I gave up writing poetry. This art became impossible for me after 1892." Poe had taught him that poetry was a sort of machine, planned and fabricated to influence others. Valéry stopped writing poetry, which he called the art of amusing oneself at the expense of others (*"l'art de se jouer de l'âme des autres"*), in order to try to work on his own intellectual understanding, to undertake *"un advancement en soi-même."*[5]

In his letter to Thibaudet, Valéry says that about this time, in 1892, he became personally acquainted with Mallarmé, whose personal example may have been of importance. In fact Mallarmé himself had gone through a period of almost complete literary silence; during the years 1867-73 he did not complete a single literary work. Not until after 1873 did he write, during a period of twenty-five years, the thirty late poems that represent his definitive and specifically Mallarméan production.

The paralysis Mallarmé experienced when faced with a blank sheet of paper has become almost proverbial; it was not for nothing that he called the empty white sheet the most beautiful poem. This same Mallarmé spoke of the feeling of poetic impotence as a necessary ingredient or precondition for the creative act. Abastado, who wrote a book about Mallarmé's experiences as poet and about his

aesthetic beliefs, calls his muse *"la Muse moderne de l'Impuissance."*
It is she, in his view, who inspired Mallarmé to some of his finest
poems.[6] Mallarmé himself maintained that the state of inspiration,
of poetic enthusiasm, is not characteristic of the *poet's* state of
mind. It is the *reader*, not the poet, who experiences *"l'état poétique,"* he explains. Later on, we find the same experience and
the same belief in Paul Valéry.

It goes without saying that Paul Valéry's poetic crisis cannot be
explained solely in literary and theoretical terms; we have to suppose an upheaval at a deeper level of his personality. In any event,
what he experienced one stormy summer night in Genoa in 1892,
while rapid flashes of lightning played over the Mediterranean, led
him to abstain from literature, that tissue of lies pertaining to our
emotional life. He published nothing in 1893 and 1894. But he
had not yet entirely severed the connection with the medium of
words, and in August 1894 he wrote *Soirée avec Monsieur Teste*,
and subsequently the odd poem and literary article. But from 1900
on his literary silence was for all intents and purposes total.

He had—to quote his own words—guillotined poetry. Poetry demands of its practitioners a certain sacrifice of the intellect, and
Valéry was no longer prepared to make this sacrifice. Like Monsieur Teste and Leonardo da Vinci, whose pictures he draws; he
wants to devote all his time to becoming an *"ésprit universel."* He
embarked on this enterprise with the aid of two then fashionable
sciences—natural science and mathematics—which he had detested
at school. He had moved to Paris in 1892 and worked at a bourgeois
occupation. He wrote to André Gide: "I beg you not to call me a
poet, big or small, any longer." And on another occasion he wrote
to Valéry Larbaud: "I am no longer in a condition to write poetry.
I have never regarded literature as a potential career." For mental
exercise he kept a diary, which he wrote early in the morning, but
without a reader in view: "The thought of a reader vanishes completely at these times."[7] His *Cahiers* were not printed in their entirety until after his death.

The productive upsurge that took place around 1913 surprised
Valéry himself. The external impulse in this instance is well known.
André Gide had urged him to collect and publish his early poems,
which were scattered in a number of different magazines. In the

end he agreed, and began revising his early poems for the projected collection. He then had the idea of composing a final poem, a sort of farewell to his youthful production as well as a farewell to poetry itself. He planned a short poem of some forty lines. This he worked on with great difficulty for four years, during which period it was reworked over a hundred times and swelled to 412 verses. This became the poem *La Jeune Parque*, published in 1917. But far from becoming his farewell to poetry, it heralded his big new collection *Charmes ou poèmes*, appearing in June 1922. His period of silence was over.

How are we to understand the strange periodicity of Paul Valéry's literary life? Scholars who have sought to trace his inner development from the psychological or psychoanalytical angle—like Aigrisse in his book *Psychanalyse de Paul Valéry*—are sure that Valéry himself in remembering events simplified and intellectualized them. It is unlikely that intellectual considerations and acts of will only can lie behind *so* unusual a creativity curve. Aigrisse hints that behind Valéry's flight into the pure world of the intellect there lay the concealed fear and repression of an emotional nature, which were not harmoniously resolved until later. Valéry's posthumously published *Cahiers* also give us a glimpse of the transformation that was under way from 1913 to 1921 and that led to his new wave of poetic creativity. The poems he wrote at this time have a double aspect: of clear, intellectual control on the one hand and of the creative power of the subconscious on the other. In his poems and discursive pieces Valéry at times personifies this mysterious power in the shape of Pythia. In the metaphoric language of his late poetry Pythia represents the primitive, the untamed, the subconscious; perhaps she even stands for rejected inspiration.[8]

This renewed experience of poetic creativity gave Valéry a new relationship to language. In the essay *Comment je reviens à la Poésie*, Valéry describes how he once more became sensitive to the inherent music of words, syllables came alive once more. "Certain expressions, certain forms of language arose sometimes as though of their own accord in the boundary-land between the soul and the voice, and craved to be given life."[9]

In some ways this second creative period represents a regression, a return to the author's youth. But at the same time it is far removed from the symbolist Narcissus period. The poet who had dwelt so long in the pure air of the intellect did not descend into the same river: both he and his language had changed. In fact Valéry's periods of silence and of lyrical creativity are so intimately connected that they represent acts in a dialectical drama.

3

Rainer Maria Rilke provides us with another extreme example of the periodicity of creative life. A richly productive stage in his life had been brought to an end with the writing of the novel *Malte Laurids Brigge* (1910). Rilke, who was born in 1875, was now thirty-five. Shortly after having completed his novel, he complained in a 1911 letter from Paris of being abandoned by the muses, of living a *"von den Musen gemiedenes Leben."* His mood was depressive. In numerous letters to, among others, Lou Salome, he bewails his productivity crisis and lack of inspiration. His friend with a name reminiscent of an operetta, Countess Marie von Thurn und Taxis Hohenlohe, gives us a detailed description of his life the following year. She writes:

> So then Rilke in December [the year is 1911 and the place Duino] started his long, lonely winter. But he continued to feel disheartened and complained about lack of inspiration. The exquisite little poems which from time to time flowed from his pen gave him no release, he did not take them seriously. Would he ever again be able to write?
> God had abandoned him . . .
> But in the middle of January the first elegy arose.
> On 23 January I received a small parcel, and in front of me lay the turquoise blue ribbon, which we had bought in Weimar *"Dolce color d'oriental saffiro."* A short letter accompanied the first elegy. Who could describe my joy, my jubilation?
> Later on Rilke told me how this elegy had arisen. He had no idea of what was in preparation within him. Admittedly he had hinted something in a letter and wrote that the nightingale was approaching. . . . Did he then feel what was to come? But the nightingale appeared to fall silent again. Deep depression overtook him, he began to believe that this winter, too, would pass without results.

Then early one day he received a troublesome business letter. He wanted to deal rapidly with the answer and had to occupy himself with figures and other dry things. There was a high wind outside, but the sun shone and the sea was bright blue, as though laced with silver. Rilke went down to the bastions which . . . were connected with each other by means of a narrow path at the foot of the castle. At this point the cliffs fall steeply some two hundred feet down to the sea. Rilke paced backward and forward, immersed in his thoughts, the answer to the letter occupying him entirely. Then, all at once, in the middle of his cogitations, he suddenly stopped, for it was as though a voice in the storm had cried out to him: *"Wer, wenn ich schriee, hörte mich denn aus der Engel Ordnungen?"* He stood still listening. "What is it," he whispered. "What is it, what is it that is coming?"

He took out his notebook, which he always carried on him, and wrote down these words, and immediately afterward some verses formed themselves without his help [*ohne sein Dazutun*] . Who was coming? Now he knew: the God.

Very calmly he returned to his room, laid his notebook to one side, and completed his business letter.

In the way he had described to me, all the opening lines of the remaining elegies arose, strangely enough, that winter in Duino. I am thinking particularly of the indescribably beautiful opening line of the last elegy. He told me this in Muzot—also that he had immediately known that among all the other opening lines this particular one would constitute the beginning of the last elegy. Some fragments followed, but after that the God fell silent.[10]

There is no reason to disbelieve this account completely, despite the mythical language employed by Rilke's friend and despite some errors of memory. Other testimony generally corroborates this version of events. After writing the first two elegies, Rilke once more relapsed into a state of unproductiveness. It is true that he was able to publish a new book, *Marienleben*, in 1913 and that he wrote the major part of the sixth elegy the same year and the whole of the fourth elegy during two days in 1915. But after this achievement he fell almost totally silent.

Some scholars have wrongly tried to explain his productivity crisis of the following years as a "crisis of expression." Rilke had in fact already in January 1912, with the first elegy, found the linguistic form of expression that was to become his definitive style.

The crisis was on another level. Rilke lived for a number of years in a permanent state of anxiety and restlessness. Up to the outbreak of World War I he was continually moving around. When the war had broken out, he could—with some justification—blame his *"Erstarrung"* on the new, unfavorable political climate. However, the end of the war and the postwar period brought no upsurge of creativity. He experienced new obstacles, new torments of unproductivity, the inner "icing over" which he complained of in his letters from the period. His poetic silence was not broken until 1922, when a new wave of creativeness began. Now during a stay in Muzot he wrote the twenty-five Orpheus sonnets, dedicated to the memory of the dancer Wera Ouckama Knoop. They were written in three days, between 2 and 5 February. They have rightly been regarded as a sort of prelude to the late elegies. Between 7 and 14 February Rilke wrote the remaining elegies, which were included in the suite. In a letter dated 11 February in the evening, he tells his friend from Duino how he wrote the elegies: "All within the space of a couple of days, it was a nameless storm, a gale in my spirit (like that time in Duino), everything inside me that is fiber and tissue was on the point of breaking."[11] After completing the elegies, he again wrote a number of sonnets, which were included in the collection *Sonette an Orpheus*. Last, on 26 February he reworked the end of the seventh elegy. His two most remarkable collections had a sort of twin birth within the space of three weeks. "I regard it as an inestimable grace that it was vouchsafed me in one and the same breath to fill both these sails, the small rust-colored sail of the sonnets, and the great, white sail of the elegies," he wrote in a letter to his Polish translator in 1925.[12] He realized that his work as a poet was now completed. The following year he died.

The ten intervening years between the stay in Duino and that in Muzot was not a period of total silence, for as we have seen, Rilke experienced short bursts of creativity in 1913 and 1915. But on the whole these middle years were dominated by physical ill-health and mental tensions, anxiety, and guilt feelings. Attempts to explain the extraordinary periodicity of Rilke's work must naturally be hypothetical. Kretschmer, who has not dealt with Rilke's life, would in all probability have indicated an underlying biological curve and would perhaps have included Rilke in the category of manic-depressives with typical fluctuations. Freudian psychologists would in all probability seek to explain productivity inhibitions on the sexual level. In her book *Psychanalyse et critique littéraire* (1973), the psychoanalytical writer Anne Clancier suggested a general connection between anxiety in the face of a blank sheet of paper and a castration complex. Sociological critics—both with and without a Marxist bent—might see Rilke as a typical example of the esoteric poet tragically alienated from his age and society.

Creative moments are as mysterious as unproductive periods. Rilke's moments of lyrical inspiration—the opening lines of the sequence of poems and later the short creative bursts leading to the elegies and sonnets—arose with a suddenness that overwhelmed him and took him by surprise.

The story of how Rilke, occupied by the highly unpoetic task of answering a business letter, was struck by a flash of inspiration, is indeed typical. There are many parallels in the careers of other writers, as well as inventors. A flash of illumination can strike at the very moment when one's mind is occupied with the most trivial matters; Poincaré stepped off a tram at the moment when the theory of the Fuchsian functions occurred to him.[13] A suggested explanation of the phenomenon runs as follows: When one's concentration is strongly engaged at a trivial or unessential level, a blockage is released, thereby enabling thought processes and word-formation processes to rise from a deep level of the subconscious and cross the threshold of consciousness.

Whatever we may think of this explanation, and its psychological imagery, the fact remains that Rilke—like many other poets—typically received *les vers donnés* (to use Valéry's phrase) only in the form of short lines or discontinuous fragments. The ensuing poetic process involves resumed effort, representing an interplay of inspiration and hard work.

It was just as characteristic of Rilke that the first short wave of inspiration, which lifted him out of his depression, soon died away. After he had composed the first two Duino elegies, "the God fell silent" once more. And after he had composed the five last elegies, the God fell silent for good.

Attempts to explain what led to Rilke's late, continuous, and intensive period of creativity in February 1922 have often suggested that his exposure to the works of Paul Valéry was an important stimulus. Rilke wrote enthusiastically, almost ecstatically, about Valéry to his friends, and several times he compared his own silent period with Valéry's years of silence—the years that preceded the Frenchman's second creative period. The similarity seemed to confirm Rilke's poetic situation. It cannot be said, however, although the suggestion has been advanced, that Valéry's poetry provided Rilke with new linguistic or thematic impulses. For as we noted, Rilke established his late style when he wrote the first elegies. In the essay entitled "Creative Subjectivity in Rilke and Valéry" Judith Ryan pointed out an important factor in this connection. Rilke's translations of Valéry's work took place *after* he had completed both his elegies and his sonnets, and these translations appear to offer linguistic proof that Rilke with his new style had influenced Valéry in the German language version rather than vice versa.[14] Insofar as Valéry can be said to have played a part in Rilke's compositions, it must be regarded more as the result of his identifying with Valéry than as the fruit of any verifiable direct influence.

4

In his novel *Doktor Faustus* Thomas Mann described an artistic fate in which the alternations between productivity and apathy were just as striking as in Rilke's career. We know that Mann made use of documentary material pertaining to past writers and artists in his "exemplary" story of the fate of Adrian Leverkühn. The hypothesis has been advanced that he also had Rilke in mind, but this is an uncertain speculation. On the other hand, we know for certain that his montage technique presented pictures and episodes from another interesting life story, that of the composer Hugo Wolff.

Wolff, too, experienced periods of creativity alternating with phases of inaction and powerlessness, which drove him to desperation. He wrote in a letter: "I am almost prepared to believe that I have reached the end of my life. . . . In fact I have reached the end."[15] His despair at a lengthy period of barrenness brought him, as it had Rilke, close to suicide. In a letter, the wording of which was introduced directly into Thomas Mann's account of Leverkühn, he wrote: "Möge sich die Hölle meiner erbarmen. . . . Und ich fühl's, ich bin auch so ein Höllensohn."[16]

Suddenly, after four years of silence and inhibited productivity, inspiration welled up within him once more. "I work," he now wrote, "as one demented, from six in the morning until dark falls."[17] For Wolff too, his productivity curve was linked to physiological factors; he suffered from the same disease that afflicted Thomas Mann's Adrian Leverkühn, and, like him, he died insane. He, too, is a manic-depressive genius. The musicologist Graf, who recounts Wolff's fate in his book *Die innere Werkstatt des Musikers*, asks himself there how we should interpret the silent periods of an artist's life, such as those experienced by Wolff. Are they times of sterility and inhibition or are they periods of inner, creative recuperation and recharging? What is quite clear is that the writers and artists concerned experienced them as profoundly depressing; countless illuminating quotations could illustrate this contention, for instance, those from the diaries of Hebbel and Grillparzer.

5

Extremely long periods of silence preceding new creative phases — a period of ten years for Rilke, twenty years for Valéry — are uncommon. It is far more usual for the unproductive troughs of a poet's creativity to be relatively short. The periodicity of the Swedish poet Gunnar Ekelöf illustrates the latter experience.

A particular period in Ekelöf's work can be said to have been completed with the collection *A Night in Otacac*, published in 1961. His next collection appeared in 1965, under the title *Diwan over the Prince of Emgión*; it was the first part of what he calls the "acrite" cycle. We know how the composition of this work progressed, partly through Ekelöf's documentary testimony, partly through his wife's account. After a two-month spell in the hospital — which appears to have represented a period of drought in more than one sense — the poet traveled to Istanbul with his wife. It was after this change of scene and atmosphere that a fresh wave of inspiration overtook him. As a young man Ekelöf had experimented with poems written in a dream state or at least on the verge of waking and sleeping. As a rule, however, his supposedly "surrealistic" poetry was the fruit of highly conscious labor based on a wealth of drafts. His collections from the 1940s and '50s show him to have been an exponent of the repeatedly reworked and intricately thought-out poem. The upsurge of inspiration that overtook him in the final phase of his creative life appears to have been unique in his experience.

"To the accompaniment of a large alcohol intake," says one of his biographers, "Ekelöf started writing with eruptive force."[18] His wife, Ingrid Ekelöf, reports that "he sat up straight . . . wrote without any hesitation, sheet after sheet, 17 poems *almost without any alterations* [author's italics], most of them during the night of 28 and 29 March."[19] What he had produced was in fact the basis of his *Diwan* cycle; fourteen of the seventeen poems were published in *Diwan over the Prince of Emgión* in October 1965. "I have been so overwhelmed here by poverty and riches that during the space of 2 days I have spouted out poems, 18 small and 1 large," he wrote in a letter some days later. In another letter, dated 31 March, he speaks of "an angel, which tears me out of bed and puts a pen in my hand. Sometimes it gives poor results, sometimes better, but never good. In Norwegian that sort of thing is called *raptus*, in other superior languages a *visitatio*."[20]

When Ekelöf speaks of what Norwegians call a *raptus*, he clearly has Holberg in mind; when he speaks of the angelic visitation, he is using religious terminology. He is creating the kind of myth used by poets down through the ages to present their inspirational experiences, whether they speak of a muse or, like Valéry, of Pythia. In psychological terms this represents an exteriorization of their poetic condition, the origins of which are placed outside the poet's self. At a later date Ekelöf repeated his remarks about an angelic visitation, in all seriousness, it would seem. Ingrid Ekelöf noted down on 29 May that he had said: "I am possessed by an angel, it's quite mad, it can't go on much longer."[21] He confides to his notebook a poem opening with the following lines:

An angel visited me
for the space of a lunar month he (or she)
has commanded me.
To disobey was unthinkable[22]

Ekelöf may have recalled Swedenborg's experience of angelic visitations; already when working on the early parts of *A Mölna Elegy*
he had periodically delved deep into Swedenborg. But he may also,
and this is perhaps more likely, have been thinking of Rilke's
poetic *visitatio*, in connection with the writing of the angel elegy.
It is worth adding that Ekelöf continued to be poetically fertile
after the passing of this abnormally powerful wave of inspiration;
he remained productive to the end of his life, which was marked
by progressive illness but also by renewed creativity.

How the transition from periods of sterility to phases of fruitful
creativity are to be understood and explained constitutes an area
of hypotheses touching various levels of psychological, biological,
and sociological speculation. Poets themselves, even sophisticated
contemporary poets, like to speak of their creative moments in the
language of myth: like Rilke, they still speak of "the muses";
like Valéry, of "Pythia"; or like Ekelöf, of "the angel." Modern
depth psychology—still using metaphoric language—tends to see
the welling up of creative power as a wellspring rising up from a
previously blocked level of the subconscious.

6

Establishing the fact of periodicity in creative life does not in itself,
of course, say anything about the genesis of individual works of
literature or art. Can we get any closer to the *individual* creative
process?

Basing their hypotheses largely on the testimony of writers and
artists, psychologists attempted a long time ago to sketch out a
generally valid theory of the stages of creativity. Edvard von Hartmann, philosopher of the unconscious, proposed one such model
in the middle of the nineteenth century. His schema contains five

stages, which he calls: (1) the productive mood, (2) the conception, (3) the inner execution, (4) the objectivization, and (5) the fixation. It is noteworthy that this early model was advanced by a philosopher who took the unconscious—in modern terminology, the subconscious—as the basis of his philosophical system. It is in the region of the unconscious that Hartmann locates a crucial part of the genesis of the creative process.

Within the field of German aesthetics scholars have simplified Hartmann's model. In Müller Freienfels's *Psychologie der Kunst*[23] and Max Dessoir's *Ästhetik* the vital stages of the process are reduced to three. For the first stage they retain Hartmann's term "produktive Stimmung." They call the second stage "conception," and the third "execution." But both these scholars stress that they have not been concerned with establishing a uniform schema, in accordance with which all creative work is assumed to proceed; rather, they note that one or other of the stages may well be missing and that both a very lengthy and a very swift genesis do not lend themselves to the chronological categories suggested.

A more recent attempt at a theory of stages was presented in Graham Wallas's book *The Art of Thought* (1925). Unlike Edvard von Hartmann and his German successors, Wallas bases his model on the experiences of scientists, discoverers, and inventors rather than on those of artists and writers. Nevertheless, it has subsequently been used by art and literary historians in many countries. That the same model has been found applicable to both inventions and linguistic invention, to scientific as well as to artistic work, is in itself an interesting phenomenon.

Wallas distinguishes four basic stages in the creative process.[24] He calls the first the preparatory stage, which is identical to the stage Müller Freienfels called *Die Vorbereitung des Schaffens*. At this stage experiences and impressions, including, of course, writers' experiences from the world of words and language, are garnered and sifted. The "creative" person receives and stores a greater quantity of material, an abundance of contradictory impressions and possibilities. The uncreative person does the exact opposite: s/he rejects the problematic material or turns it into stereotyped forms and patterns. The creative person—and naturally the creative writer—possesses a degree of mobility that allows him/her to absorb what is new, to reshape and reorganize it. To use the terminology of the creativity psychologist: the creative person is a divergent thinker who perceives divergently. Or to use biblical terminology: with the creative person, the seeds fall on good ground: with the noncreative person, they fall on stony ground.

According to Wallas, the incubation stage comes next. Just as an illness has a certain incubation period, so an idea is not immediately realized—it takes time. In metaphorical terms, the incubation period is the time during which the seed lies in the earth. The artist or poet stores an idea in his/her memory or in a notebook, where it rests awhile. The incubatory stage is the most elastic of the creative phases in terms of time.

Some works never "went under ground" but were executed in practically the same breath as the one in which they arose. These are the improvisations we looked at earlier. Other works led a subterranean life for years or decades before coming up into the light of day. H. C. Andersen had personal experience with both slow and swift literary creation. One morning he received a letter with the now famous drawing by Lundbye of a little girl with a handful of matchsticks. The very same day he wrote his story of *The Little Match Girl* and made his fair copy of it the following day. But months and years could also pass between idea and execution. He comments on a volume of his stories in a letter: "The ideas behind them all arose in Portugal, long concealed, not forgotten, they sprang forth here at home."[25] Concealed, not forgotten this is the formula of the incubation period.

There is practically no limit to the length of time an artistic seed can lie buried. In his account *Die Entstehung des Doktor Faustus*, Thomas Mann quotes an entry in his diary from 1942: "Morning with old notebooks. Looked at the three-line plan for *Dr. Faustus* from 1901. *Kommt alte Lieb' und Freundschaft mit herauf.* Forty-two years had passed since I mentioned an artist's contract with the devil as a possible idea in my notes."[26] This incubation period embraced over four decades, the whole of Thomas Mann's time as a productive writer. The Faust theme had waited for him and he for it—until they caught up with one another one morning during the second world war. He reflects on his return to the theme, with every justification, by quoting a famous line from Goethe's

Zueignung, which also represented a return to an earlier poetic plan.

Naturally, the period of incubation also applies to writers of poetry, and earlier in this chapter we spoke of the genesis of Rilke's *Duino Elegies*. Only the first two elegies were written in Duino in 1911, but the opening lines of each of the following eight elegies presented themselves the same year. Presumably they never entirely vanished from the poet's consciousness or memory. However, not until ten years later did Rilke succeed, using these lines as nuclei, in writing his last elegies. The incubation—or gestation—period coincided with Rilke's lengthy phase of lyrical unproductiveness.

During the third stage of the genesis of the work of art, called "illumination" by Wallas, the work is suddenly, like a flash, grasped or seen as a totality: the poem or play intuitively within the writer, the painting to the inner eye of the painter, the form to the sculptor, the melody to the composer. The term illumination, common in religious psychology, was introduced by Rimbaud in the title of his work *Les Illuminations* (1886). One single moment of this kind can by no means always be found in the development of a work of art. Just as frequently, there is a series of illuminations, interrupted by periods of work or waiting. The psychological differences between individual artists' manner of conceiving and shaping their material vary so greatly that no one theory of stages can embrace the whole of this complex phenomenon.

The best example of a moment of illumination was provided in our case history of Ibsen's *Brand*. During the preliminary stages Ibsen experimented with a narrative exposition of his subject. After a period of discouragement and stagnation—an incubatory stage—came the day when he visited St. Peter's, when "all at once" he became aware of "a powerful and clear form" for what he had to say. It was on this day that *Brand* was conceived as a play. After this sudden revelation the artistic problems of form were solved without further delay, and the play was finished in less than three months, i.e., faster than any other comparable work by Ibsen.

As already noted, scholars have wondered in what way St. Peter's, with its architectural perfection and completeness, can have impressed Ibsen so as to provide in symbolic form a solution to his artistic problems. For it is a fact that the sought-after solution to a problem occasionally manifests itself in the shape of "symbol equivalence," both to scientists and to composers. The image represents an idea, is pregnant with significance.

When Kekulé, the great innovator in the field of organic chemistry, dreamed of a snake biting its own tail, he conceived an idea of the molecular nature of certain organic unions.[27] When Carl Maria von Weber, at a German spa, saw a pile of tables and chairs that had been turned upside down because it was raining, he conceived the idea for the march he later used in the music for the tragedy *Henry IV* and, subsequently, for *Oberon*. The anecdote of the incident is wellknown: Weber, seeing the upturned tables and chairs, turned to his friend and said, "Look at that, Mr. Roth, doesn't it look like a triumphal march. By jove what trumpets. I can use that." Then in the evening he composed his great march of victory.[28] The story must surely be taken to imply that Weber had already, consciously and subconsciously, occupied himself with the march. What he saw, he interpreted symbolically; he absorbed the visual image and transposed it into notes and rhythms. We can guess that Ibsen experienced the architecture of St. Peter's and transposed it into a dramatic structure in a similar way.

After the stage of illumination follows the fourth and last stage of Wallas's schema. For poets, this is the stage of execution and artistic verification. It might seem natural to regard it as a period of conscious, reflective work. But, as Liviu Rusu so strikingly emphasized in his book *La création artistique*: conscious, methodical work by no means excludes continued work on the part of the subconscious. The stage of completing a work is certainly one of disciplined imagination, but ideas can still be abundant. Imagination and the critical faculty also function together in the final stage of a work of art.[29]

It is natural to conceive of the four stages in Wallas's schema as being successive, chronologically separate. I. A. Taylor objects to this view, however, in his essay "The Nature of the Creative Process," and maintains that the stages do not necessarily follow each other in a given order but are often integrated or overlapping. In addition, of course, one or another of the stages can in practice be missing.[30]

Other reservations about Graham Wallas's stage theory can be advanced. We can ask, how shall we define the inception of a literary work? As we know, Paul Valéry maintained that a work of literature or art has no clearly definable chronological beginning. And T. S. Eliot supported this view by including in the preparations for a poem everything the poet has ever read, learned, or experienced. External circumstances play a part in deciding when a writer or artist breaks off or sells his/her work. But a literary work continues to exist and develop for as long as it lives on in its creator. It can be changed long after it has been printed and made public. Valéry is one of the poets—as are W. H. Auden and Ekelöf— who regard every poetic product as mutable, as a work in perpetual progress, and hence linked to the aesthetic of the unfinished.

Traditionally, of course, poets embracing the classicist aesthetic, from Horace to Gautier and beyond, took a different view. They regarded it as the poet's goal to strive for a definitive, rounded form, which could not be improved upon. In this final shape the literary work was to challenge the ravages and changes of time. The difference between the two aesthetic judgments outlined above are probably ultimately dependent on a different basic view of the place of a work of art in time and history. Beethoven formulated the older aesthetic's requirement of definitive form when he wrote, in a letter dated February 1813 (to G. Thomson, Vienna): "It is not my habit to change my compositions, once they are completed. I have never done so, since I am firmly of the opinion that the least alteration would alter the character of the composition."[31]

The same view is often encountered in the audience, be it listener or reader. We are prone to regard the form in which we become acquainted with a work of art as final. It bears for us, to quote Dessoir once more, the *"Gepräge der Unabänderlichkeit."* The finality of the form becomes a criterion of value: the fact that a work cannot be and should not be changed implies that it cannot be improved upon. Out of respect for the inner autonomy and finality of the work, the reader or listener will not tolerate impertinent alterations, the intervention of other people's ideas into the given text. Our modern copyright laws, which protect the autonomy of works of art, have provided a legal basis for this aesthetic doctrine.

An abstract model like Graham Wallas's, and every other schema of the stages of creativity, provoke the following questions: Do they in fact constitute an effective instrument of investigation into the creative process? To what extent are they verifiable by reality, i.e., by the objective testimony of manuscripts and the subjective testimony of authorial pronouncements?

We can perhaps claim that a model of this kind at least helps us to ask the right questions, to use preserved source material in the correct sequence. It is the aim of all genetic research to reach as far back as possible toward the origins of an individual work, to follow its roots as far as possible. The notebooks and sketchbooks of writers, artists, and musicians are the ground to be explored for this purpose, since they represent the source material in which we hope to find the earliest ideas, whether noted down in words, lines, or musical annotation. As we have already seen, the notebooks of Shelley, Stephen Spender, or Beethoven show the preliminary stages of many works that were subsequently completed. But fragments of early ideas can also be discovered elsewhere—for instance, in a metaphor or a striking phrase in a poet's letter. The earliest seeds of a poem or painting can occasionally be found in the works of previous writers or artists, a phenomenon examined by art historian Ragnar Josephson in *The Birth of the Work of Art*, under the title "The Transformed Model." Many comparative literature studies illustrate the same process. The preparatory stage is, in other words, often imitative. One need only have studied the manuscripts of one or two poets from the period *before* they published their first work to know that.

The stage Graham Wallas calls that of incubation is also one of silence. The manuscripts themselves are silent. So one must find out what has been happening within the poet up to the time when the work appears again in visible or audible form.

Nor can the stage of illumination be directly perceived in a manuscript—other than in exceptional circumstances. For information about this, we normally have to rely on the testimony of the writers themselves, like that of Rousseau, Ibsen, and Lagerlöf. Yet in a way, this moment or stage is the most important in the whole process, for it is in a real sense *the* creative element. It often involves the liberation of the work from a tradition, or from its own past. It represents a breakthrough in the work's developmental course. But by no means all works have so discontinuous and uneven a genesis that this phase can be discerned.

Many scholarly manuscript studies focus on the final phase of the work, its elaboration, artistic verification, and testing. It is normally in the late stages of development that alterations, interpolations, and crossings out allow us to perceive or assume the poet's successive—or successively altered—verbal intentions.

There are, of course, as already indicated, works of art that cut across the boundaries of the phase or stage model. These are improvisations in various mediums. With these works, all the stages—preparation, incubation, illumination, and elaboration—have been telescoped into one. Such works appear to have arisen in a sequence other than that of temporal succession. This could be paradoxically expressed by saying that with improvisational poems or music, the labor of elaboration belongs to a stage that *precedes* conception and execution. For no improvisation of artistic magnitude can exist without previous technical training. The improviser's consciousness must have passed into a "structured unconscious"[32] in order to produce this artistic automatism. Manuscripts of spontanist poetry are uninteresting, or so they would seem, because they resemble corrected fair copies. But in fact it could be claimed that the moment of illumination is codified in these very manuscripts.

Inspiration Disputed

And it shall come to pass afterward,
that I will pour out my spirit upon all
flesh, and your sons and your daughters
shall prophesy, your old men shall dream
dreams, your young men shall see visions.

Joel 2:28

There is undoubtedly an element of inspiration in
all real literary creation. This in itself need
imply neither mysticism nor mystification, simply
something partially unknown, a function which cannot
be rationally surveyed and controlled.

Artur Lundkvist
The Author and His Method of Work

1

A theory of creative stages, like the one advanced by Graham Wallas, systematizes a complicated process and thus helps demystify it. But it still leaves us with an irrational factor in the creative process, namely the decisive stage, which Wallas terms illumination. We already noted that the word belongs to the vocabulary of the psychology of religion. *Illuminatio interna*, the inner light, expresses the sudden experience of inner enlightenment that mystics so often speak of. Graham Wallas's systematization is based not on the experiences of religious mystics but rather on those of discoverers and inventors, in whose lives he often finds a precisely definable moment of illumination.

The word "illumination" itself, however, has no real standing in the history of aesthetics, even though it occasionally occurs there. Paul Valéry uses the word, speaking of verbal illuminations of commanding power: *"ces illuminations impérieuses qui imposent tout à coup une certaine combinaison des mots."* The word that partly— but only partly—covers the same psychological phenomenon and that is better known in the aesthetic context is "inspiration." The terms are related insofar as "inspiration" is a word that also originally belonged to the religious sphere. The word contains a faint

159

image. The Latin word *"spiritus"* means breath, and in primitive religious beliefs the breath was believed to be the spirit in visible guise. When a foreign, divine power blew its breath or spirit into a human being, she/he became a partaker of the divine, became inspired. Now that metaphysical explanations of the phenomenon of inspiration have been abandoned, the state of being inspired is normally interpreted as emanating not from above but from below, from the subconscious.

In the Vulgate version of the New Testament (*Peter* II, 1:21), the prophets are referred to as *Sancto Spiritu inspirati*, "moved by the Holy Ghost" in the Authorized version. In *St. Paul's epistle to Timothy* (II, 3:16) we read that "all scripture is given by inspiration of God," *theopneustos* or *divinitus inspirata*. This gave rise in the Middle Ages to the dogma of the Bible's verbal inspiration. If its inspiration was wholly or partly divine, it must also be infallible. So here, too, inspiration became a criterion of value.

The word "inspiration" appears to have come into general use rather late in secular contexts, i.e., in connection with art, poetry, and poets. There are solitary examples of French usage from the seventeenth century. But according to Heidsieck, who wrote a book about the word and the phenomenon, entitled *L'Inspiration*,[1] it did not come into general use until the following century, when it became part of the apotheosizing myth of the poet, a myth being built up then, as it had been during the renaissance. The word has survived the romantic era, signifying a phenomenon that has never been wholly demystified.

The ideas about the nature and manifestations of inspiration, which over the centuries have become common in Western aesthetic philosophy, rest on a double tradition, Platonic and biblical. In a series of dialogues—*Ion, Meno,* and *Phaedrus*—Plato refers to poets as being divinely inspired, possessed by the deity—*entheoi*—and he says, as in *Meno*, that they are "inspired by the breath of the God, by whom they are possessed." In *Phaedrus* he dissociates himself from writers who put their trust solely in artistic skill and technique. They become bad poets. So already in Plato we find the origin of the conflict between the aesthetic of work and that of inspiration which we rediscover in Young and the early romantics.

Writers of varying temperaments and ages have expressed the most contradictory views on the phenomenon of inspiration, its existence and possible significance. Some of them deny absolutely the existence of anything that might be covered by this word, Edgar Allen Poe, for instance, in his account of how he wrote *The Raven*, resolutely excludes all foreign influences and declares the poem to be the fruit of rational deliberation, and we have seen many writers follow his example. As opposed to this, there are others who see the whole of their work as being dependent on inspiration.

William Morris's words on the subject are well known: "The talk of inspiration is sheer nonsense; there is no such thing. It is a mere matter of craftmanship."[2] The opposite extreme is represented by Herbert Read, who was close to the surrealist painters of his day: "I can aver that all the poetry I have written which I continue to regard as authentic poetry was written immediately, instantaneously, in a condition of trance."[3] For Read, not only was inspiration synonymous with the creative, poetically productive state, but it also determined the value of poetry produced in this state.

It would be possible to regard these two contradictory points of view as proof of the existence of a psychological difference between two types of poet and artist. And there may be some truth in this. But as we have already seen, the extreme cases are rare, or only momentary, in the aesthetic universe. Coleridge was not always the poet who composed *Kubla Khan* in a dream or trance; Poe was not always the Poe who followed the engineering recipe he had propounded in *The Philosophy of Composition*. The activity of poetic creation is carried out within a wide range of possibilities found between the two extremes.

Another way of explaining the disagreement between the views of William Morris and Herbert Read would be to claim that it is based on a semantic misunderstanding. Maybe they do not mean the same thing by the word "inspiration"?

The word is undoubtedly ambiguous. If we look at its use during the nineteenth century as well as during our own time, we can establish several different meanings. Stephen Spender writes in his well-known essay *The Making of a Poem* that the word can be understood to mean two quite different things. On the one hand, it

can denote that something occurs to one, that a thought or a line
"is given to one." On the other hand, it can be used about the
state of mind in which a poet writes his/her best poems.[4]

Julius Bahle illustrates varied uses of the word, in his study of the
creative psychology of modern musicians. For the composers interviewed, the word was evidently sometimes equivalent to the emotional experiences that *precede* fortunate musical ideas and represent a precondition for them. At other times, the composers used
the word as *synonymous with a fortunate idea* or a whole series of
fortunate ideas. Finally it was also used to indicate the emotionally
heightened state in which a composer works at and executes his/her
musical ideas; i.e., it covered the working frame of mind that is also known as creative intoxication, or *Schaffensrausch*.[5]

2

The fact of inspiration has been examined by psychologists from
what might be called the phenomenological angle, as opposed to
the semantic and the linguistic. They have asked what discernible,
recurrent elements are included in the accounts given by poets,
musicians, and visual artists of their experiences of inspiration. In
his *Psychologie der Kunst,* Müller Freienfels has noted, in the chapter on inspiration, three recurring phenomena in the work reports
of artistically creative individuals: first, the *suddenness* of the occurrence; second, *the particular, unusual state of mind (Gemüths-
verfassung)* of the inspired poet; third, that inspiration involves
what he calls an *impersonal consciousness (Unpersönlichkeitsbe-
wusstsein)*, that is, the poet feels as though she/he were speaking
on behalf of someone else.[6]

A similar but rather more detailed model is presented by Abrams
in his book on eighteenth-century aesthetics, *The Mirror and the
Lamp*. Based largely on ideas he found in the theories and poetic
reality of the romantics, the book attempts to isolate the elements
that—singly or collectively—constitute part of the experience of inspiration. He notes, in addition to the suddenness of the state, that
creative activity takes place without effort. He describes the inspired
act as spontaneous and automatic. Like Freienfels, he says that the

poet-artist feels enthusiastic during his/her creative act; the word "enthusiasm" has its counterpart in descriptions of the inspired artist in Plato's dialogues. But, adds Abrams, this exceptional state, which has so often been described as one of delight, can also be experienced as unbearable and painful, or as both delightful and unbearable at one and the same time. When the work—or the day's work—is done, it is followed by a feeling of relaxation and liberation. As a final element Abrams, too, notes the impersonal consciousness that the poet-artist often experiences in creative moments, a phenomenon which can later have the effect of making him/her feel a stranger to (and not responsible for) what she/he has produced in an inspired state.[7]

The prototype of accounts of the startling suddenness of literary inspiration are Rousseau's descriptions, scattered in his works, of what happened to him the day he was on the road to Dijon with a copy of *Mercure de France* in his pocket. When he glanced through it, he discovered the Dijon Academy's famous question. In his second letter to Malesherbes, he describes the experience in the following words:

> If anything ever resembled a sudden inspiration, it was the inner emotion that took place within me on reading this. I suddenly felt my soul blinded by a thousand lights. Myriads of living ideas presented themselves to me at the same time, with a power and in a chaos that threw me into unspeakable confusion; I felt my head seized by a dizziness that resembled intoxication.[8]

Rousseau enlarges on the physiological symptoms that accompanied his state. In a later work—*Rousseau juge de Jean Jacque*—in which he reverts to the incident, he continues: "From the living flame that was lit in his soul on that occasion, came all the sparks of genius that have been seen to flash from his writings during the course of ten years of delirium and fever."[9]

Rousseau's experience of this literary vocation has a great deal in common with stories of religious conversion, as scholars have not been slow to point out. Its suddenness and violence, as well as the phenomena of light, are ingredients in many religious documents. It is well known that pietist mysticism influenced the romantic movement in many ways, and equally, that Rousseau himself had close links with mysticism and pietist religiosity. The inspiration—or illumination—experienced by Rousseau leads us once more back to the religious origin of the phenomenon and the word.

Many of Rousseau's contemporaries doubted that Rousseau actually had experienced his call to literary activity in this way. Marmontel had heard another story of how Rousseau wrote the answer to the Dijon Academy's question, his famous first-prize essay. In his memoirs Marmontel ironically commented on Rousseau's own description: "Behold, that's what you can call an ecstacy, eloquently described. But listen now to how it all actually happened in reality";[10] and he proceeds to explain that it was Diderot who gave Rousseau the idea for the paradoxical answer to the question posed by the Academy, which overwhelmed both Rousseau and the judges.

Recent scholarship has tended to side with Rousseau in this disagreement. *"L'illumination de Vincennes n'est pas une légende,"*[11] Pierre Trahard assures us in his book on French eighteenth-century sensibility, and he points to Rousseau's repeated assurances that he, on the road to his Damascus, "saw another universe and became another person."[12]

Now whether Rousseau described with psychological realism an actual experience, or whether he created a myth about his literary calling, based on stories of religious conversions, the fact remains that his account was so effective that it became a typical—or archetypical—model for many descriptions of the inspirational state. The suddenness of the experience is almost always stressed in such descriptions. In answer to an interviewer's question about how the creative impulse first arises, the modern German writer Hans Erich Nossak answered: "It comes from nowhere, suddenly, *like lightning*" [author's italics].[13] The composer Gustav Mahler seizes upon the same image or topos when he describes the inception of the last movement of his second symphony in a letter. He heard the Klopstock choral *Auferstehen* in a church and explains what happened next: "It struck me like lightning, and everything appeared clearly and distinctly to my soul. The creative person waits for this flash of lightning; this is 'holy inspiration' [—*heilige Empfängnis*]."[14]

The first flash of inspiration, the sudden initial impulse, can appear as an intuitive conception of the whole or as a shorter sequence of images, words, or notes, i.e., as a continuum or as a fragment. Mozart's experience of creative work is well known: he saw the totality in a synoptic moment. He describes this in a letter: "I do not hear the various parts [of the work] successively, one after the other, but, if one can say so, all at once."[15] Many modern composers have similarly stressed that the first stage of the creative act embraces an anticipation of the whole, of the work's future shape. F. v. Weingartner says of the moment when a musical work first makes itself known to the composer's consciousness, a moment he calls that of conception: "Suddenly, apparently for no reason [*ohne Veranlassung*], the picture of the coming work appears before me. Without at all demonstrating any individual traits, it already possesses distinguishing characteristics, the type of the whole [*—den Typus des Ganzen*]. This picture, once seen, can no longer be erased from the mind."[16] Honegger expresses himself in similar terms: "First I always have to see the total construction [*—die Gesamtkonstruktion—*] even if only schematically."[17]

Many similar experiences of authors could be quoted, instances when the whole—to speak in the language of Gestalt psychologists—appears to have come before the parts. These famous words of Racine's can probably be interpreted in that light: "*Ma pièce est terminée, je n'ai plus à l'écrire.*" (My play is ready, all that remains is to write it down.)[18] Gottfried Benn uses an equally paradoxical formulation of a similar experience when he writes in an essay quoted in this book: "The poem is completed even before it has been started on."[19] The Swedish writer Hjalmar Bergman (1883-1931) refers to this type of total view in a letter to his philosophy teacher Hans Larsson, in which he has just discussed the term intuition. He writes: "If one at this moment of intuition could ask the dramatist for the tenth line in the seventeenth scene of the second act of the unwritten play, he would answer with somnambulist certainty."[20] If we subtract from this remark its jocular exaggeration, it still retains a belief in an intuitive conception of the whole as the first phase of the creative process. The same Hjalmar Bergman wrote in another letter: "The disadvantage of my inspiration is actually that I can never alter anything. I am quite prepared to admit that I sometimes almost feel that I am taking down a dictation when I write my things, but at the same time I am convinced that neither am I a prophet nor is there a demon standing over me whispering in my ear."[21]

The sudden first moment of inspiration by no means always, however, appears as a vision of the total work. Just as often, it consists of a limited sequence of words or notes. In his investigations, particularly the essay "Zur Psycholgie des Einfalls und der Inspiration im musikalischen Schaffen," Julius Bahle deals with the interesting question of the scope of the first concrete ideas. He asked a number of contemporary composers to what extent concrete musical ideas were represented in their compositional work. Richard Strauss affirmed that "the melodic idea as a rule extends to only two or three bars. The following bars are the result of very deliberate work."[22] This answer was confirmed by a number of other composers including Vittorio Gnecchi, Ernst Krenek, and H. Neal. Bahle consigns to the realm of the fairy tale traditional beliefs that the musician receives whole, complete melodies—*ganze Tonstücke*— in a moment of inspiration. He maintains that the study of composers' notebooks, including Beethoven's, confirms that concrete musical ideas (*Einfälle*) are initially very limited in extent.

These musicological results provide useful background and comparative material for the study of the same question in literature. A good deal of evidence points to the fact that the first concrete ideas of poets also are limited in scope. If Poe is to be believed, the first *word* that occurred to him when he prepared to write *The Raven* was "Nevermore"—other considerations about the overall character of the poem having preceded it. When Marianne Moore was asked how she composed poetry, she replied "that a well turned phrase suddenly sprang to mind—just a word or two," and she provided examples of phrases of this kind, "*objets trouvés*," including a rhythmic and rhyming word sequence: "Its leaps should be set/to the flageolet."[23] Marianne Moore's experience has been confirmed by many writers, among them the contemporary Swedish poet Johannes Edfelt, who answered a query about *his* experiences of writing poetry in the following way: "A phrase, a few words, *in my case generally rhythmically ordered* [author's italics], provide the cell out of which the tissue of the whole poem is then developed. Sometimes a phrase like this proves to be illusory or trivial and leads to nothing. But sometimes it refuses to be dismissed, returns and grows. A 'lyrical idea' of this kind consists of one line generally speaking, perhaps occasionally a couple of lines. In exceptional cases the poem grows quite swiftly out of these original lines."[24]

The type of impulse or idea that Marianne Moore and Johannes Edfelt described would have been called "*vers donné*" by Paul Valéry. We can often guess or establish such "given" lines when studying the notebooks and drafts of poets. We already noted that Stallworthy in his careful study of Yeats's manuscripts found that a phrase, two acoustically linked words, or a whole verse line often constitutes a sort of nucleus, out of which the poem develops.

The line that represents the inception of a poem sometimes also becomes its first line. When Rainer Maria Rilke heard a voice speaking in the storm, it was the first line of the *Duinoelegien: Wer wenn ich schriee* etc., which reached him through this verbal inspiration. Sometimes the first verbal idea of a poem is the closing line, and often the original line only gradually finds its "rightful" place in the growing poem.

3

The aesthetic worth of spontaneously given ideas is a point of some interest. Is their suddenness in itself a guarantee of value? Hardly. If we try to examine how contemporary writers and musicians regard spontaneous ideas or inspired flashes, we find a divided front. Writers who subscribe to a surrealistic aesthetic work very largely— as do psychoanalysts—by the method of free association. But outside the surrealist circle writers are ambivalent toward or downright suspicious of suddenly arising word or note sequences. The same Valéry who coined the expression "*les vers donnés*" frequently expressed doubts about the fruits of spontaneity, and in the preface to *Le Cimetière marin* he says he suspects that all sudden ideas can be improved upon. Poets like Ezra Pound, T. S. Eliot, and Robert Lowell share this opinion and are united in the view, expressed by Pound, that technique and not spontaneity is the "test of sincerity."[25]

The same ambivalent attitude toward sudden ideas is seen in

many of the modern composers interviewed by Julius Bahle, whereas the opposite view is propounded by the musicologist and composer Pfitzner. Bahle summarizes the attitude of the interviewed composers in the following words: "The . . . fact that the ideas arise suddenly does *not* tell us anything about their value, for the most valuable and the most worthless—and the latter are by no means rare in the creative process and most often appear as *musical reminiscences*—arise in the artist's mind in exactly the same way, phenomenologically speaking."[26] As a parallel to this we can remind ourselves that the poems composed by professional improvisers—who were dependent on momentary inspiration alone—to some extent consisted of ready-made formulas with frequent reminiscences from earlier poetry. The creative artist—i.e., the original and innovative creator—as a rule needs something the improviser lacks: time to choose and reject, to cross out and reformulate.

Among the answers received by Julius Bahle on the value of spontaneous flashes, the Italian Gnecchi's contained the following observation: "When I feel musical ideas fermenting inside me, the only difficulty lies in choosing the best among the ones that arise and thereby sacrificing the mistaken ones or those that do not adequately express the intended feelings [—*Empfindungen*]. I often write down four or five ideas before I decide on one of them. I never use the rejected ones again."[27] We can compare this with the method described by Stephen Spender in *The Making of a Poem.* Spender explains that his method was to write down as many ideas as possible in his notebooks, irrespective of whether they were unfinished or not. After this he started his critical appraisal of them. A notebook of a hundred closely written pages might result in six completed poems.[28] There is an undeniable similarity in the methods of the composer Gnecchi and the poet Spender.

Gnecchi pointed out—after he had spoken of the necessity of *choosing* between the mass of ideas—that it sometimes seems impossible to distinguish between the original "inspiration" and artistic self-criticism. A spontaneous idea can be modified by critical considerations—or by a new improvisation that adds something to the first. Richard Strauss testified that it is very exceptional for an absolute melody to arise spontaneously: in the vast majority of instances it is altered during the course of being written out, as a result of reflection. *"Ich feile an ihnen"* (I file away at them), said Strauss about his musical ideas,[29] providing an image used ever since Horace, the father of the aesthetics of work, employed it to illustrate the laborious creative process.

Several composers interviewed by Bahle explained that ideas and work go hand in hand during the creative process, and the same experience appears to underlie Stephen Spender's essay, referred to above. Many poetic manuscripts lead scholars intuitively to interpret them in this light. A reservation should also be voiced about the frequent claim that musical—or poetic—ideas arise spontaneously without any act of will. "The best ideas arise out of previous deliberations," says one of Bahle's interviewees,[30] and another spoke of "disciplined ideas." These are ideas that Edgar Allen Poe could have confirmed. The idea of the poet as a *passive* medium, as a receiver of spontaneous impulses from the subconscious, is in some measure a relic of romantic mythology, with few counterparts in reality outside the field of surrealistically influenced writers.

The relative consensus of opinion on artistic inspiration and ideas which we noted between a group of composers and poets should not be exaggerated or converted into some sort of aesthetic law with general relevance in creative life. The consensus undoubtedly derives from the fact that the answers were given in a particular historical context, an "age of criticism" which regards artistic self-consciousness and artistic criticism as a precondition of art and which sees positive value in work—including artistic work. Writers and musicians can no more free themselves from the self-evident aesthetic assumptions prevalent in a particular period in a particular part of the world than they can free themselves from their own shadow.

It is unlikely that the value of spontaneous flashes would have been assessed in the same way in twentieth-century Latin America, where Huidobro named a literary school *il creaconismo* and where Neruda with his volcanic imagination wrote visionary poems on a grand scale. We can also ask ourselves if the answers would have been the same if an interview of Bahle's type had been conducted a century or a century and a half earlier. There is reason to believe that the then dominant aesthetic belief in inspiration would have colored both attitudes and wording.

"Genie blitzt, Genie schafft, veranstaltet nicht," wrote Lavater, one of the precursors of German romanticism, and he also maintained that all creativity wells up from within and is given from above—*"quillt von innen heraus, und wird von oben her gegeben."*[31] Let us once more, to round this off, quote from Shelley's *A Defence of Poetry*: "Poetry is not like reasoning, a power to be exerted according to the determination of the will. A man cannot say: 'I will compose poetry.' . . . I appeal to the greatest poets of the present day whether it is not an error to assert that the finest passages of poetry are produced by labour and study."[32]

4

It is natural that the artists of the romantic era, in view of the aesthetic beliefs prevalent in their day, were particularly interested in products of "spontaneous birth." It is likewise a fact that both the musical and literary histories of the age contain a great many accounts of musical compositions and poems that arose with astonishing speed in a definitive shape needing no subsequent alteration. This is not a question of a mere musical phrase presenting itself in a flash, not a question of a *vers donné* but of a *poème donné*. The suddenness governs the *whole* creative process, the speed of which overwhelms and astonishes poets as well as musicians.

Striking examples of improvisational conceptions and of speedy musical "deliveries" are found in Schubert's experiences as a composer. As he sat in the garden of the inn *"Zum Biersack"* in Pötzleinsdorf reading a drinking song in Shakespeare's *Anthony and Cleopatra*, he exclaimed: *"Mir fällt eine schöne Melodie ein, hätte ich nur Notenpapier bei mir!"* And he scribbled down his music for the song on the back of a menu card. A similar anecdote is told of how he set the music to Goethe's *Erlkönig*. Some of his friends found him reading the poem for the first time with great enthusiasm. He paced backward and forward a few times, sat down suddenly, and—says our spokesman—"in the shortest space of time, as quickly as it at all is possible to write, the lovely ballad was set on paper."[33]

There is no reason to doubt the veracity of these and similar stories of Schubert's creative powers. But historians of music seem agreed that "inspiration" of this kind occurs only in natures organized in a special way and then only on exceptional occasions. We may also note in our two examples above that the actual creative impulse arose out of a poetic text, i.e., from an already completed work of art. The composer is already "magnetized," to use Plato's image in *Ion*, by the power emanating from the poem. The anecdotes are no less instructive for that: in these instances the inspiration did not consist solely of two or three bars; it was not fragmentary but flowed as a continuous stream.

Many parallel examples are provided by the literary history of romanticism in practically all European countries. Goethe, who on many occasions referred to the conditions of his literary creativity, describes in his conversations with Eckermann the suddenness with which—particularly during his youth—poems occurred to him. "They suddenly came over me and demanded to be made instantly, so that I felt compelled to write them down on the spot."[34]

From the English romantic era we have similar but more detailed testimony of an inspired stream of words immediately being turned into a poem. Coleridge was already referred to at length. William Blake presents himself, in a famous letter to Thomas Butts,[5] as a passive medium: "I have in these years composed an immense number of verses on One Grand Theme. . . . I have written this poem from immediate Dictation, twelve or sometimes thirty lines at a time, without Premeditation and even against my Will." Like Shelley, he discounts the value of "labor and study," adding: "An immense Poem Exists, which seems to be the Labour of a long Life, all produc'd without Labour or Study.[35] Blake's remarks are of particular interest since his experiences—and the way in which he interprets them—sum up many of the elements that appear to be typical of inspired creativity: in addition to the swift stream of words, unintentional and unpremeditated, there is the impersonal consciousness, the feeling of being a channel for an outside power.

From the French romantic era we have the well-known story of how Musset wrote *La nuit de mai*: how the poet after a whole month of unproductiveness was suddenly overwhelmed by inspiration and completed the poem about the muse of the May night with astonishing speed. The source of this account is Alfred de

Musset's brother Paul, who is also the authority for the information that the poet—once the poem was written down—found nothing in it to alter. The actual manuscript, the objective documentary proof, appears to have been lost; not even the organizers of the exhibition arranged by Bibliothèque nationale for their centenary exhibition on Musset were able to trace a manuscript. But a manuscript fragment for one of the other *Nuits* was found—ironically enough in a version that differed substantially from the one finally printed.[36]

From Scandinavia we have Oehlenschläger's account of how he wrote his poem *The Golden Horns,* both the first and the central work of Danish romanticism. The composition took place during the space of one night, after a day-long conversation with the philosopher Henrik Steffens. For this particular poem we are well served by source material, for in addition to Oehlenschläger's *Memoirs* we have Henrik Steffens's *Recollections.*

All these examples are from the same period—the romantic era—and skeptics might for this reason feel that they rightly belong to the category of romantic myths. So let us augment our examples by similar reports from times subject to other aesthetic conventions and conditions. Samuel Johnson, who certainly cannot be regarded as a romantic mystifier, is reported in Hawkins's *Apothegms* to have said of his poem *The Vanity of Human Wishes*: "I wrote . . . the first seventy lines in The Vanity of Human Wishes in the course of one morning in that small house beyond the church in Hampstead." This is confirmed by Boswell, who adds: "The fervid rapidity with which it was produced is scarcely credible. I have heard him say that he composed seventy lines of it in one day, without putting down one of them upon paper till they were finished."[37] The wording of the poem suggests that Dr. Johnson's method may have been a perfected mnemonic technique rather than a form of direct improvisation. It is nevertheless noteworthy that a poet of the classicist Augustan era was capable of producing poetry with such extraordinary speed.

From later periods this side of romanticism, we can also find a good many examples of improvisationally swift composition. Fontane says that one of his poems arose "Literally *stante pede*. As I was getting dressed it suddenly came over me and with one shoe on and one in my left hand I leaped up and wrote down the poem in one swoop."[38]

Long before the age of structuralism, the American psychologist June Downey introduced the concept "structured unconscious" in her book *Creative Imagination*. She drew attention to the fact that all so-called inspiration functions strictly within the bounds of the particular individual's capabilities, training, and previous intellectual performance.[39] No poems arose from Schubert's subconscious, no music from that of Coleridge; it was Poincaré, not Rilke, who hit upon the Fuchsian functions in a moment of distraction. In other words: the precondition for such phenomena of inspiration as we have been discussing is the training, practice, and preparation the artist has acquired through years of contact with his/her medium—be it language, music, or color. To quote Tchaikovsky: "Inspiration is a guest that does not willingly visit the lazy."[40]

Studying the lives of creative geniuses, we are constantly reminded of the dichotomy idea/technical skill, inspiration/work. Not until after a year of hard, to outward appearances fruitless, work could Ibsen say of his project, after that day in St. Peter's: "[it] went ahead at a pace, which nothing else hitherto has ever done for me."[41] Many years of effort and experiment passed before Selma Lagerlöf discovered her own style and could say: "See, this was really writing! . . . The pages were filled with a speed she had never dreamed of."[42]

Poets like to use the word "inspiration" to cover occurrences of this kind, i.e., experiencing a continuous stream of words in a prestructured form.

5

In addition to the suddenness of the ideas and the speed of the creative process, the inspired state includes, according to psychologists researching this question, the "peculiar state of mind" that writers experience during their creative act.

Ever since Plato and Plotinus, the idea of the poet seized by divine enthusiasm has been a standing element, a topos, in descriptions of inspiration. It is a state that also has physiological manifestations, such as a heightened pulse rate and increased tension in the whole organism. On his way to his desk to write down *La nuit de mai*, Alfred de Musset was described by his brother as though he were set for a lover's meeting. Schubert struck his friends as being *"ganz glühend"* at the moment when the melody for Goethe's *Erlkönig* suddenly took shape in his mind. It is not always a tolerable state. "It's quite mad, it can't go on much longer," said Ekelöf of the angelic visitations to which he was subjected.[43]

Many writers have compared the extreme state of inspiration to having a fever. Grillparzer does this when he describes the composition of "Die Ahnfrau"; he lay one night tossing from side to side, and felt as though he had a sudden temperature—*"Fieberhetzen überfielen mich."* When he got up the next morning he had a feeling of "an approaching, severe illness." in this tense and feverish state he wrote the first act of the play with exceptional speed.[44]

In an author interview Strindberg related that his first work had been written in "an extraordinary fever." The image of a fever is one of Strindberg's favorites when speaking of creative moments. In a letter from the 1880s he writes: "And I believe that the writer in his fever is led in the right direction, even if he in a sober state afterward feels that one or two things might have been different. That is why I hardly ever dare alter anything, and when I do alter, then I ruin everything. The long and the short of it: 'What I have written I have written.' "[45]

Strindberg was one of those authors who produce work with surprising ease and speed. An eyewitness from an admittedly late stage in his life—the spring of 1907 when Strindberg was occupied with his *Chamber plays*—wrote: "He wrote at top speed, pulled aside the completed sheets and threw them onto the floor, where I picked them up and then sat down to read them."[46] On the whole, Strindberg's manuscripts confirm these and similar accounts of his working methods: once he had left his youthful efforts behind him, he was not a man for many versions, deletions, and emendations.

On the other hand, it would be incorrect to present him as a carefree improviser. Before writing his works, at the planning and organizing stage, he worked carefully and methodically, almost like a civil servant. Notices about real events, rough outlines of situations and verbal exchanges, a division of the material into chapters or acts—all this preceded the writing of the work. His working papers tell us this, but he himself seldom refers to it. It has rightly been pointed out that being still somewhat enthralled by the romantic world picture, he overemphasizes inspiration, at the expense of craftsmanship and technical work, when speaking of his own authorship. He also has the predilection, so typical of the romantics, for using images from organic or biological life when discussing creative work. "His poems grew freely in his head like grapes or mold," he wrote about himself in a letter.[47]

In addition to the link with the romantic-organic view of authorship—the poems growing in his head—he has a need to demystify and reduce, hence the grapes or *mold*. Strindberg often reverts to a view of the creative process colored by scientific determinism or medical science, as in a remark from 1909, in which he again speaks of a fever: "It starts with a ferment or a sort of pleasant fever, which passes into ecstacy or intoxication."[48]

Both ecstacy and intoxication are standing images employed by poets when faced with the necessity of describing the state of mind linked to inspiration. Already the Platonic aesthetic spoke of the ecstatic state as being a precondition for composing poetry. The best-known and fullest statement on the subject is found in the dialogue *Ion*: "So is it also with the good lyric poets; as the worshiping Corybantes are not in their senses when they dance, so the lyric poets are not in their senses when they make these lovely lyric poems. No, when once they launch into harmony and rhythm, they are seized with the Bacchic transport, and are possessed—as the bacchants, when possessed, draw milk and honey from the rivers, but not when they are in their senses. So the spirit of all lyric poets works, according to their own report." Very soon the notion of ecstacy was linked to that of dionysian fervor.[49]

If the inspired state is experienced as a form of intoxication, the logical question arises whether other states of intoxication produced by alcohol or drugs can be conducive to creativity. Since the French renaissance, the idea has been current that intoxication really can produce an inspiring contact with the divine, and Scaliger cites two types of poets in his *Poetics*: those who receive their powers directly from above and those who are inspired by the vapor of strong wine. The question has been discussed down through the centuries by doctors, psychologists, and, of course, writers themselves.

These three categories are all represented in the book *On Intoxication and Inspiration*, published by the Swedish Authors' Association as its yearbook for 1948. Per Henrik Törngren, psychologist and psychoanalyst, notes in one of the essays that the affinity between creation and intoxication is as old as poetry itself and that alcohol, the most universal of poisons, transforms the mind and emotions so swiftly that it has come to be regarded "as a shortcut to the creative state."[50] He quotes the piece from *Ion* given above, in which poets are compared to those followers of Dionysus, the Corybants and Bacchantes, and he writes: "With all due respect to Corybants and Bacchantes, artists are also professionals; and art faces not only onto inspiration and chaos, but also onto science and cosmos. And since the majority of higher or acquired skills enter a danger-zone in the alcoholic state, the question of alcoholic debit and credit cannot be answered unless the premises have first been established."[51] On the credit side, Törngren notes the livelier associative reactions and playfulness with phonetic-acoustic effects that are a product of alcohol. But his closing observation is that most artists and writers are themselves skeptical of the so-called inspiration induced by alcohol: *"During actual work* it must be said that alcohol takes with one hand what it gives with the other."[52]

Törngren is no preacher of teetotalism; note the qualification *"during actual* work." For the problem concerns the creative moments themselves—not the experiences contributing to them. The majority of the book's contributors point out that the changed outlook that results from an increase of alcohol in the bloodstream has at times involved an extension of their experiental resources and field of consciousness. The Swedish twentieth-century poet Bertil Malmberg, no stranger to Dionysian inspiration and its problems, represents an extreme yet interesting point of view. He dismisses the belief in incidental intoxication as a stimulant. But on the basis of his own and other people's experiences, he believes that addiction can play the same part in artistic creativity as certain mental illnesses. In the addictive condition the writer can discover a "hallucinatory truth," linked to what he in his aesthetics calls "hallucinatory realism."

The problem of the role of hallucinogenic drugs in the life of the imagination and creativity was posed in connection with Coleridge's *Kubla Khan* and Baudelaire's poetry by Alethea Hayter in her book *Opium and the Romantic Imagination,* referred to earlier. The myth of opium intoxication as a positive, creative factor has been largely abandoned or reduced by critical modern research. But the role of hallucinogenic drugs in the life of the imagination has recently been discussed with new intensity by medical experts, creativity psychologists, and writers and artists having personal experience with new types of stimulants.

Aldous Huxley, notable in this context as author of *The Doors of Perception*, declared in an interview that it is difficult to generalize about these matters, for experience has shown that people's reactions to hallucinogenic drugs can vary enormously. As an answer to a question in The Paris Review Interviews he said: "Some people probably could get direct aesthetic inspiration for painting or poetry out of such drugs as lysergic acid. Others I don't think could. For most people it's an extremely significant experience, and I suppose in an indirect way it could help the creative process. But I don't think one can sit down and say, 'I want to write a magnificent poem, and so I'm going to take lysergic acid.' " Asked if the drug would be of more help to a poet than a novelist, Huxley answered that the poet undoubtedly would get an extraordinary view of life, which she/he would not find in any other way, and that this might help him/her a great deal. But he pointed out that during the experience itself the subject is not interested in undertaking anything practical—not even writing lyric poetry. Huxley adds: "During the experience you're not particularly interested in words, because the experience transcends words and is quite inexpressible in terms of words." However, Huxley does suggest that the experience might be of use retrospectively; the writer would see the universe in a very different way and might be inspired to write something about it.[53]

It appears that the experience can to some extent be revived afterward, in particular the changed appearance of the outside world.

Experts claim that from time to time it is possible to catch a glimpse retrospectively of the hallucinogenic world, although with feebler intensity. It enables one to understand much more clearly the very special way artists like van Gogh or Blake experienced the world. But Huxley believes that it is unlikely that a writer's or painter's talent in itself would be changed as a result of hallucinogenic experiences. Scientists have experimented with painters to see what the latter could achieve under the influence of drugs. The results were disappointing. It proved impossible for them to reproduce fully the incredible intensity of the colors they saw in their drugged state. It is another matter that these drugs, as Huxley sees it, can have a "liberating and widening" effect, which he compares to the release of power and personality resulting from a completed psychoanalysis.

Allen Ginsberg has spoken in some detail about the consciousness-expanding effects of certain drugs; they can be experienced as cosmic-ecstatic or cosmic-demonic. The actual state of power expansion or vast expanses of time are certainly reminiscent of similar states of inspired *poetic* intoxication, described for instance by Nietzsche. Summing up his experiences, Ginsberg says that the drugs were useful in exploring perception, the potentialities of the sensory organs, and various possibilities or kinds of consciousness. He believes that these experiences are also useful for writing poetry and that poetry sometimes is written under their influence. He cites examples of his own poems written in a drugged state; the second part of *Howl* was apparently written "during peyote vision," and *Kaddish* was written under the influence of amphetamine injections.[54]

It is impossible for a nonmedical critic to decide to what extent descriptions like Allen Ginsberg's should be regarded as objective proof of a link between hallucinogenic intoxication and "creative intoxication." Nor is it possible to discuss in detail whether poems written in a drugged state differ in any significant way from poems inspired or created *without* the help of hallucinogenic drugs. The interesting point is the unequivocal likeness between the euphoric or ecstatic, transcendental state described by certain poets and mystics as being typical of the timeless moment of illumination, and the experiences equally remote from the everyday world that have been recorded by writers and artists while under the influence of drugs.

It is clear that hallucinatory states *as such* cannot be called *creative* moments. The precondition for the creation of a work of art is—let us repeat it once more—constant preparation and technical training. For the mystic to reach his/her goal she/he must not neglect the stages of preparatory training. The drug or pill that would enable everyone to produce works of art will remain an illusion. Whatever we may believe about the importance of opium for Coleridge, it is clear that he would never have written *Kubla Khan* had he not been an accomplished poet—thanks to diligent study of the poetry of others and sustained production of his own.

6

It is not only emotional, more or less physiological phenomena that characterize the inspired phase of the creative process. A variety of sensory phenomena often belong to sensory areas far removed from the subject's creative medium. Composers often have experiences of light and color while they are working. Musical ideas and moods sometimes affect painters, as do tactile feelings of space and volume, and authors experience both optical and acoustic phenomena.

In his essay *The Logic of Imagination*, Verner von Heidenstam, literary leader in the circle of Swedish poets of the 1890s, lets one of the artists say: "A feeling of cheerful relief fills me in the moment of execution. I feel warm and excited and hear a sound as though of churchbells. Sometimes I interrupt myself and ask: Is it possible that they are ringing the bells so late at night?" These words are very reminiscent of what Heidenstam wrote in a letter of his own experiences of poetic inspiration: "There is a sound in my ears as though of music or churchbells, and I round my lips as though to sing along with it."[55]

During a stage of the creative process, lyric poets often note an auditory element that is musical-rhythmic. It is noteworthy that professional improvisers—of the eighteenth-century Italian variety—regularly depended on music as an inspirational impulse, and the same is true of the Swedish poet Bellman.

Friedrich Schiller's words in a letter from 1792 have often been quoted to illustrate poetic composition accompanied by musical intimations: "The musical element of a poem is far more often present in me, when I sit down to write it, than a clear idea of the content, which I am scarcely aware of."[56] Eduad Sievers, verse theoretician in this century, has examined more closely the connection between rhythmical-musical impulse and poetic composition. He writes: "It is clearly the case that poetic conception and poetic shaping are linked in the poet with a certain musical, i.e., rhythmic, melodic mood."[57] We already saw how certain poems by Shelley and Valéry arose out of pure, wordless, rhythmic impulses. Not only Valéry's *Le Cimetière marin* but also his *La Jeune Parque* began this way; Valéry said of the latter that "like the majority of my poems," it was born of "the unexpected presence in my mind of a particular rhythm."[58] Stephen Spender provides similar testimony about rhythmic inspiration in his essay *The Making of a Poem*. Evidently there are moments during composition when the music behind the words is more important than the words themselves. "I am conscious of a rhythm, a dance, a fury, which is as yet empty of words," he writes.[59] We will presently in another connection examine examples of the fact we have now established, that rhythmic impulses sometimes take musical form and that many poets compose to the accompaniment of an inner melody.

The acoustic element in literary composition can flow directly into verse—as rhythm and acoustic pattern. Visions, on the other hand, have to be transferred into the medium of language first. The ability to see images and visionary experiences appears to have been particularly prevalent in the romantic generation of poets— which may confirm that the psychological bases for the emergence of romantic poetry and for the experiences of the mystics were similar. We can undoubtedly take the following lines from Coleridge's *Kubla Khan* literally:

> A damsel with a dulcimer
> *In a vision once I saw*[60]

His account of the composition of the whole poem, an intense acoustic-visionary experience merging sight and sound, is even more telling. People in whom the spontaneous capacity for seeing images is very strongly developed are called "eidetics." Coleridge must have belonged to this category, and so must Blake, whose visions were so vivid that they could fill him with terror—Milton, Moses, and the prophets visited him in the shape of gray or colorless shadows. Shelley called his poems "visions," and we know that Goethe considered it essential for an artist to be able to conjure up "idols from things." Both the word "imagination," derived from "image," and the term "fantasy," derived from a stem also meaning "image," "a making visible," indicate the way in which a visionary quality has been associated with the idea of artistic creation.

There are poems that originated in acoustic, rhythmic, and linguistic impulses. There are also those that are just as clearly derived from the field of vision and image. In his play *To Damascus*, Strindberg demonstrated most strikingly how impulses from both sensory areas overlap each other. The passage is a dialogue between The Stranger and The Lady. The Stranger speaks first:

> Hush, I hear a poem approaching . . . that's what I call it when an idea starts germinating in my brain . . . *but I hear the rhythm first* . . . this time it resembles the sound of horses' hoofs, and the jingle of spurs and clatter of armour . . . but as well there's a flapping sound as of a wind-filled sail—that's the banners . . .

The Lady thinks she can explain the whole thing in terms of a simple auditory delusion and replies: "No, it's the wind, which you can hear rustling in the tree." But The Stranger is adamant, and a vision emerges:

> *Hush—now they are riding over a bridge, but it's only a wooden one and there is no water in the river, only pebbles* . . . but wait! Now I hear a rosary being recited, men and women; the angelic greeting; *but now I can see, guess where? in your crochet work*—a large kitchen, white, the walls white-washed, there are three small, deep windows with bars and flowers, in the left-hand corner there's the fire-place, to the right the dining-table with pine-wood benches, and in a corner above the table there's a black crucifix.[61]

In our context it is of little significance that Strindberg goes on to interpret the image seen by The Stranger on the crochet work as clairvoyance. The interesting point is the intersection of acoustic-rhythmic and visionary elements. Strindberg would scarcely have written the scene in this way had he not based it on personal literary experience. Image flow and word flow, rhythmic-acoustic-visionary impulses (doubtless including other sensory phenomena), are continuous and more or less clearly discernible stimuli and factors in the creative process.

7

We already referred to Strindberg's reply to an interview in 1909, in which he spoke of the fever, ecstacy, or intoxication of creativity. He continues: "There are times when I feel that I am a medium, for it's so easy, half unconscious, hardly calculated at all."[62] Strindberg is stressing that aspect of the state of inspiration which psychologists have isolated and termed "impersonal consciousness," the feeling of being a spokesman or medium for some outside power. This brings us back to the original meaning of the word "inspiration," *inspiratio.*

The particular experience is often seen in religious or quasi-religious terms. Goethe expresses the romantic interpretation of it when he says in his conversations with Eckermann: "In cases like this the person is most commonly to be regarded as an instrument of a higher world order, as a vessel which has been found worthy of absorbing a divine influence [*als ein würdig befundenes Gefäss zur Aufnahme eines göttlichen Einflusses*]."[63]

The outside power that inspires the poet is often concretized in his/her mind. The poet sees himself/herself as listening to a stranger's voice:

> *On ne travaille pas—on écoute—on attend.*
> *C'est comme un inconnu qui vous parle à voix bas.*[64]

In these lines Musset still gives the experience the form of a simile, an "as if" situation. But often the voice has the status of transcendent reality. William Blake in a letter to Thomas Butts wrote: "I hope to . . . be a Memento in time to come and to speak to future generations by a Sublime Allegory, which is now completed into a Grand Poem. I may praise it since I dare not pretend to be other than the Secretary; the Authors are in Eternity."[65]

Admittedly the poet's invocation of a muse, with the prayer that she will graciously let her voice speak through him/her, has become a formula, a topos. But it is likely that its psychological roots are found in the experience of and belief in the poet as spokesman or *Mundstück* for a being of another order.

A demythologized version of the same belief or idea was prevalent long after the aesthetic philosophy of classical antiquity and the romantics had ceased to be binding. Flaubert quotes George Sand as saying: "When she wrote, it was not she herself but another being which overwhelmed and occupied her. If this experience was absent, then her inspiration also remained silent."[66] We could easily suppose that this interpretation of the creative experience had by now been abandoned. But in the aesthetic doctrine of the New Criticism, the notion of an authorial voice or self manifested in the literary text, and separate from the private voice or self of the writer can be seen as a lingering reflection of the old theory of inspiration, the idea that the poet at work is separate from—indeed another person than—the writer's self.

Of the accounts of "impersonal consciousness" we have discussed so far, Selma Lagerlöf's is the most interesting psychologically. Whenever her inspiration failed her, she deliberately assumed the role of listener. She then let her old grandmother, storyteller of her childhood, or Miss Salvius, fictional governess in one of her works, take over—she let them speak, while she wrote down what they dictated. The result was texts written in the Värmland dialect she had heard the old people speak. On rare occasions she actually listened to the voice of God, transforming herself into the unwritten page on which God himself wrote down his thoughts.

It is a strange fact that experiences of "impersonal consciousness" appear to be limited to a distinct category of creative persons— to prophets, seers, mystics, and writers—and never seem to occur in the lives of scientists and inventors, or even painters and musicians. It was not God who whispered the secret of the law of gravity in Newton's ear. Neither God nor the muse revealed the names of flower and animal species to Linnaeus. Nor did an outside voice dictate the formula of the Fuchsian functions to Poincaré at the decisive moment when he stepped off the tram.

If we were to seek a psychological explanation of why writers, alongside prophets and seers, experience and interpret their states of inspiration in a unique way, the following hypothesis might be advanced. They all create in and with words. Once upon a time, in their early childhood, they obtained their words from other people. Cradle songs have been sung by women down through the ages. Nursery rhymes and jingles, their first structured poems, all were conveyed to them by human voices. If it is true that creative states constitute a regression to a more spontaneous phase, the explanation follows automatically. Not only Selma Lagerlöf deliberately returns to an earlier stage, that of the listening child. By analogy, it should be possible to explain similar experiences on the part of Musset, Rilke, or anyone else, as a regression to an age when the first structured word-masses constituted an auditive experience communicated not by words on a page but by a human voice. This would explain why poets and writers listen or listened to the muse, who was a hidden mother figure—often with erotic undertones,—whereas prophets, who pronounce judgment and exhortation to their people, listen to the voice of a male God—the voice of a projected father figure. The less intellectualized a literary creative process, the more directly the writer reverts to an earlier situation. And the more intellectualized and conscious the creative process, the more untenable the whole inspirational doctrine appears, particularly the idea of the writer as spokesman for someone else.

But the poet's linguistic capacity during the creative moments cannot, of course, be reduced to —and can be only metaphorically compared with—early stages in a child's experience. It has recently been suggested by one of the structuralists that the poet's utterance during the act of creation comes from "a different sign-system than that employed by the ordinary speaker."[67] The concept of regression is not sufficient. We should perhaps also talk of "progression" up to the highest level of linguistic capacity and strategy. Here—as on so many other points of the psychology of creativity—we may find a dichotomy behind the complex phenomenon of "inspiration."

8

Unlike improvisers, creative writers are not placed face to face with audiences but work in the privacy of their own rooms. In spite of this, they are engaged in a communicative process. They can experience — or simulate — their role in this process in two ways: by adopting the stance of listener or by choosing the role of speaker. They can shape their poems or texts as spoken words, before they set them down on paper. Many writers feel the need of the spoken word in its physical, oral manifestation.

This is particularly true of poets, who often find they need to try out word tones and sequences orally. We know that a great many poets of different nationalities and ages used and use their voices when composing. A visitor to the Swedish romantic poet Esaias Tegnér, K. A. Adlersparre, wrote: "The fact is that Tegnér, when he was composing poetry, generally walked backward and forward with rapid steps, and he shaped his verse half singing it, after which he straightway wrote it down. It is strange," continued Adlersparre, "that the manuscripts written in this way seldom have any alterations or crossings out."[68] William Butler Yeats tells a very similar story. "Like every other poet, I spoke verses in a kind of chant when I was making them, and sometimes, when I was alone on a country road, I would speak them in a loud, chanting voice," he writes in his essay *Speaking to the Psaltery*.[69] E. A. Karlfeldt and Wordsworth represent another Swedish and English example respectively.

The explanation, suggested above, of such behavior is that the writer, through the spoken word, experiences or simulates an original communicative process. If literary creation is held to be a process of moving back to earlier stages of speech, another hypothesis could alternatively be advanced, namely, that speech without an external listener corresponds to another well-known aspect of a child's speech development — the purely phonetic "prattling" stage during which the child tries out his/her powers of speech and word formation, without reference to an outside audience. This latter explanation would seem reasonable for certain extreme literary movements like Dadaism and Lettrism, where the writer is far less interested in the communicative function than in the phonetic and expressive aspects of his/her activity. But this of course holds true only for extreme situations. As a rule, literary communication— including the lyrical monologue—presupposes the implied listener, the implied reader.

If we were to wish for an authentic account that both summarizes and concretizes various aspects of the experience of inspiration, our purpose would be admirably served by a quotation from Nietzsche's autobiographical work *Ecce Homo*, in which he describes how he wrote *Also sprach Zarathustra*.

> Has any one at the end of the nineteenth century any distinct notion of what poets of a stronger age understood by the word inspiration? If not, I will describe it. If one had the smallest vestige of superstition left in one, it would hardly be possible completely to set aside the idea that one is the mere incarnation, mouthpiece, or medium of an almighty power. The idea of revelation, in the sense that something which profoundly convulses and upsets one becomes suddenly visible and audible with indescribable certainty and accuracy—describes the simple fact. One hears—one does not seek; one takes—one does not ask who gives: a thought suddenly flashes up like lightning, it comes with necessity, without faltering—I have never had any choice in the matter. There is an ecstasy so great that the immense strain of it is sometimes relaxed by a flood of tears, during which one's steps now involuntarily rush and anon involuntarily lag. There is the feeling that one is utterly out of hand, with the very distinct consciousness of an endless number of fine thrills and titillations descending to one's very toes;—there is a depth of happiness in which the most painful and gloomy parts do not act as antitheses to the rest, but are produced and required as necessary shades of colour in such an overflow of light. There is an instinct for rhythmic relations which embraces a whole world of forms (length, the need of a wide-embracing rhythm, is almost the measure of the force of an inspiration, a sort of counterpart to its pressure and tension). Everything happens quite involuntarily, as if in a tempestuous outburst of freedom, of absoluteness, of power and divinity. The involuntary nature of the figures and similes is the most remarkable thing; one loses all perception of what is imagery and metaphor; everything seems to present itself as the readiest, the truest, and simplest means of expression. —This is my experience of inspiration.[70]

All the elements we noted earlier as being characteristic of the inspired state—suddenness, spontaneity, the specific mood, impersonal consciousness, physical reactions—are included in the description. Nietzsche is also clearly aware of the paradoxical contradictions inherent in the experience, such as the mingling of joy and pain, of conscious and unconscious states. He has captured all this in prose, which in its original language, by virtue of its very syntax and its stormy, rhythmic splendor, is designed to express the state it is describing.

Nietzsche was aware that he was living in an age in which inspiration was beginning to lose ground. He was, or felt he was, one of the last representatives of the romantic prophetic tradition. In fact, not even *his* view of inspiration was as firmly based or unequivocal as the passage from *Ecce Homo* might lead us to suppose. In his earlier works with their more intellectual stance, we find pronouncements diametrically opposed to this song of praise to inspiration. He declares in *Menschliches Allzumenschliches* that the artist's methods do not differ fundamentally from those of the inventor, scientist, or historical scholar. To create, he says, is the same as to combine, and all the groups mentioned are equal masters of this technique. He plays out *work* in contradistinction to *inspiration*, and writes: "All great men have been great workers, indefatigable not only in invention but also in their ability to reject, sift, reshape and organize'" And he adds; "No one, face to face with a work of art, can discover how it arose [*wie es geworden ist*] ; this is an advantage, for in all the cases where one can observe the formative process [*das Werden*] it cools one's interest somewhat."[71] It is obvious that Nietzsche was conscious of the paradoxical nature of creativity, even though he never in his writings clearly formulated an awareness of the dialectical relationship between inspiration and work.

If we ask ourselves why the belief in and myth of inspiration was so passionately adhered to by the romantics, it is scarcely sufficient to refer exclusively to psychological typologies or aesthetic traditions. Another factor is likely to be the new situation that had arisen for writers—and this was particularly true of poets—leading to a strong sense of isolation from their own age and surroundings.

In previous centuries writers had occupied legitimized positions in the society of their day—as civil servants or attached to the courts of aristocrats and royalty. In the eighteenth century, as has often been pointed out, the writer's position changed. S/he now stands alone, or, to use a fashionable phrase, becomes alienated. When seeking to legitimize his/her precarious position and gain authority for his/her words and work, it proves an advantage to the writer to utilize the myth of being a spokesperson for an external, superhuman power, an authority above that of contemporary society. The extrapersonal consciousness experienced during creative activity is dignified with a metaphysical interpretation. The poet becomes a prophet.

9

Since Nietzsche wrote *Ecce Homo* and after several succeeding stages of romantic prophecy and cult of genius have been left behind, the majority of writers and artists have become more and more skeptical about inspiration as a phenomenon and about the fruits of an uncontrolledly inspired state. Reading interviews with recent generations of prose writers in *The Paris Review Interviews* or similar series, one seldom comes across the word "inspiration." The present-day Swedish poet Artur Lundkvist speaks for many contemporaries when he says that "the term inspiration has become too romantically elevated, too emotionally exalted, even too pretentious."[72] A socially aware writer who wishes to communicate a message—whether social or political—is unlikely to seek sanction for his/her task by invoking metaphysical or subconscious powers. A generation of intellectualist writers who regard writing as work or even as a service to society are far more attracted to an aesthetics of work than to the myth of inspiration.

It is probably true to say that lyric poets clung the longest to some form of mystic belief in inspiration, yet many of them, too, have during this century voiced skepticism about, and at times even ridiculed, the faith in inspiration. No one has more unequivocally and consistently opposed the thoughtless, vulgar cult of inspiration than the poet Paul Valéry.

Valéry objects to "this naive conception of a strange breath or almighty spirit, which suddenly for a period of time replaces our own,"[73] and he expresses ironic surprise that so many writers have been prepared to accept the notion. He himself rejects the idea of spontaneous literary creation, for as he says in his *Lettre sur Mallarmé*, already referred to in a previous chapter, "If I were to write, I would much prefer to write something which was weak with my consciousness fully turned on and in complete clarity [*dans une entière lucidité*], than create a masterpiece in a trance and outside myself."[74] Ecstasy or enthusiasm is not the right state for the creative writer, as Platonic and romantic aesthetics would have us believe. The literary work is shaped by a lucid consciousness, and the writer's natural state is what distinguishes him/her most clearly from the dreamer. *Exactitude* and *style*—two key words in Valéry's aesthetic—invoke and underline the exact opposite of dreams.

Valéry demonstrates the absurdity of the romantic belief in inspiration with murderous logic. "Assume that inspiration were that which one believes it to be and which is absurd and entails that a *whole* poem could be dictated to a writer by some deity. This would necessarily entail that an inspired person could write as well in a foreign language as in his own, but that he would not be aware of it. . . . The inspired writer would be capable of forgetting both the period flavor of the age in which he was living, and the works his predecessors and contemporaries had created."[75]

If not—Valéry points out—we are forced to reinterpret the word "inspiration" and see it as a force so deft, well articulated, clever, well informed, and calculating that it should instead be termed "intelligence and knowledge." Valéry's recasting of the concept of inspiration in terms of control and precision brings it close to the idea of intuition advanced by the Swedish philosopher Hans Larsson in his book *The Logic of Poetry* (1899). Larsson was anxious to free the overworked concept of intuition of its metaphysical associations, and he, in contrast to and in open controversy with Henry Bergson, saw it as a logical and cognitive function of consciousness in its highest coordinating activity.

Distrust of "inspiration" both in the sense of spontaneous, unreflected impulse and unchecked creative intoxication followed

Valéry down through the years. He wrote to Pierre Louÿs in 1890 that his ideal writer—i.e., he himself—would never be able to abandon himself to the caprices of inspiration—*aux hasards de l'inspiration*—never write a poem during a night of fever. After which he adds the words: "Je n'aime pas Musset."[76]

Denial of the value of spontaneity and inspiration is the cornerstone of Valéry's aesthetic, to which he adhered more or less consistently throughout his works. But being a skillful dialectician with profound insight into the processes of poetic creation, he saw the necessity of introducing an antithesis into his aesthetic system.

Having exposed the false mythological and metaphysical pretentions of inspiration, he found that he could not dispense with them *altogether*. Pythia, he says, thereby introducing into his argument a mythological figure which had hitherto figured only in his poetry, would never be able to dictate a whole poem. A whole poem—never; but a line here and a line there. It is clear that Pythia, oracle priestess, figures not only in Valéry's poetry but also in his logical discourse as a symbol of the subconscious, of levels he only gradually came to include in his conscious personality.[77]

In his aesthetic arguments Valéry also borrowed ideas and concepts from theology which are markedly different from the notions and images present in his "engineering philosophy," as Hytier pointed out. It appears that a line can come as a gift from above and surprise the poet, and this Valéry calls *"ce cas d'une grace soudaine."* He writes on another occasion that "the Gods in their grace and favor give us a first line for nothing but it rests on us to fashion the next one so that it harmonizes with and answers to the first one."[78] Here Valéry clearly demonstrates the contrast between what he elsewhere calls *les vers donnés* and *les vers calculés*.

However, what Valéry on one occasion calls "grace," he calls "chance" on another. *Le hasard*, it has been claimed, is Valéry's true muse. But if so, it is chance of another type and magnitude than the one Poe banished from his theory of poetry.

The spontaneity rejected by Valéry returns to his discourse in connection with the final stage of the creative process. He speaks of *"la merveille d'une improvisation de degré supérieure,"* placed not at the beginning but at the end. He writes in the same essay: "That which is spontaneous is the fruit of a victory."[79] This fruit

is by no means available to everyone, but only to those who have
the power to carry out an artistic assignment using all the resources
available to them. Not until their intellectual effort has been pushed
to its uttermost extreme are poets finally accorded the grace of
becoming the instruments of their own final discoveries—*"ils peu-
vent à présent improviser en pleine possession de leur puissance."*
Here we see Valéry having carried his dialectical argument to the
point of reversal; the earlier poet-engineer, poet-calculator, has
been transformed into his opposite, a creative improviser! Stravinsky sees the process of musical composition in the same light when
he writes: "I have no intention of denying a decisive role to inspiration; I only maintain that it is not a precondition for creative activity, but that in the temporal sequence it is a product of a secondary
nature."[80]

The phenomenon of improvisation has already been described
in an earlier chapter as a form of psychic automatism. Its distinguishing mark is a spontaneous and continuous flow of words or
music. In addition, improvisation involves an element of surprise—
the unexpected turn, the fortunate chance solution of an artistic
problem.

It is well known that many composers have exercised their improvisational talents at the keyboard as a preliminary to composing
music. What Stravinsky and Valéry are referring to is, however,
something different. They have in mind the final phase of composition, when the artist suddenly by means of a spontaneous action
brings the work to completion, maybe even to perfection.

In the section on Italian *improvvisatori* we noted the gap between improvisation on the one hand, this art of the unprepared,
with all that it entails of provoked spontaneity and verbal acro-
batics, and the artistically more distinguished phenomenon known
as inspiration on the other hand. Having noted Valéry's remarks,
we now have reason to reconsider the terms somewhat. The
"improvisation de degré supérieur" that Valéry speaks of is clearly
identical with the experience he has called *"inspiration"* or *"illumination"* in other connections. Here consciousness and noncon-
sciousness have merged. The spontaneity and airy improvisation
Valéry wished to banish from his aesthetic system are ultimately
readmitted and rehabilitated.

Valéry's aesthetic system houses strong contrasts and contradictions. As Ince pointed out, his dialectic is not merely the play of contrasts on one and the same temporal plane. There is also a chronological development of his aesthetic ideas when thesis and antithesis form a higher synthesis, for at a late stage in his life Valéry, undoubtedly strengthened by his personal literary experiences, reaches the stage when he reinstates into his system the inspiration he had so forcibly denied.

But this inspiration is never to be taken in the facile vulgar-romantic sense of a sort of psychic automatism. Valéry does not believe in poetic composition as a continuous, steady process; he stresses its fragmentary and discontinuous nature, as he had himself experienced it. He does not believe that a poem suddenly and of an instant presents itself on the poet's blank sheet of paper. Time and again he stresses the long preparatory processes that form the basis of every serious work of art. If we revert to Graham Wallas's schema of stages, it becomes apparent that the first stage, that of preparation, is in many ways the most important for Valéry. This involves for him not only self-knowledge but in equal parts linguistic knowledge and reflection. Valéry knows better than most that poems are written not with feelings but with words.

Against an exaggerated belief in spontaneity he pits his conviction that every great work of art is created by struggle, by the artist overcoming resistance. He goes so far as to believe that it is a poet's task to seek out—and even to heighten—resistance. The rules of the game have to be demanding, and writing becomes a form of problem solving. By making use of ready-made forms, rhythmic or rhyming, the poet turns a linguistic adventure into a mere steeplechase: Readily accessible and easy solutions are the enemies of art. Charles Du Bos notes in his *Cahiers* a characteristic remark by Valéry from the 1920s: "It worries me that I nowadays write poetry with too great facility."[81]

Like Poe, the mentor of his youth, Valéry is above all anxious that a poem should work—on the reader. He contends that we recognize the true poet by the fact that s/he inspires *the reader*, or as he puts it: *"On reconnait le poète . . . à ce simple fait, qu'il change le lecteur 'en inspiré.' "*[82] The true state of the poet—let us recapitulate—is not lyrical ecstasy, for that is the fortunate lot of the reader. The poet can and possibly should remain aloof from the emotions s/he is able to evoke, just as the actor should stand aloof, according to Diderot. It is the reader who should feel inspired when confronted with great art.

By means of this argument Valéry pursues his dialectic to a brilliant culmination. In so doing, he has also indirectly indicated an idea that has played a central role in recent aesthetic discussions, namely the idea of the reader as coauthor of all literary communication.

If we pursue Valéry's argument a step further, we find that the reader transmits his/her own "inspired state" to the poem or poet who has evoked it. By means of false or mistaken logic, the ingenuous reader convinces himself/herself of the magical powers the poet must have commanded and of the poem as a product of spontaneous inspiration.

10

It is an undeniable fact that perfect art often *looks* as though it had been effortlessly produced. This is as true of intellectual and artistic products as it is of successful sporting achievements. Seen from this point of view, it is the art of the poet to make the difficult look easy. But that which appears self-evident and artistically inevitable is, as we have already seen, most frequently produced with great labor. If we return to manuscripts, they provide a surfeit of evidence, but we will content ourselves with a couple of examples. When some of Heinrich Heine's poetic manuscripts were published under the typical title *Aus der Werkstatt der Dichter* (From the poet's workshop), it was natural for the introduction to contain the following remarks: "There is something self-evident, flowing, in Heine's language, which may give the impression that if flowed with equal ease from the writer's pen. . . . But a glance at his manuscripts and the products of his workshop show that such a conclusion regarding his method of work overestimates his talent, or rather, it underestimates his powers of writing [*Dichtertum*]. . . . With a true feeling for language and a poetic sense of responsibility he works away at his poems . . . until he finds the definitive expression, the final form, which strikes the reader or listener as though it could not be otherwise."[83]

A Swedish example that naturally springs to mind in this connection is Gustav Fröding. His poems, too, with their virtuosity and ostensibly self-evident form, might indeed appear to have been composed with consummate ease, to have been improvised. When some of Fröding's manuscripts were published in facsimile in 1924, they probably surprised many an artless reader. The manuscripts were crammed with alterations and suggested alterations in the margin, with variants, with lists of rhymes—in short, they bore witness to hard, methodical linguistic work, of which the final version gave no indication.

It might seem reasonable, at least to those not experienced in the art of writing, to suppose that modern poets who use freer forms and are free from the constraints of rhyme and stanza would also be able to compose more easily and that the distance between conception and execution would be shorter. Yet if we exclude a group of improvisers and dogmatic surrealists, this is hardly true. "The increased demand for ambiguity and 'density' in a poem, places new and increased demands on the poet's ability to organize his material and it increases his need to experiment and seek new solutions to his problems of expression."[84] This is the conclusion of a Swedish scholar after having examined a number of manuscripts of modern Swedish poems. Similar observations and conclusions are invited by the manuscript collections of contemporary English and American poets which have from time to time been exhibited, for instance, in the exhibition organized by the British Museum Library in 1967 under the title "Poetry in the Making." The exhibit included manuscripts by Auden, Spender, Philip Larkin, and Dylan Thomas, and gave ample evidence of how modern poems proceed along a laborious path to completion.

The incontrovertible evidence of the manuscripts can be reinforced by accounts of work progress and interviews provided by the same generation of writers. They confirm that most poets regard composition as a process of work. Either literally or in spirit they agree with Robert Frost's words: "I look upon a poem as a performance,"[85] and the corollary, that the poet, like the athlete, is a skillful professional. A good example of a modern extremist, a poet who almost outdoes Paul Valéry's distrust of spontaneity, is Robert Lowell. He states in *Writers at Work* that he does not believe he has ever written a formal poem in which he retained a single one of the original lines in their initial form. Asked how he went on revising his poems, he gave the expressive reply: "Endlessly."[86]

Paul Valéry advised poets to have no hesitation in publishing several different versions of a poem, and many contemporary poets have practiced this method. Robert Lowell in particular has followed this practice. During the six years 1967-73 he published three different versions of a particular volume of poems. His collection *Notebook 1967-68* was published as a book in the spring of 1969. When he published an entirely new edition of it in 1970, he had altered almost a hundred poems and had added some new ones. He explained in a commentary that he had treated his published work as thought it were a manuscript. In 1973 he published a collection entitled *History*, which at the time was designed to be the final form of *Notebook*.

Lowell's example is in many ways instructive. Here we meet a poet who spreads out before us not only his poems but also a considerable portion of the compositional process. Gottfried Benn once said that the modern poet often takes as great an interest in the process of composing as in the final product. By the same token Lowell, when he shows version upon version to his readers, might be said to demand of them as great an interest in the creative process as he himself feels.

In any case, Lowell represents an interesting and extreme example of poetic psychology. If it is true that he has never written a formal poem in which he retained a single line in its original shape, he has undeniably moved as far away as possible from the inspired experience of *le vers donné* or *le poéme donné*. For poets of earlier generations, a feeling of certainty was often an important element in the initial inspired stage, and it guaranteed that a poem or line had a definitive, unchanging shape more or less from the start. For Lowell—and no doubt a considerable number of contemporary poets—this feeling of certainty has been replaced by an ambiguous consciousness which grants a poem the right to a fluctuating and changeable shape.

Yet the conviction appears ineradicable that a poem can be improved in the direction of aesthetic perfection, which is perhaps ultimately a belief in the poem's inherent "finality." Robert Lowell himself demonstrates his allegiance to it when he declares that he has reached his last and final version of *Notebook* with the volume *History*. "I hope," he writes, "that I have cut the waste marble from the figure."[87]

The universe of aesthetics is full of contradictions. Side by side with the belief in the perfectability of a poem, that the final stage is also the best from the artistic point of view, we find the reverse notion. There are poets who, having published their poems in what appeared to be definitive versions, reverted to an *earlier* version, sometimes even to the original draft. This process can be observed in many, perhaps all, literary periods. Long before depth psychology had given writers renewed faith in original impulses, we find poets who had the transhistoric experience of the circular movement or crablike gait of the compositional process. Their original linguistic impulse proved to have superior staying power and the strength to rise up to the surface through layers of subsequent accretions. Fundamentally this means that there is no simple developmental law governing the history of literary genetics. Both advancing and retreating play a part in the writer's aesthetic strategy.

Concluding
Unscientific Postscript

Da steh' ich nun, ich armer Tor.
Und bin so klug als wie zuvor.
  Faust's first monologue

A literary, artistic or musical work can be looked at from two opposite vantage points. We can consider it the result of a particular
creative activity, which is the point of view we have largely applied
so far. But we can of course also regard it as a stimulus to an experience or a series of experiences on the part of reader, listener,
or viewer. In short, we can see it either in relation to producer or
to consumer.

The man who introduced these two terms into the field of literary theory was not, as might be supposed, a modern communica-
tions expert. Paul Valéry used them in a lecture given at Collège
de France in 1937, later published under the title *Première leçon
du cours de poétique.* He demonstrates there, with customary conviction, that these two points of view never coincide.

There are, he says, literary, artistic, and musical works that
represent the culmination of lengthy preparatory work; behind
them lie many attempts, resumed efforts, deletions, and choices.
They may have entailed months or even years of thought and ideas;
they may incorporate the experiences of a whole lifetime. Yet the
paradoxical fact is, he points out, that the effect of a work of this
kind can be instantaneous or at least very rapid. A glance may be
sufficient for the spectator to experience the aesthetic impact of a
sculpture or a painting. It takes no more than two hours to witness

197

the result of all the calculations and painstaking work that went into a tragedy or the shaping of each of its lines of verse. It takes just as short a time, or even shorter, to listen to all the combinations of harmonies and orchestral effects that a composer uses in a musical composition. In short, says Valéry, there is a total incongruity between the work of the producer and the consumer.

In the main, we have to grant that Paul Valéry is right and admit that there is a high degree of inconsistency between the processes of creation and appreciation. Finally we have to ask ourselves whether research on the genesis of a literary work has anything to impart to readers, listeners, or interpreters, or whether it is simply an end in itself. Can and does research of this kind help us interpret a work?

The question brings us to the heart of the hotly debated problem of the writer's intention when creating a work. In their famous essay from 1946, *The Intentional Fallacy*, Monroe Beardsley and W. K. Wimsatt argue against the whole idea of the genetic approach. They maintain that the intention underlying a literary work can only be divined from the finished product and cannot be isolated from it. If a writer revises his original plan as s/he goes along, or produces one version after another, this merely shows that s/he has not succeeded in realizing his *real* "intention" in all the preparatory stages. The writer evidently intended to write a better work, or a different kind of work—which s/he finally did. If we were to try to concretize Beardsley and Wimsatt's arguments with the help of our earlier examples, we could say that Ibsen intended to write not a lengthy, undramatic epic but a worthy work on the subject that had possessed him. Neither, by the same token, was it Selma Lagerlöf's "intention" to produce a poor romance cycle or a bad play. Neither of them succeeded in realizing their respective "intentions" in a manner satisfying to them in the genres they originally chose.

One of the weaknesses of Beardsley and Wimsatt's reasoning is, however, that they argue as though there were only *one* intention behind a literary work. Moreover, they have a tendency to merge the initial and the concluding intentions. It is true that there may be instances when they coincide. We have, for instance, already quoted a passage by Stephen Spender in which he explains that by producing a number of successive texts in his notebooks he was finally able to "recreate his vision." But the process is usually more complex. The material dealt with in this book has clearly shown us that a writer can change his/her intentions as the work proceeds. The writer can develop new ideas and find new solutions to formal problems, none of which were present in the original version or plan.

The study of a literary work in the making enables us to follow *changing intentions*. An author has a choice, that is, a series of choices. They embrace both ends and means, planning the work, its ideational structure, its formal structure, and linguistic considerations of an acoustic, euphonic, or metrical nature. An "intention" cannot be postulated as an abstract entity in the opening or final phase of a work. The author's intentions develop as the work proceeds.

In the visual arts the most important developmental phases are recorded by concrete evidence on paper or in clay. It is precisely these changes of direction and plan or intention that the Swedish art historian Ragnar Josephson so graphically lets us follow in his book *The Birth of the Work of Art*. Similar transformations can be observed in literary manuscripts, albeit this material is less graphic, and we also have to reckon with several invisible stages (a great deal is both written and erased in the mind).

Despite all that has been said at various times about the uselessness of establishing the authorial intentions behind a given work, there can be little doubt that knowledge of the early stages of the work can aid our understanding of it, can allow us to follow its underlying associative chain. In this way an early version of a poem can be read as a commentary to a later version. A metaphor, a symbol, or a series of associations, half hidden or compressed in the final version, are often more easily spotted by the interpreter if s/he is aware of what lies behind them. Also important for manuscript studies is what a writer rejects and crosses out. Indeed, as Karl Shapiro puts it, no poem in its final version tells us as much about the intention of the poet or about his/her mind as do the rough drafts s/he almost systematically *destroys*. To interpret or understand is to choose.[1] To choose is to exclude. Manuscripts can help us in this respect too.

There is another important point that can be adduced in defense of the genetic approach. The actual creative process can in a very specific way be mirrored in the final product, i.e., in its symbolism. For the writer, the ebb and flow of creativity are as central as many other personal experiences and she/he can disguise creative problems with images and symbols from totally different spheres— those of religion, love, and philosophy. Literary scholars have all too seldom been prepared to note this aspect of metacreativity. In order for it to be intelligible, it is essential for us to accompany the writer as she/he wrestles with material.

We come now to the last and perhaps most difficult question: can investigations of the genesis of a work of art help shed light on the mysterious phenomenon known as creativity?

All writers work with words. According to a contemporary view which has Chomsky as an adherent, every act of speech can be seen as a creative act. Every time we utter words we "create" something new, a sentence which neither we nor anyone else has ever said in exactly the same way before. But in order to "create" and be understood, we have to observe the given rules of the language system.

Behind every literary work or creation there stands an individual who has shaped words into a cosmos according to certain rules, rules not only of language but also of literary conventions and genres and of poetic grammar. The writer's linguistic inventiveness must, in other words, be adapted to a system of rules determined individually or by tradition. All literary creativity takes place between the poles of rules and chance, of technique and impulse. Valéry strikingly describes the dialectic we have touched on a number of times in this book when he says that: "very strict and even severe conditions free the artist from a number of subtle decisions and a great deal of responsibility in regard to form, whilst these very conditions sometimes encourage discoveries to which total freedom would not have led him."[2] Neither a great poet nor a computer can produce poetry without having been fed a strict set of rules—in its absence, the random number generator or the factor called inspiration produces nothing resembling poetry.

Much imaginative literature, indeed the major part of it, is produced *within* the boundaries of literary traditions, conventions, and genres. All writers and artists who can be subsumed under "schools" or "groups" are to some extent reproductive in their work. Big breakthroughs and innovations in art and literature arise when traditions and conventions are overstepped and broken down, from both within and without. A big literary and artistic breakthrough is also a breakthrough for the personality.

Friedrich Nietzsche formulates this idea of resistance as the precondition for all innovatory creativity when he describes in *Ecce homo* how he wrote *Also sprach Zarathustra*. Everything seemed to have conspired against him: the cold winter in Rapallo, with rain and sickness. He sums it up in this way: "These circumstances were surely the very reverse of favorable; and yet, in spite of them, and as if in proof of my belief that everything decisive comes to life in defiance of every obstacle, it was precisely during this winter and in the midst of these unfavorable circumstances that my Zarathustra originated."[3]

Probably many modern creativity psychologists would be prepared to extend the validity of Nietzsche's dictum. New and decisive achievements, they would claim, are seldom if ever produced except by people with strong inner tensions. The histories of art, literature, and music of recent centuries provide overwhelming evidence that outstanding creative and innovative artists were complex personalities, in whom destructive forces were held in check by or struggled for supremacy over creative powers. Moreover there is something like a dialectic relation between creator and work. Not only does the author create his/her work; the work creates its author. Montaigne wrote: "Je n'ai pas plus fait mon livre que mon livre m'a fait." Reformulating Descartes's "Cogito ergo sum," Paul Valéry stated: "J'invente, donc je suis."

Creative life is not without its tragedy, primarily on the personal level. "No real artist writes except from a profound awareness of the dark void which lies behind everything human." The sentence quoted is an aphorism, formulated by a Swedish writer from this century, Vilhelm Ekelund. The true creative artist is not only a renewer but also a destroyer, at times a self-destroyer. She/he is an iconoclast, ruthless toward traditions and accepted forms and values. Literary history is not only the history of literary traditions but to an equal degree that of literary overthrowings.

Today there is still no accepted definition of the term "creativity."

But there exists a host of varied interpretations of creativity as a psychological phenomenon. According to one of these, the human creative drive can be regarded as a manifestation of the "tendency to duplication" found at different levels of organic life, from the biological cell upward. If there is *any* truth in the bold view that all creativity, including the artistic variant, results from a "tendency to duplication," it is perhaps not entirely unreasonable to seek traces of the artist in his/her work. *"Non omnis moriar,"* I shall not die entirely, said Horace, thinking of his poetry.[4]

But creative ability is more than a tendency to duplication, just as a work of art is more than a copy of its maker. The truly creative artist has a transcendent drive that disregards normal boundaries. The majority of philosophers and psychologists who have taken an interest in the creative process—from Bergson to Jacques Maritain and on to contemporary American creativity researchers—have stressed that freedom is integral to creativity and leads to unpredicted and unpredictable results.[5] Writers themselves just as frequently stress the inner compulsion associated with creativity. The contradiction is significant.

It is held that creativity, in the sense of innovation, is something uniquely human. The songbird builds its intricate nest in the same way now as at the time of the flood. Humans alone transform and are transformed. Man's way of living and building and shaping his environment—including his aesthetic environment—has changed from century to century, from decade to decade. The song of a bird is the same from one spring to the next. That of man is renewed.

Notes

Notes

Preface

1. English-language works of general interest include Brewster Ghiselin, *The Creative Process, a Symposium* (Berkeley: University of California Press, 1952); Rosamond Harding, *An Anatomy of Inspiration*, 3rd ed. (Cambridge: W. Heffer, 1948); Wallace Hildick, *Word for Word, A Study of Author's Alterations* (London: Faber and Faber, 1965; Arthur Koestler, *The Act of Creation* (London: Hutchinson, 1964).

Documentation and Experimentation

1. Quoted in *Criticism, The Foundations of Modern Literary Judgment*, ed. Mark Schorer, Josephine Miles, Gordon McKenzie (New York: Harcourt Brace, 1948), p. 13.

2. Alfred de Vigny, *Journal d'un poète, Oeuvres complètes*, vol. IV (Paris: C. Delagrave, 1906), p. 107.

3. Quoted by Hans Pfitzner, *Über musikalische Inspiration* (Berlin-Grunewald: Adolph Fürstner, 1940), p. 44-45.

4. Quoted in Julius Bahle, *Eingebung und Tat im musikalischen Schaffen* (Leipzig: Hirzel, 1939), p. 347.

5. Edward Young, *Conjectures on Original Composition*, in *Criticism*, p. 13.

6. Gustave Flaubert, *Correspondence*, vol. III (Paris: G. Charpentier, 1891), p. 110.

7. For Valéry's imagery, see Jean Hytier, *La poétique de Paul Valéry* (Paris: Armand Colin, 1953), pp. 132, 168.

8. Quoted in Konrad Krause, *Werkstatt der Wortkunst* (Munich: Oldenburg, 1942), p. 93.

9. Gottfried Benn, *Probleme der Lyrik* (Wiesbaden: Limes, 1951), pp. 132, 168.

10. For analogy between poet and cosmic creator, see also Milton Charles Nahm, *The Artist as Creator* (Baltimore: Johns Hopkins, 1956).

11. Rudolf Arnheim's essay is published in *Poets at Work. Essays Based on the Modern Poetry Collection at the Lockwood Memorial Library, University of Buffalo*, ed. Rudolf Arnheim, Karl Shapiro, et al. (New York: Harcourt Brace, 1949), pp. 125-62.

12. Quoted in Willy R. Kastborg, *I kunstnerens verksted* (Trondheim: Cappelen, 1967), p. 127.

13. For Lawrence Durrel's and T. S. Eliot's work habits, see *Writers at Work*, the Paris Review Interviews, second series, prepared for book publication by George Plimpton (New York: Viking Press, Compass Books, 1965), pp. 268 and 101.

14. On Yeats's manuscripts, see Jon Stallworthy, *Between the Lines* (Oxford: Oxford University Press, 1963), p. 99; cf. his book *Vision and Revision in Yeats's Last Poems* (Oxford: Oxford University Press, 1969).

15. Quoted in Neville Rogers, *Shelley at Work* (Oxford: Clarendon Press, 1956), p. 1.

16. Igor Stravinsky, "Der schöpferische Akt in der Musik," *Universitas, Zeitschrift für Wissenschaft, Kunst, und Literatur* 6 (1951), p. 1089.

17. Stephen Spender, *The Making of a Poem*, in *Criticism*, p. 189.

18. Frank Barron, *Creative Person and Creative Process* (New York: Holt, Rinehart and Winston, 1969); Barron, *Artists in the Making* (New York: Seminar Press, 1972), particularly p. 145.

19. Barron, *Artists in the Making*, p. 145. Cf. Barron, *Creative Person and Creative Process*, where part of the same material has been used.

20. For synectics, see William J. J. Gordon, *Synectics, the Development of Creative Capacity* (New York: Harper, 1961).

21. Viktor Shklovskij [Sklovskij] is here quoted after the Swedish translation in *Form och Struktur*, texter valda av Kurt Aspelin och Bengt Lundberg (Stockholm: Norstedt, 1971), p. 51.

22. Shklovskij, *O Teorii prozy* (Moskou, 1925).

23. See Louis T. Milic, "The Possible Usefulness of Poetry Generation," in *The Computer in Literary and Linguistic Research*, ed. Roy Albert Wisbey (Cambridge: Cambridge University Press, 1971), pp. 169-82; R. L. Widmann, "Recent Scholarship in Literary and Linguistic Studies," in *Computers and the Humanities* (Flushing, New York: Queens College Press, 1972), vol. 7, no. 1.

24. For type and duration of inspirational ideas, see J. Bahle, "Zur Psychologie des Einfalls und der Inspiration im musikalischen Schaffen," in *Acta psychologica*, The Hague 1 (1936), p. 10.

25. Pfitzner, *Über musikalische Inspiration*; on Max Reger, p. 35; on Goethe, Schopenhauer, and Ibsen, pp. 43-47.

26. *Ibid.*, p. 80.

Improvisation—Rite and Myth

1. Ernst Ferand, *Die Improvisation in der Musik* (Zurich: Rhein-Verlag, 1938), p. 25.

2. See *ibid.*, p. 20.

3. *Die Musik in Geschichte und Gegenwart, Allgemeine Enzyklopedie der Musik*, vol. 6 (Basil-London: Verlag Kassel), p. 1123.

4. See Adele Vitagliano, *Storia della poesia estemporanea nella letteratura italiana* (Rome: Loescher, 1905); E. Bouvy, "L'improvisation poétique en Italie, d'aprés un livre recent," in *Bulletin italien* 6 (1906), pp. 2-20; Wilhelm Herrman, *Deutschlands Improvi-*

satoren, ed. with an introduction by Oswald Berkhan (Braunschweig: H. Sievers, 1906); Wiktor Weintraub, "The Problem of Improvisation in Romantic Literature," *Comparative Literature* 16 (1964), pp. 119-37.

5. Charles de Brosses on Bernardo Perfetti, in *Le Président de Brosses en Italie*, 3rd ed. (Paris: Didier, 1869), pp. 302-4.

6. Tobias Smollett on improvisation, in *Travels through France and Italy*, part II (London, 1756), p. 56.

7. See Allardyce Nicoll, *The World of Harlequin* (Cambridge: Cambridge University Press, 1963), p. 35-39.

8. Voltaire, *Oeuvres complètes*, new edition by L. Moland, vol. XVII (Paris, 1878), pp. 238-40 and vol. XXVI (Paris, 1880), pp. 340-41.

9. Carlo Goldoni, *Memorie del signor Carlo Goldoni*, nuova traduzione dal francese (Piacenza: Dai Torchi del Majno, 1823), p. 292

10. Gudmund Göran Adlerbeth, *Svenska Memoarer och Bref. Gustaf III:s Resa i Italien*, annotations by G. G. Adlerbeth, vol. V ed. by Henrik Schück (Stockholm: Bonniers, 1902), pp. 52-53.

11. Schack Staffeldt on Fortunata Fantastici, in *Levned II*, p. 349, quoted in Hakon Strangerup, *Schack Staffeldt* (Copenhagen: Gyldendal, 1940), p. 125.

12. Per Daniel Amadeus Atterbom, *Minnen från Tyskland och Italien*, vol. II (Örebro: Beijer, 1863): on Rosa Taddei, pp. 76-89.

13. Karl August Nicander, *Minnen från Södern, efter en resa i Danmark, Tyskland, Schweitz, och Italien*, vol. II (Örebro: Beijer, 1863), p. 80.

14. August von Platen, *Die Tagebücher*, vol. II, hrsg. von E. v. Laubmann and L. v. Scheffler (Stuttgart: Cotta, 1900), p. 827.

15. Martin Persson Nilsson, *Homer and Mycenae*, Methuen's Handbooks of Archaeology (London: Methuen, 1933), p. 202.

16. Carl Michael Bellman as improvisor: Carl Fehrman, "Bellman och improvisationens konst," in *Bellmansstudier*, ed. Bellmanssällskapet (Stockholm: Nyblom, 1966), pp. 9-40. Bellman's formulas: Carol Clover, "Improvisation in Fredman's Epistlar," *Scandinavian Studies*, 44, no. 3 (1972), pp. 310-35.

17. Geneviève Gennari, "La part du Midi," in *Le premier voyage du Madame de Staël en Italie, et la genèse de Corinne* (Paris: Boivin, 1947), pp. 135-44.

18. Quoted in *ibid.*, p. 140.

19. Madame de Staël, *Corinne ou l'Italie*, new edition, H. Nicolle (Paris, 1843), p. 284.

20. *Ibid.*, p. 221.

21. *Ibid.*, p. 116.

22. H. C. Andersen, *Romaner og Rejseskildringer*, vol. I: *Improvisatoren*, ed. Knud Bøgh (Copenhagen: Gyldendal, 1943), p. XL.

23. H. C. Andersen, *Levnedsbog*, ed. Helge Topsøe-Jensen (Copenhagen: Schönberg, 1962), p. 62.

24. Quoted in Helge Topsøe-Jensen, *H. C. Andersen og andre studier*, ed. Odense Bys Museer (Odense: Odense Bys Museer, 1966), p. 328.

25. H. C. Andersen, *Romerske Dagbøger*, ed. Paul Rubow and Helge Topsøe-Jensen (Copenhagen: Gyldendal, 1947), p. 60.

26. Andersen, *Improvisatoren*, p. 280.

27. Andersen, *Romerske Dagbøger*, p. 35.

28. Andersen, *Improvisatoren*, p. 145.

29. Paul Rubow *H. C. Andersens Eventyr*, 2nd ed. (Copenhagen: Gyldendal, 1943), p. 95.

30. Andersen, *Improvisatoren*, p. 200.

31. See Edvard Collin, *H. C. Andersen og det Collinske Hus* (Copenhagen: Reitzels Forlag, 1882), p. 95.

32. H. C. Andersen's own commentaries in *Eventyr og Historier* (Copenhagen: Reitzels Forlag, 1863), p. 415.

33. H. C. Andersen, *Brevvexling med Jonas Collin den aeldre og andre medlemmer af det Collinske Hus*, vol. I, ed. Helge Topsøe-Jensen (Copenhagen: Munksgaard, 1945), p. 253.

34. H. C. Andersen, *Brevvexling med Edvard og Henriette Collin*, vol. IV, ed. C. Behrend and Helge Topsøe-Jensen (Copenhagen: Levin og Munksgaard, 1936), p. 24.

35. Andersen, *Improvisatoren*, p. 253.

36. See Ferand, *Die Improvisation in der Musik*.

37. Quoted in Weintraub, "The Problem of Improvisation in Romantic Literature," p. 120.

38. Adlerbeth, *Gustaf III:s Resa i Italien*, p. 53.

39. See Lutz Winckler, *Kulturwarenproduktion, Aufsätze zur Literatur und Sprachsoziologie* (Frankfurt on the Main: Suhrkamp, 1970), pp. 46-53.

40. Quoted from *Modern French Poets on Poetry*, compiled by Robert Gibson (Cambridge: Cambridge University Press, 1961), p. 235.

Coleridge and His Dream Poem

1. Percy Bysshe Shelley, *A Defence of Poetry* (written in 1821, first published in 1849), quoted in *Criticism, the Foundations of Modern Literary Judgment*, ed. Mark Schorer, Josephine Miles, Gordon McKenzie (New York: Harcourt Brace, 1948), p. 468.

2. Quoted in Stanley Edgar Hyman, *The Armed Vision* (New York: Knopf, 1952), p. 360.

3. See Elisabeth Schneider, *Coleridge, Opium, and Kubla Khan* (Chicago: University of Chicago Press, 1953), p. 24.

4. *Ibid.*, p. 84

5. *Ibid.*, p. 82.

6. *Ibid.*, pp. 10 and 77.

7. Samuel Taylor Coleridge, *Anima Poetae*, ed. E. H. Coleridge (London: William Heinemann, 1895), p. 206.

8. See John Livingston Lowes, *The Road to Xanadu* (New York: Vintage Books, 1959), chapter 20.

9. See Walter Silz, "Otto Ludwig and the Process of Poetic Creation," *Publications of the Modern Language Association of America* 60 (1945), p. 865.

10. Albert Béguin, *L'âme romantique et le rêve* (Marseille: Cahiers du Sud, 1937), p. 174-90.

11. Jean Bosquet, *Le thèmes du rêve* (Paris: Didier, 1964), p. 372.

12. F. v. Hausegger, *Gedanken eines Schauenden* (Munich: F. Bruckmann, 1903).

13. Quoted in J. Bahle, *Der musikalische Schaffensprozess* (Leipzig: Hirzel, 1936), pp. 160-61.

14. See *Grove's Dictionary of Music and Musicians*, 5th ed., vol. VIII, ed. Eric Blom (London and New York: Macmillan, 1954), p. 313.

15. Quoted in J. Bahle, *Eingebung und Tat im musikalischen Schaffen* (Leipzig: Hirzel, 1939), p. 274.

16. Quoted in Bahle, *Der musikalische Schaffensprozess*, p. 62.

17. Quoted in Lowes, *Road to Xanadu*, p. 394.

18. Charles Baudelaire, *Correspondance générale,* vol. III (1860-61), ed. and annotated by Jaques Crepet (Paris: Conrad, 1948), p. 38

19. Maud Bodkin, "The Archetype of Paradise—Hades," in *Archetypal Patterns in Poetry* (New York: Vintage Books, 1958), pp. 87-93.

20. Marshall Suther, *The Dark Night of Samuel Taylor Coleridge* (New York: Columbia University Press, 1960), p. 64.

21. Alethea Hayther, *Opium and the Romantic Imagination* (London: Faber and Faber, 1968), p. 224.

22. See Paul Valéry, *Au sujet d'Adonis, Oeuvres,* vol. I, Bibliothèque de la Pleiade, ed. Jean Hytier (Paris: Gallimard, 1957), p. 476; Valéry, *Pièces sur l'art* (Paris: Gallimard, 1936), p. 180; Valéry, Swedenborg quotation, *Études philosophiques, Oeuvres,* vol. I, p. 881.

E. A. Poe and the Aesthetics of Work

1. E. A. Poe and his *Philosophy of Composition*: G. Woodberry, *The Life of Edgar Allan Poe, Personal and Literary,* 2 vols. (Boston and New York: Houghton Mifflin, 1909), particularly vol. II, the chapters "Poe on Poetry" and "The Author of the Raven"; James S. Wilson, "Poe's Philosophy of Composition," in *North American Review* 223 (1927), pp. 675-84; Margaret Alterton, "Origin of Poe's Critical Theory," *University of Iowa Humanistic Studies* 2, no. 3 (1925); Summerfield Baldwin, "The Aesthetic Theory of Edgar Poe," *Sewanee Review* 26 (1918), pp. 210-21; May Garretson Evans, *Music and Edgar Allan Poe* (Oxford: Johns Hopkins, 1939). Editions of Poe's works: *Complete Poems of E. A. Poe,* ed. J. H. Whitty (New York: Houghton, 1917) and *Collected works of E. A. Poe,* vol. I, *Poems,* ed. Thomas Olive Mabbot (Cambridge, Mass: Harvard University Press, 1969).

2. See commentaries to the poem in Whitty's *Complete Poems of E. A. Poe,* pp. 224-26.

3. See Woodberry, *Edgar Allan Poe,* vol. II, p. 111.

4. See Whitty, *The Complete Poems of E. A. Poe,* p. 224.

5. See Woodberry, *Edgar Allan Poe,* vol. II, pp. 111-15.

6. See Mabbot, *Collected Works of E. A. Poe,* vol. II, p. 364.

7. Letter to Frederick W. Thomas in *The Letters of Edgar Allan Poe,* vol. 1, ed. John Ward Ostrom (Cambridge, Mass: Harvard University Press, 1948), p. 287.

8. Quoted in Woodberry, *Edgar Allan Poe,* p. 425.

9. *The Complete Works of Edgar Allan Poe,* vol. 14, ed. James A. Harrison, Essays Miscellanies (New York: Crowell, 1902), p. 195.

10. *Ibid.,* p. 195.

11. *Ibid.,* p. 194.

12. *Ibid.,* pp. 194-195.

13. *Ibid.,* p. 195.

14. *Ibid.,* pp. 195-96.

15. *Ibid.,* p. 197.

16. *Ibid.,* p. 198.

17. *Ibid.,* p. 199.

18. *Ibid.,* p. 201.

19. *Ibid.,* pp. 202-3.

20. *Ibid.,* p. 203.

21. *Ibid.,* p. 204.

22. *Ibid.*, p. 207.

23. Mallarmé's remarks on *Le Corbeau* and quotation from Madame Suzan Achard Wirds's letter, in *Les Poèmes d'Edgar Poe*, trans. Stéphane Mallarmé (Paris: Gallimard, 1928), pp. 173-74.

24. "an essay of 1839" ("Song-writing"): *The Complete Works of Edgar Allan Poe*, vol. 10 (New York, 1902), p. 41.

25. Paul Valéry, *Oeuvres*, vol. I, Bibliothèque de la Pleiade, ed. Jean Hytier (Paris: Gallimard, 1957), p. 1483.

26. Quoted in Julius Bahle, "Zur Psychologie des Einfalls und der Inspiration im musikalischen Schaffen," *Acta psychologica*, The Hague 1 (1936), p. 17.

27. Mary Garretson Evans, *Music and Edgar Allan Poe* (Baltimore: Johns Hopkins, 1939), pp. 1 and 6.

28. Friedrich Schlegel, *Charakteristiken und Kritiken*, vol. I, ed. Hans Eichner (Paderborn: Verlag Ferdinand Schöningh, 1967), p. 161.

29. Manfred Windfuhr, *Die barocke Bildlichkeit und ihre Kritiker* (Stuttgart: Carl Ernst Poeschel Verlag, 1966).

30. *Ibid.*, pp. 119-20.

31. *Ibid.*, pp. 120-21.

32. Hugo Friedrich, *Die Struktur der modernen Lyrik* (Hamburg: Rowohlt, 1956), p. 38.

33. *Ibid.*, pp. 30 and 36.

34. Mallarmé's letter to Cazalis, quoted in *Modern French Poets on Poetry*, compiled by Robert Gibson (Cambridge: Cambridge University Press, 1961), p. 261.

35. Quoted by Jean Hytier, *La poétique de Paul Valéry* (Paris: Armand Collin, 1953), p. 133, n. 5.

36. Paul Valéry's six conditions in *Tel quel, Oeuvres*, vol. II, Bibliothèque de la Pleiade, ed. Jean Hytier (Paris: Gallimard, 1960), p. 676. Hytier's reflection in his book *La poétique de Paul Valéry*, p. 221.

37. Vladimir Mayakovsky, "How to Make Verse," in *Vladimir Mayakovsky and His Poetry*, compiled by Herbert Mashall (London: Pilot Press, 1942).

38. The succession Valéry-Mayakovsky-Benn is outlined by Hans Meyer in his essay "Inspiration und Gestaltung. Zu einigen Fragen der Poetik im 20 Jahrhundert," *Actes du IV:e Congrès de l'Association de Littérature Comparée* (The Hague and Paris: Mouton, 1968), pp. 940-51.

39. See Walter Silz, "Otto Ludwig and the Process of Poetic Creation," *Publications of the Modern Language Society of America* (1945), p. 822.

40. Marie Bonaparte, *Life and Works of Edgar Allan Poe* (New York and London: Anglobooks, 1949); for Poe's retrospective rationalizations, see pp. 96, 135, 156.

41. See John Esten Cooke, *Poe as a Literary Critic* (Oxford: Johns Hopkins, 1946), particularly p. 64, and J. S. Wilson, "Poe's Philosophy of Composition," *North American Review* 223 (1927), p. 680.

42. André Breton, *Les manifestes du surréalisme* (Paris: Edition du Sagittaire, 1946), p.54.

Paul Valéry and *Le Cimetière marin*

1. Lloys-James Austin, "La Genèse du Cimetière marin," in *Cahiers de l'Association Internationale des Études Françaises* (Paris: La Librairie Française, 1952); Austin, "Paul Valéry compose Le Cimetière marin," *Mercure de France*, April and May 1953, nos. 1067,

1070; Paul Valéry, I: *Le Cimetière marin*, preface by Henri Mondor (Grenoble: Roissard, 1954); II: *Le Cimetière marin, Facsimilés* (Grenoble: Roissard, 1954).

2. Paul Valéry, *Au sujet du Cimetière marin, Oeuvres*, vol. I, Bibliothèque de la Pleiade, ed. Jean Hytier (Paris: Gallimard, 1957), p. 1500.

3. Quoted in Jean Pommier, *Paul Valéry et la création littéraire* (Paris: Edition de l'Encyclopédie française, 1946), p. 17.

4. See Neville Rogers, *Shelley at work* (Oxford: Clarendon Press, 1956), p. 204.

5. See Felix Gatz, *Musik-Ästhetik in ihren Hauptrichtungen* (Stuttgart: F. Enke, 1929), p. 70.

6. Valéry, *Oeuvres*, vol. I, p. 1503.

7. Paul Valéry, "La création artistique," in *Vues* (Paris: La Table Ronde, 1948), p. 300.

8. Valéry, *Oeuvres*, vol. I, p. 1504.

9. Jean Hytier, *La poétique de Paul Valéry* (Paris: Armand Collin, 1953), p. 168.

10. Austin, "Paul Valéry compose Le Cimetière marin," no. 1076, p. 582.

11. J. Lawler, *Form and Meaning in Valéry's Le Cimetière marin* (Melbourne: Carlton, 1959).

12. See Max Graf, *Die innere Werkstatt des Musikers* (Stuttgart: F. Enke, 1910), pp. 185-86.

13. C. M. Weber, quoted in Julius Bahle, *Eingebung und Tat im musikalischen Schaffen* (Leipzig: Hirzel, 1930), p. 294.

14. Paul Valéry, *Oeuvres*, vol. II, Bibliothèque de la Pleiade, ed. Jean Hytier (Paris: Gallimard, 1960), *Tel quel, Rhumbs*, p. 674.

15. *Ibid.*, p. 628.

16. Lawler, *Form and Meaning*, p. 13.

17. Hytier, *Poétique de Paul Valéry*, p. 150.

18. See Lawler, *Form and Meaning*, p. 15; and Austin, "Paul Valéry compose Le Cimetière marin," p. 597.

19. Valéry, *Oeuvres*, vol. I, p. 1500.

20. *Ibid.*, p. 1499.

21. Pommier, *Paul Valéry et la création littéraire*, p. 9.

22. See Lawler, *Form and Meaning*, p. 13, n. 23; and Paul Valéry, *La Jeune Parque, manuscript autographe*, texte de *l'édition de 1942, états succesifs et brouillons inédits de poème. Présentation et étude critique par Octave Nadal* (Paris: Club du meilleurs livres, 1957).

23. See Marcel Raymond, *Du Baudelaire au surréalisme*, new revised edition (Paris: J. Corti, 1947), p. 163.

The Writing of Ibsen's *Brand*

1. Henrik Jaeger's words about *Brand* quoted in the introduction to Karl Larsen's *Henrik Ibsens episke Brand*, edited after the original manuscripts (Copenhagen and Kristiania, 1907), p. 10; Jaeger, *Henrik Ibsen, 1828-1888*, Et Literært Livsbillede (Copenhagen: Gyldendal, 1888), p. 200.

2. Lorentz Dietrichson, *Svunde Tider*, vol. I (Kristiania: Cappelens, 1896), p. 339.

3. Letter to Bjørnson, 12 September 1865, in Henrik Ibsen, *Hundreårsutgave, Samlede Vaerker*, vol. XVI, ed. Francis Bull, Halvdan Koht, Didrik Arup Seip (Oslo: Dreyer, 1940), p. 110.

4. Letter to Peter Hansen, 28 October 1870, in *ibid.*, p. 317.

5. See Halvdan Koht, "Henrik Ibsens digt Til de medskyldige," *Nordisk Tidskrift* (1908), particularly pp. 422-28.

6. Larsen, *Henrik Ibsens episke Brand*, p. 98.

7. *Ibid.*, p. 88.

8. *Ibid.*, p. 110.

9. Ibsen, *Hundreårsutgave*, vol. XVI: *Brev [Letters]*, p. 110.

10. Quoted in Halvan Koht, *Henrik Ibsen. Eit diktarliv* (Oslo: Aschehoug, 1928), p. 323.

11. *Ibid.*, p. 399.

12. See Larsen, *Henrik Ibsen episke Brand*, p. 193.

13. Dietrichson, *Svundne Tider*, vol. I, p. 339.

14. Just Bing, *Henrik Ibsens Brand* (Oslo: Steen, 1919), p. 20.

15. Åse Hiorth Lervik, *Ibsens verskunt i Brand* (Oslo: Universitetsforlaget, 1969), pp. 32 and 40.

16. Koht, *Henrik Ibsen*, p. 252.

17. Hallvard Lie's objections to Koht's arguments are in his opposition to Åse Hiorth Lervik's disputation, *Edda* 72 (1972), pp. 262-63.

18. Hans Brix, *Om grundformen af "Brand,"* in the periodical *Det ny Aarhundrede,* Copenhagen 6 (1908), p. 404.

19. Quoted in Francis Bull, *Norsk Litteraturhistorie* (Oslo: Aschehoug, 1960), p. 355.

20. Larsen, *Henrik Ibsens episke Brand*, p. 48.

21. Max Dessoir, "Das Schaffen des Künstlers," in *Ästhetik und allgemeine Kunstwissenschaft* (Stuttgart: F. Enke, 1906), p. 234.

22. Ibsen, *Hundreårsutgave*, vol. XIII, p. 229.

23. See Koht, "Henrik Ibsens digt Til de medskyldige," pp. 422-32, especially p. 427.

Gösta Berlings saga and Its Transformations

1. Helge Gullberg, *Stil och manuskriptstudier till Gösta Berlings saga,* Göteborgs Kungl. Vetenskaps- och Vitterhetssamhället Handlingar (Göteborg: Wettergren and Kerbers, 1948); Gullberg, *Hur Gösta Berling växte fram, Lagerlöfstudier,* vol. 1, ed. Lagerlöfsällskapet (Malmö: Allhem, 1958); Gullberg, "Ett Gösta Berlingkapitel på vers," in *Samlaren,* Tidskrift för svensk litteraturhistorisk forskning (Uppsala: Almqvist and Wiksells, 1958).

2. Erland Lagerroth, *Landskap och natur i Gösta Berlings saga och Nils Holgersson* (Uppsala: Bonniers, 1958), p. 92.

3. Selma Lagerlöf, *En saga om en saga* [A story about a story] in *När vi började,* ungdomsminnen af svenska författare, ed. Sveriges författarförening (Stockholm: Aktiebolaget Ljus, 1902), pp. 143-44.

4. Pierre Audiat, *La Biographie de l'oeuvre littéraire* (Paris: Champion, 1924), p. 116.

5. Lagerlöf, *En saga om en saga*, p. 145.

6. *Ibid.*

7. *Ibid.*

8. *Ibid.*

9. Gullberg, "Ett Gösta Berlingkapitel på vers," pp. 53-63.

10. See *ibid.*, p. 64.

11. Lagerlöf, *En saga om en saga*, p. 146.

12. Selma Lagerlöf, *Dockteaterspel*, with introduction and commentary by Ying Toijer-Nilsson, *Lagerlöfstudier*, vol. 2., ed. Lagerlöfsällskapet (Malmö: Allhem, 1959).

13. See Stellan Arvidsson, *Selma Lagerlöf* (Stockholm: Bonniers, 1932), pp. 16-17.

14. Fréderic Paulhan, *Psychologie de l'invention*, 3rd ed. (Paris: F. Alcan, 1923).

15. Lagerlöf, *En saga om en saga*, p. 146.

16. *Ibid.*, p. 147.

17. *Ibid.*, pp. 147-48.

18. *Ibid.*, p. 148.

19. *Ibid.*, p. 149.

20. *Ibid.*, p. 154.

21. Selma Lagerlöf, *Ur Gösta Berlings saga*, Presentupplaga (Stockholm: Frithiof Hellberg, 1891), p. 43.

22. *Ibid.*, p. 43.

23. Selma Lagerlöf on Carlyle in *Höst, Berättelser och tal* (Stockholm: Bonniers, 1933), pp. 58-61. More information about the Carlyle-Lagerlöf relationship is in Vivi Edström, *Livets stigar* (Stockholm: Scandinavian University Books, 1960), pp. 328 ff.

24. Selma Lagerlöf, *Brev*, vol. I, ed. Lagerlöfsällskapet, selected by Ying Toijer-Nilsson (Lund: Gleerups, 1967), p. 59.

25. *Ibid.*, p. 71.

26. Lagerlöf, *En saga om en saga*, p. 150.

27. Valborg Olander, *En blick i verkstaden*, in Svenska Studier dedicated to Gustaf Cederschöld, 25 June 1914 (Lund: Gleerups, 1914), p. 202.

28. *Ibid.*, p. 202.

29. *Ibid.*, p. 203.

30. Lagerlöf, *Brev*, vol. 1, p. 78.

31. *Ibid.*, vol. 2, p. 217.

32. See Gunnel Weidel, *Helgon och gengångare* (Lund: Gleerups, 1964), p. 118.

33. See Lars Ulvenstam, *Den åldrade Selma Lagerlöf* (Stockholm: Bonniers, 1955), pp. 18-22.

34. Weidel, *Helgon och gengångare*, p. 109.

35. Quoted in Elin Wägner, *Selma Lagerlöf*, vol. I (Stockholm: Bonniers, 1942), p. 19.

36. The manuscript is in the Selma Lagerlöf collection in the Royal Library, Stockholm.

37. Quoted in Nils Afzelius, "Selma Lagerlöfs manuskript och något om August Strindbergs," in *Selma Lagerlöf, den förargelseväckande* (Lund: Gleerups, 1969), p. 37.

38. Afzelius, "Selma Lagerlöfs manuskript," p. 36.

39. Lagerlöf, *Brev*, vol. 1, p. 83.

40. Letter to Stella Rydholm, quoted in *Mårbacka och Övralid*, ny samling (Uppsala: Lindblads, 1941), p. 79.

41. Sigvard Lindqvist, "Om Selma Lagerlöfs konstnärliga medvetenhet," in *Samlaren*, Tidskrift för svensk litteraturhistorisk forskning (Uppsala: Almqvist and Wiksells, 1962).

42. Lagerlöf, *Brev*, vol. 1, p. 225.

43. Lindqvist, "Om Selma Lagerlöfs konstnärliga medvetenhet," p. 127.

44. *Ibid.*, p. 133.

45. Letter to Stella Rydholm, quoted in *Mårbacka och Övralid*, p. 79.

46. Lagerlöf, *Brev*, vol. 1, p. 225.

47. *Ibid.*, p. 83.

48. Letter from Sophie Elkan, quoted in Lindqvist, "Om Selma Lagerlöfs konstnärliga medvetenhet," p. 132.

49. Afzelius, "Selma Lagerlöfs manuskript," p. 22.

50. Letter to Henriette Coyet, quoted in Lagerlöf, *Brev*, vol. 2, p. 227.

51. Olle Holmberg, *Dagens Nyheter*, 20 November 1928.

52. Edström, *Livets stigar*, p. 143.

Periodicity and the Stages of Literary Creativity

1. Friedrich Hebbel and his productive phase, in Gottfried Keller, *Tagebücher*, vol. II, p. 170, quoted in Otto Behagel, *Bewusstes und unbewusstes im dichterischen Schaffen* (Leipzig: Freytag, 1906), p. 54.

2. Quoted in Nils-Olof Franzén, *Hur stora författare arbeta* (Stockholm: Natur och Kultur, 1947), pp. 87 f.

3. T. S. Eliot's essay was originally printed in 1928; it is now the introduction to Ezra Pound, *Selected Poems* (London: Faber and Faber, n.d.).

4. Ernst Kretschmer, *Geniale Menschen* (Berlin: Springer, 1929). p. 109.

5. For Valéry's productivity crisis and resumed creative activity, see Paul Valéry, *Oeuvres*, vol. I, Bibliothèque de la Pleiade, ed. Jean Hytier (Paris: Gallimard, 1957), particularly commentaries on pp. 1620-39; F. Rauhut, *Paul Valéry, Geist und Mythos* (Munich: Max Hueber, 1930); Paul Aigrisse, *Psychanalyse de Paul Valéry* (Paris: Editions Universitaires, 1964).

6. Claude Abastado, *Expérience et théorie de la création poétique chez Mallarmé* (Paris: Minard, 1970), pp. 8-9.

7. Paul Valéry's letter to André Gide, quoted in Rauhut, *Paul Valéry*, p. 22; letter to Valéry Larbaud, *ibid.*, p. 21; words in his diary, *ibid.*, p. 23.

8. See Aigrisse, *Psychanalyse de Paul Valéry*, p. 138.

9. Valéry, *Oeuvres*, vol. I, p. 1492, originally printed under the title *Comment je reviens à la Poésie* in April 1927.

10. For Rilke's experience in Duino, see Marie von Thurn und Taxis Hohenlohe, *Erinnerungen an Rainer Maria Rilke* (Frankfurt: Insel Verlag, 1966), pp. 48-50.

11. Rainer Maria Rilke, *Briefe* (Wiesbaden: Insel, 1950), p. 742.

12. *Ibid.*, p. 900.

13. See Arthur Koestler, *The Act of Creation* (London: Hutchinson, 1964), p. 115.

14. Judith Ryan, "Creative Subjectivity in Rilke and Valéry," *Comparative Literature* 25 (1973), pp. 1-16.

15. Quoted by Max Graf, *Die innere Werkstatt des Musikers* (Stuttgart: F. Enke, 1910), p. 47.

16. Quoted by Gunilla Bergsten, *Thomas Manns Doktor Faustus*, Studia litterarum Upsaliensia, vol. 3 (Lund, 1963), pp. 84-85.

17. Graf, *Die innere Werkstatt*, p. 50.

18. Bengt Landgren, *Ensamheten, döden och drömmarna*, Studia litterarum Upsaliensia, vol. 7 (Lund, 1971), p. 183.

19. Ingrid Ekelöf's report is quoted in Landgren, *ibid.*, p. 183.

20. *Ibid.*

21. Gunnar Ekelöf, *En självbiografi*, efterlämnade brev och anteckningar, ed. Ingrid Ekelöf (Stockholm: Bonniers, 1971), p. 227.

22. See Landgren, *Ensamheten*, p. 184.

23. Richard Müller Freienfels, *Psychologie der Kunst*, 2 vols. (Berlin: Teubner, 1923).

24. Graham Wallas, *The Art of Thought*, new edition by May Wallas (London: C. A. Watts, 1945). Walter Newcombe Ince used Wallas's schema in the chapter "The Stages of Creation" in his book *The Poetic Theory of Paul Valéry, Inspiration and Technique* (Leicester: Leicester University Press, 1961).

25. Quoted by Helge Topsøe-Jensen in *Buket til Andersen*, Bemærkninger til femogtyve Eventyr [Notes to Twenty-Five Fairy Tales] (Copenhagen: Gad, 1971), p. 231.

26. Thomas Mann, *Die Entstehung des Doktor Faustus* in *Gesammelte Werke in zwölf Bänden*, vol. XI (Oldenburg: Fischer, 1960), pp. 155-56.

27. See Koestler, *Act of Creation*, p. 118.

28. See Freienfels, *Psychologie der Kunst*, vol. II, p. 144.

29. Liviu Rusu, *Essai sur la création artistique* (Paris: F. Alcan, 1935), pp. 240-42.

30. I. A. Taylor, "The Nature of the Creative Process," in *Creativity. An Examination of the Creative Process* (New York: Art Directors Club of New York, Hastings House, 1955), pp. 61 ff.

31. Beethoven's letter is quoted in Sam Morgenstern, *Composers on Music, an Anthology of Composers' Writings* (London: Faber and Faber, 1958), p. 86.

32. The term "structured unconscious" is from June Downey, *Creative Imagination* (Cambridge: Cambridge University Press, 1925).

Inspiration Disputed

1. F. Heidsieck, *L'inspiration. Art et vie spirituelle* (Paris: Presses Universitaires de France, 1961).

2. Quoted in J. Bowra, *Inspiration and Poetry* (Cambridge: Cambridge University Press, 1955), p. 3.

3. Quoted in Walter Newcombe Ince, *The Poetic Theory of Paul Valéry, Inspiration and Technique* (Leicester: Leicester University Press, 1961), p. 9.

4. Spender's *The Making of a Poem*, which appeared first in *Partisan Review* in 1946, is quoted after *Criticism, The Foundations of Modern Literary Judgment*, ed. Mark Schorer, Josephine Miles, Gordon McKenzie (New York: Harcourt Brace, 1948), pp. 190-91.

5. Julius Bahle on the various applications of the word "inspiration," in "Zur Psychologie des Einfalls und der Inspiration im musikalischen Schaffen," *Acta psychologica*, The Hague 1 (1936), pp. 7-29.

6. Richard Müller Freienfels, *Psychologie der Kunst* (Berlin: Teubner, 1923), vol. II, chapter VI on inspiration, pp. 141 ff.

7. M. H. Abrams, *The Mirror and the Lamp. Romantic Theory and the Critical Tradition* (New York: Norton, 1958), p. 159.

8. Letter to Malesherbes, quoted in Gerhard Gran, *Jean Jacques Rousseau*, vol. II (Oslo: Aschehoug, 1911), pp. 1-2.

9. *Ibid.*, p. 4.

10. *Ibid.*, p. 5.

11. Pierre Trahard, *Les maîtres de la sensibilité française*, vol. III (Paris: Boivin, 1939), pp. 52-53.

12. *Ibid.*

13. Hans Erich Nossak's remark "Das Thema fällt mir schon blitzartig ein," in Horst Bienek, *Werkstattgespräche mit Schriftstellern* (Munich: Carl Hauser Verlag, 1962), p. 80.

14. See Julius Bahle, *Eingebung und Tat im musikalischen Schaffen* (Leipzig: Hirzel, 1939), pp. 186 ff.

15. Mozart's words about his experience, quoted in Rosamond Harding, *An Anatomy of Inspiration*, 3rd ed. (Cambridge, Heffer, 1948), p. 11.

16. *Ibid.*, p. 18.

17. *Ibid.*, p. 197.

18. Quoted in Heidsieck, *L'inspiration*, p. 115.

19. Gottfried Benn, *Probleme der Lyrik*, in *Gesammelte Werke in vier Bänden*, vol. I, ed. Dieter Wellershoff (Wiesbaden: Limes, 1962), p. 506.

20. Hjalmar Bergman's letter to Professor Hans Larsson, in *Hjalmar Bergman Samfundets årsbok* (Stockholm: Bonniers, 1963), p. 12.

21. Hjalmar Bergman, *Samlade Skrifter*, vol. I, ed. Johannes Edfelt (Stockholm: Bonniers, 1949), pp. 491 f.

22. See Bahle, "Psychologie des Einfalls und der Inspiration," p. 10.

23. Marianne Moore on rhyming word sequences, in *Writers at Work*, The Paris Review Interviews, second series, prepared for book publication by George Plimpton (New York: Viking Press, Compass Books, 1965), p. 39.

24. Swedish author Johannes Edfelt, in a letter to the author, 21 July 1963.

25. Quotation from Ezra Pound, in *Writers at Work*, p. 39.

26. See Bahle, "Psychologie des Einfalls und der Inspiration," p. 12.

27. *Ibid.*, p. 12.

28. Stephen Spender, *The Making of a Poem* (1946), reprinted in *Criticism, the Foundations of Modern Literary Judgement*, ed. Mark Schorer, Josephine Miles, Gordon McKenzie (New York: Harcourt Brace, 1948), p. 189.

29. Quoted in Bahle, "Psychologie des Einfalls und der Inspiration," p. 13.

30. *Ibid.*

31. Quoted in Bruno Markwardt, *Geschichte der deutschen Poetik*, vol. II (Berlin: Walter de Gruyter, 1956), p. 420.

32. Shelley's "A Defence of Poetry," reprinted in *Poets on Poetry*, ed. C. Norman (New York: Free Press, 1965), p. 206.

33. Max Graf, *Die innere Werkstatt des Musikers* (Stuttgart: F. Enke, 1910), p. 206.

34. Quoted in Otto Behagel, *Bewusstes und unbewusstes im dichterischen Schaffen* (Leipzig: Freytag, 1907), p. 13; cf. R. Meyer, "Goethes Art zu arbeiten," in *Goethejahrbuch*, vol. 14, ed. L. Geiger (Frankfurt Am Main: Rütter und Loening, 1893), p. 187.

35. *The Writings of William Blake* ed. Geoffrey Keynes (New York: Random House, Nonesuch Press, 1957), p. 824.

36. Information provided by Paul de Musset, *Biographie de Alfred de Musset, sa vie et ses oeuvres* (Paris: G. Charpentier, 1879).

37. See Carl Fehrman, "The Moment of Creation, Two Methods of Composition, Two Metaphors, Two Approaches," *Orbis Litterarum*, Copenhagen 2 (1967), p. 16.

38. Fontane's story "Von Zwanzig bis Dreissig," quoted in Behagel, *Bewusstes und unbewusstes im dichterischen Schaffen*, p. 13.

39. June Downey, *Creative Imagination* (New York: Harcourt Brace, 1929), particularly Book IV, "Springs of the Imagination."

40. Quoted in Bahle, "Psychologie des Einfalls und der Inspiration," p. 12.

41. See p. 109 of this volume.

42. See p. 126 of this volume.

43. Bengt Landgren, *Ensamheten, döden och drömmarna*, Studia litterarum Upsaliensia, vol. 7 (Lund: Gyldendal, 1971), p. 184.

44. Quoted in Richard Müller Freienfels, *Psychologie der Kunst*, vol. II, 2nd ed. (Berlin: Teubner, 1923), p. 147.

45. August Strindberg, *August Strindbergs Brev*, vol. VII, ed. Torsten Eklund (Stockholm: Bonniers, 1961), p. 184.

46. See August Falck, *Fem år med Strindberg* (Stockholm: Wahlström and Widstrand, 1935), p. 81.

47. Strindberg, *August Strindbergs Brev*, vol. VIII, ed. Torsten Eklund (Stockholm: Bonniers, 1964), p. 97.

48. From a 1909 interview, quoted in Nils-Olof Franzén *Hur stora författare arbeta* (Stockholm: Natur och Kultur, 1947), p. 97.

49. Quoted after *The collected Dialogues of Plato*, ed. Edith Hamilton and Huntington Cairns (New York: Random House, Pantheon Books, 1961), p. 220.

50. Per Henrik Törngren, *Anden i flaskan*, in *Vintergatan 1948*, ed. Sveriges författarförening (Stockholm: Norstedts, 1948), p. 208.

51. *Ibid.*, pp. 209-10.

52. *Ibid.*, p. 221.

53. *Writers at Work*, second series, pp. 202-5.

54. Quoted in *Writers at Work*, third series, pp. 312-17.

55. Verner von Heidenstam, *Inbillningens logik*, in *Samlade skrifter*, vol. 9, ed. Böök and Bang (Stockholm: Bonniers, 1943), p. 59.

56. Quoted by Harding, *Anatomy of Inspiration*, p. 65.

57. Eduad Sievers, "Ueber Sprachmelodisches in der deutschen Dichtung," in *Rytmische Studien* (Heidelberg: Carl Winther, 1912), pp. 58-60.

58. Quoted in Frédéric Lefèvre, *Entretiens avec Paul Valéry* (Paris: Chamontin, 1926), p. 62.

59. Spender, *The Making of a Poem*, quoted after *Criticism*, p. 194.

60. Quoted in Jon Bernard Beer, *Coleridge the Visionary* (New York: Macmillan, 1959), p. 141.

61. August Strindberg, *Till Damaskus*, in *Samlade Skrifter*, vol. 29, ed. John Landqvist (Stockholm: Bonniers, 1922), pp. 58-59.

62. Quoted in Franzén, *Hur stora författare arbeta*, p. 97.

63. Goethe's conversation with Eckerman, 11 March 1828, quoted in Freienfels, *Psychologie der Kunst*, p. 150.

64. Musset's poem "On ne travaille pas," *Dédicace, La Coupe et les Lèvres*, quoted in *Modern French Poets on Poetry*, compiled by Robert Gibson (Cambridge: Cambridge University Press, 1961), p. 219.

65. Keynes, *The Writings of William Blake*, p. 825.

66. Quoted in Freienfels, *Psychologie der Kunst*, p. 154.

67. See Robert Schooles, *Structuralism in Literature* (New Haven: Yale University Press, 1974), p. 29.

68. C. A. Adlersparre, "Anteckningar om bortgångna samtida," in *Essaias Tegnér sedd av sin samtid*, an anthology, ed. Nils Palmborg (Lund: Gleerups, 1958), p. 124.

69. W. B. Yeats, *Speaking to the Psaltery*, in *Essays and Introductions* (London: Macmillan, 1961), p. 14.

70. Friedrich Nietzsche, *Complete Works*, vol. 17, ed. Oscar Levy (Edinburgh and London: J. A. Foulis, 1911), pp. 101 f.

71. Friedrich Nietzsche, *Menschliches Allzumenschliches*, in *Werke* (Leipzig: C. G. Naumann, 1897), p. 163. For Nietzsche's view of inspiration see Elrud Kunne-Ibsch, *Die Stellung Nietzsches in der Entwicklung der modernen Literaturwissenschaft* (Assen: Van Gorcum 1972), pp. 122-23.

72. Artur Lundkvist, in *Författaren och hans arbetsmetod*, Dagens Nyheter (Stockholm: Skriftserie, 1950).

73. Paul Valéry, *Lettres à Quelques-uns* (Paris: Gallimard, 1957), p. 160.

74. Paul Valéry, *Oeuvres*, vol. I, Bibliothèque de la Pleiade, ed. Jean Hytier (Paris: Gallimard, 1957), p. 640.

75. Paul Valéry, *Oeuvres*, vol. II, Bibliothèque de la Pleiade, ed. Jean Hytier (Paris: Gallimard, 1960), p. 628.

76. Quoted in Jean Hytier, *La poétique de Paul Valéry* (Paris: Armand Collin, 1953), p. 133.

77. Valéry, *Oeuvres*, vol. II, p. 628.

78. *Ibid.*, vol. I, p. 482.

79. *Ibid.*, vol. II, p. 1317.

80. Igor Stravinsky, "Der Schöpferische Akt in der Musik," *Universitas, Zeitschrift für Wissenschaft, Kunst, und Literatur* 6 (1951), p. 1089.

81. Charles du Bos, *Cahiers, Le Figaro*, 17 April 1973.

82. Valéry. *Oeuvres*, vol. I, p. 1321.

83. Heinrich Heine's poetic manuscripts are in *Veröffentlichungen des Landes- und Stadtbibliothek Düsseldorf*, Eberhard Galley, *Heine, Aus der Werkstatt des Dichters*, Faksimiles nach Handschriften Düsseldorf, 1956.

84. Gerhard Arfwedson, *Diktens födelse* (Stockholm: Norstedts, 1964), p. 138.

85. Robert Frost on the poet as craftsman, in *Writers at Work*, second series, p. 30.

86. Quoted in *Writers at Work*, p. 350.

87. Quotation from *Newsweek*, 16 July 1973, p. 47 (Walter Clemens, "Carving the Marble").

Concluding Unscientific Postscript

1. Karl Shapiro's paradoxical formulation is in *Poets at Work, Essays Based on the Modern Poetry Collection at the Lockwood Memorial Library, University of Buffalo*, ed. Rudolf Arnheim, Karl Shapiro, et al. (New York: Harcourt Brace, 1949), p. 121.

2. Paul Valéry, *Oeuvres*, vol. I, Bibliothèque de la Pleiade, ed. Jean Hytier (Paris: Gallimard, 1957), p. 1342.

3. Friedrich Nietzsche, *Werke*, vol. II: *Ecce Homo*, ed. K. Schlechta (Munich: Hanser, 1960), p. 1132.

4. See Ellen Bach, *Kreativitet i teori og praxis* (Copenhagen: Gyldendal, 1972), and the valuable annotated bibliography in A. Eza Arasteh, *Creativity in the Life-Cycle*, vol. I (Leiden: Brill, 1968).

5. Jaques Maritain, *Creative Intuition in Art and Poetry* (New York: Meridian Books, 1955).

Index

Index

221